CHILD DEVELOPMENT

The Basic Stage
of Early Childhood

THE CENTURY PSYCHOLOGY SERIES

Richard M. Elliott, Gardner Lindzey, & Kenneth MacCorquodale

Editors

CHILD DEVELOPMENT

The Basic Stage
of Early Childhood

BY
Sidney W. Bijou
UNIVERSITY OF ARIZONA

Prentice-Hall, Inc., Englewood Cliffs, New Jersey

Library of Congress Cataloging in Publication Data

BIJOU, SIDNEY WILLIAM, (date)
    Child development.

    (The Century psychology series)
    Includes bibliographies and index.
    1. Child psychology. I. Title. [DNLM: 1. Child
development.   WS105 B594ca]
BF721.B4242   155.4′23   75-40137
ISBN   0-13-130419-4

PRENTICE-HALL INTERNATIONAL, INC., *London*
PRENTICE-HALL OF AUSTRALIA PTY. LIMITED, *Sydney*
PRENTICE-HALL OF CANADA, LTD., *Toronto*
PRENTICE-HALL OF INDIA PRIVATE LIMITED, *New Delhi*
PRENTICE-HALL OF JAPAN, INC., *Tokyo*
PRENTICE-HALL OF SOUTHEAST ASIA PTE. LTD., *Singapore*

TO MY WIFE, JANET,
WHOSE ASSISTANCE AND
SUPPORT WERE INDISPENSABLE

CONTENTS

PREFACE

Most of a child's complex behavior originates during the ages from two to five, making this stage of development an analytical challenge to a behaviorally oriented child psychologist. His main task is to relate the well-known facts of early development to probable observable conditions. The result of this effort would be a clearer understanding of early childhood behavior within the framework of a scientific analysis and, equally important, would provide a basis for the analysis of development at the succeeding stages. For example, a behavior analysis of initial moral development in terms of the family's practices can be extended to an analysis of moral behavior in a middle childhood child when peer interactions become important.

The analysis presented here is *theoretical* but not in the sense of explaining a preschool child's behavior in terms of hypothetical mental events such as cognitive structures and processes (Piaget), ids, egos, and superegos (Freud), or hypothetical physiological events such as the physical dimension of the mind (Gesell). It is theoretical in interpreting behavior in terms of the empirical concepts and functional laws that have been generated by laboratory and field experimental research in the last fifty years and organized into a system founded on the assumptions embodied in the philosophy of modern behaviorism presented by B. F. Skinner and J. R. Kantor.

Preparation of this volume followed this general procedure: 1. We selected for analysis the significant behaviors of a preschool child. No attempt was made to be exhaustive. 2. We speculated on the observable conditions and empirical processes that might account for these behaviors. 3. Our speculations centered on the behavior of an individual child with a particular history, interacting with environmental events, with all terms functionally defined. From time to time we described how an analysis might contribute to our understanding of him as an interrelated behaving system or "personality." 4. Lastly, we showed how the style of the analysis can be applied to practical pursuits: child rearing, child behavior treatment, and preschool education. We also noted some of the problems and issues such applications might generate, such as ethical problems in treatment, and parental issues revolving around responsibility for determining goals in child rearing and preschool education.

A review of the research literature on each topic discussed was deliberately excluded because it is unprofitable to integrate concepts and principles derived from data collected in myriad ways and purposes. It is not meaningful to try to integrate concepts and principles on abilities when some of the data are based on correlations among response classes and some are based on functional relations among response classes and environmental events. A survey of theoretical formulations for each area was also excluded, but descriptions of major theories were added so that they may readily be contrasted with those offered here. For example, although there are at least four prominent theories of intelligence, only the statistical theory is described and contrasted with the behavioral theory.

This book has been written for the undergraduate and graduate college student interested in a scientific analysis of human development. It is designed to extend the analysis presented in Child Development, Volumes 1 and 2, by Bijou and Baer and is coordinated with the collection of readings by the same authors. Yet it is the hope of the author that this volume will by itself be comprehensible. All technical terms and analyses are explained and illustrated in the text and the glossary.

Many people have contributed most generously to the final production of this volume. I wish to thank the hundreds of undergraduates who studied and commented on the material when it was offered as part of a course in child development, and the graduate students in psychology and education who scrutinized it critically in seminars. I owe a debt of gratitude to my graduate students who devoted time and energy "beyond the call of duty," among them Edward K. Morris, Joseph A. Parsons, Howard S. Rosen, Colleen F. Surber, and Grover J. Whitehurst. The same is true for many of my colleagues—Robert K. Bijou, Bruce W. Gladstone, Jeffrey A. Grimm, Arthur L. Miller, Robert F. Peterson, and William H. Redd—all of whom offered helpful suggestions for changes in the content and form of particular chapters. Finally, I wish to express my appreciation to Rodger K. Bufford, the American University, Kenneth MacCorquodale, University of Minnesota, Joseph A. Parsons, University of New Mexico, and Bernard Spodek, University of Illinois at Urbana-Champaign for their critical evaluation of the entire manuscript.

I wish to thank Morton W. Weir who, during his tenure as Head of the Department of Psychology, made possible a semester's appointment to the University of Illinois's Center for Advanced Study which enabled me to concentrate my efforts on this book. I also wish to express my appreciation to the Bureau of the Handicapped, U.S. Office of Education, and the National Institute of Mental Health, U.S. Public Health Service, for supporting research pertaining to several aspects of this work.

Last, but not least, I am indebted to Mrs. Dorothy M. Whalen for her enthusiastic interest in the venture and her untiring work at the typewriter and duplicating machine.

S.W.B.

The Basic
Stage of
Early Childhood

This volume, picking up where *Child Development II: Universal Stage of Infancy* (Bijou & Baer, 1965) leaves off, is devoted to a behavior analysis of the development of a child from approximately two to five years of age which we shall refer to as the *basic* stage. In terms of developmental landmarks, it spans the period from the time a child begins to talk to the time he enters kindergarten or first grade. It is the stage in which he learns a unique set of skills, perceptions, and motivations that make him a "personality" and equip him to adapt to others. Although he may attend a preschool, his interactions are mainly with members of his family; consequently, his assorted behaviors evolve primarily from the specific childrearing practices of his parents. The basic stage is the period in which he develops into a *distinctly socialized individual.*

We refer to development between the ages of two to five years as the basic stage because the behavioral repertoires acquired during this period play significant roles in determining a child's future interactions.

. . . the basic reactions are among the most fundamental of the individual's psychological equipment. Upon them as a basis are developed the great mass of psychological responses which constitute the individual's behavior patterns. Unless the person becomes wholly reformed, we have here the substructure of his future character and intelligence (Kantor, 1933, p. 94).

Longitudinal studies show that personality patterns are fairly stable by the age of five, and, barring drastic changes in the child brought about by previous illness, accident, or radical changes in his external environment, persist along the lines observed at this time (Hurlock, 1972).

A few words about developmental stages or stage theories. In psychology, one finds that stages of human development are generally related to (1) age, (2) changes in hypothetical structures and processes, or (3) changes in observable conditions, depending upon the point of view of the proponent. The concept of stages based on age is exemplified by those who hold a maturational theory of development. Gesell and Ilg (1949), for example, refer to age-stages that begin at 4 weeks and progress to 16 weeks, 28 weeks, 40 weeks, one year, 15 months, 18 months, 2 years, $2\frac{1}{2}$ years, 3 years, 4 years, 5 years, the primary school years, the pre-adolescent years, and the adolescent years.

Stages based on changes in hypothetical structures and processes are found in cognitive and psychoanalytic theories of development. Piaget (1970), for example, divides the development of behavior into major stages designated as sensorimotor involving reflex behavior and simple sensory-motor coordinations (from birth to about 2 years), representative intelligence involving simple forms of reasoning in terms of concrete objects and events (from 2 years to about 12 years), and propositional or formal operations involving all forms of thinking, reasoning, and logic (from 12 years to maturity). This succession of stages is dependent upon qualitative changes in hypothetical cognitive structures or schemata. To classical psychoanalytic theorists, the stages of psychosexual development are related to the areas of the body in which hypothetical libidinal energy is dominant. They would say, for example, that before two years of age libidinal energy is concentrated in the oral region; between two and three years of age, it is concentrated in the anal area; and between three and six years of age in the phallic zone. The pre-two-year-old period is referred to as the oral stage, the two-to-three-year-old as the anal phase, and three-to-six-year-old period as the phallic phase of psychosexual development (Freud, 1949).

Stages formulated on the basis of changes in observable conditions and events, either in the physiological structure or functioning of the child or in his external environment, are found in empirical behavioral theories of development. Kantor, for example, divides development into universal, basic, and societal stages (1933). The universal stage begins some time before birth (where the fetus responds as a unitary system) and continues until the beginning of verbal behavior (about the first year and a half). It is the preverbal stage of development. The basic stage begins with the onset of verbal behavior and ends with enrollment in school, and the societal stage begins with enrollment in school, representing the occasion for contacts with groups of individuals outside of the family, and continues through the adult years.

The *only* justification for dividing the human life span into stages is to simplify the analysis of the extraordinarily complex relationships that are involved in development (Baer, 1970; Bijou, 1968; & Piaget, 1970). When stages are conceptualized on the basis of hypothetical states, structures, and processes, the analytical task becomes even more involved, because it becomes necessary to conduct research not only to demonstrate empirically the lawful relationships among variables but also to validate the postulated network of hypothetical terms. Considering that a workable general theory of human psychological development is just beginning to emerge, the field needs, more than anything else at present, research devoted to demonstrating functional relationships between environmental events and behavior (Lipsitt, 1967). The construction and use of hypothetical or formal concepts (such as qualitative changes in cognitive structures) must wait until developmental theory is firmly established on an empirical foundation (Skinner, 1947).

The basic stage of early childhood may be analyzed along a variety of dimensions. We shall concentrate on those that are considered important and at the same time are amenable to a functional analysis. They include exploratory, cognitive, intellectual, play, and moral development. Social development, which includes all of verbal development (Skinner, 1957), is not treated as a separate chapter topic. It is, instead, woven into the fabric of all the chapters because social variables are inextricably intertwined with practically every aspect of a child's behavior. However, aspects of social development, social abilities, and social knowledge are emphasized as categories of cognitive behavior and social values, and social self-controlling techniques are emphasized in the treatment of initial moral development. Nor is personality development treated separately because personality is defined here as the total organization of all the child's repertories. Each aspect of development—exploratory, cognitive, intellectual, and moral—is viewed as a facet of the child's personality.

Although the behaviors acquired during the universal stage (e.g., body management, locomotion, manual dexterity, initial socialization, and verbal behavior) are complex, those that evolve during the basic stage are infinitely more so. Nevertheless, we shall attempt to analyze each class of behavior in terms of the empirical concepts and principles presented in the first volume of *Child Development*, Bijou and Baer (1961). Thus, in Chapter 2, exploratory behavior is treated as behavior that is reinforced by the consequences from interactions with physical events under prescribed circumstances. Exploratory behavior provides a behavioral foundation that enables a child to acquire more complex cognitive, intellectual, social, emotional, moral, and aesthetic behaviors. In the same chapter, play is considered a term that may be applied to any class of operant behavior.

Cognitive behavior, the topic of Chapters 3 and 4, is treated as operant behavior involving knowing *how to do things* and *knowing about things* (Skinner, 1968). Knowing how to do things (usually referred to as abilities) and knowing about things (usually referred to as knowledge) are analyzed functionally in terms of antecedent stimulus, operant behavior, consequent stimulus, and setting factor. To say that these terms are analyzed functionally means that they are analyzed in terms of their influence on the child's behavior rather than in terms of their physical properties. For example, a change in a traffic light as an antecedent stimulus is studied in relation to its influence on a child's behavior in crossing the street rather than in relation to changes in the spectrum of waves produced. How can abilities and knowledge be distinguished if they have the same analytical components? The answer is that a distinction can be made on the basis of the component with the dominant role. In analyzing knowing how to do things, or abilities, the emphasis is on the form of the response and the reinforcing contingency. In knowing about things, or knowledge, the focus is on the antecedent stimulus and the reinforcing contingency. In addition to ability and knowledge, cognitive behavior includes problem-solving behavior. It, too, is operant behavior, but it is distinguished from both abilities and knowledge by the interactions that precede the final or solution response rather than on the form of the response or the characteristics of the antecedent stimulus.

Intellectual behavior, considered in Chapter 5, refers to cognitive behavior repertoires generally sampled on intelligence tests. The conditions that determine a child's score on an intelligence test are the same as those that determine any of his other cognitive behaviors; that is, they are a function of the individual's genetic and personal-social history, and the stimulating situation. There is no need to raise meaningless questions about the relative influence of heredity and environment. The meaning of a child's score on an intelligence test is derived from its relationship with the performance of other children of the same age (the sample of children who were used to standardize the test), and that, in turn, derives meaning from the correlation between scores on the test and some practical life activity. Since intelligence tests are usually correlated with progress in schoolwork, a child's intelligence test score is best interpreted as an indicator of his school aptitude in the schools as we know them today. Intelligence tests, therefore, are satisfactory for grade placement, but are of little or no value in planning a teaching program for a child. Inventories, formal or informal, of the child's competence in relation to a criterion task are far more serviceable; they at least provide the teacher with information for planning teaching objectives.

The development of moral behavior is analyzed in Chapter 6 focusing on how a young child comes to respond to the moral standards and prohibitions laid down by the members of his family, particularly his mother. The childrearing practices of a family, with respect to teaching the child to adhere to the family's moral code, are analyzed in terms of the major behavioral processes that are reliably known to strengthen desired behavior and to weaken undesired behavior. Practices that attempt to establish self-controlling and moral problem-solving techniques are also considered. Finally, a procedure based on the application of behavior analysis to education and therapy is suggested as a way parents might train their child in initial moral behavior.

The last two chapters, Chapters 7 and 8, deal with the application of behavioral principles and analyses to the educational and remedial practices of preschool children. Chapter 7 examines methods of diagnosis and the treatment of young children. Chapter 8 considers the objectives and methods of preschool education and the techniques of parent training.

To acquaint the student who is unfamiliar with the behavior analysis approach we include here a brief summary of the theory as it relates to human development. A comprehensive treatment of the concepts and principles is presented in Bijou and Baer (1961).

I. General formulations
    A. Psychological behavior evolves from interactions between the behavior of an individual and his environment. Psychological development is a special case of psychological behavior consisting of progressive changes in interactions between a biologically maturing child and the successive changes in his environment. Hence a child's development depends on the specific ways in which past and present biological, physical, and social events systematically alter his behavior, transforming him from complete helplessness to relative independence.
    B. The child is conceptualized as a unique biological structure having the capacity for a wide variety of activities characteristic of his species, including verbal behavior, who is in continuous interaction with stimuli that constitute his environment. The unique biological structure, or makeup, of a child results from a

combination of his genetic history and his individual history from the time of conception: prenatal nutrition and care of his mother, postnatal nutrition, physical injuries, and disease processes.

C. The environment is conceptualized functionally as the *stimuli that interact with a child.* Some of these stimuli originate from the child's external environment (physical and social stimuli), some from his own behavior (self-generated stimuli from what he does and says), and some from the functioning of his biological makeup (organismic stimuli). The child, then, is viewed here both as a source of all of his psychological behavior and as a source of part of his own environment. He is, of course, also a source of stimulation that alters his physical and social environment; his presence in the home generally prompts the mother to rearrange the household and to center her activities on caring for her child.

D. Stimuli, whether from the internal or external part of a child's environment, are assessed in terms of (1) their *physical* dimensions, such as intensity and duration of a child's scream from a hurt, and (2) their *functional* meanings for an *individual child.* The functional meanings of stimuli fall into two categories: (a) *specific functions,* such as the *reinforcing* function or the power to strengthen or increase the probability of occurrence of the preceding behavior (A mother observes that when she complimented her son for dressing himself one morning—the reinforcement—he did it again the following morning) and the *discriminative* function, or the power to signal a change in behavior (A mother calls out that it is time to come in to dinner—the signal—and her daughter stops playing and comes into the house); and (b) the *setting factors,* such as deprivation of food (an organismic setting factor), a prolonged anger reaction (an emotional setting factor), or the religious atmosphere of a church service (a social setting factor).

E. A child's genetic endowment is such that some classes of his behavior are influenced primarily by *preceding* stimulation and are largely insensitive to consequent stimulation. These are known as *respondent* behaviors. Respondent behaviors are involved in many kinds of behavior, especially in emotional reactions such as fear, anger, and love. Some classes of a child's behavior are influenced by consequent stimulation but through conditioning become sensitive to preceding stimulation. These are called *operant* behaviors and are involved in what are traditionally called verbal, social, intellectual, motor, and academic behaviors. Finally, some of a child's behaviors are influenced by both preceding and consequent stimulation, as, for example, sphincter reactions. Stimuli may, of course, produce the simultaneous occurrence of both respondent and operant behavior. The threatening approach of a vicious looking dog may produce changes in respiration and heart rate (respondent behavior), and running away (operant behavior).

II. Changes in respondent interactions

A. The number and kinds of preceding stimuli that elicit respondent behavior change many times during development. These changes come about through *classical* or *Pavlovian conditioning*, which follows this formula: A stimulus that initially has no power to elicit respondent behavior (neutral stimulus) may acquire this power (conditioned stimulus) if it is consistently associated with a stimulus that does have the power to elicit respondent behavior (unconditioned eliciting stimulus). The functional power acquired through conditioning may be weakened or eliminated by discontinuing the pairing or association of the stimuli by repeatedly presenting the conditioned stimulus without the eliciting stimulus. This well-known procedure is called *respondent extinction*.

B. Conditioned respondent behavior may be elicited by stimuli other than the conditioned stimulus. Stimuli that resemble the conditioned stimulus automatically acquire the functional power to elicit respondent behavior. Such interactions are called *respondent generalization*. The greater the resemblance between the conditioned stimulus and any other stimulus, the greater the strength (magnitude) of the conditioned respondent behavior. Stimuli that have acquired the functional power to elicit respondent behavior because of their resemblance may lose it by differential conditioning, that is, by continuing the pairing of the unconditioned stimulus with the conditioned stimulus while presenting the generalized stimulus without the unconditioned stimulus. When this procedure results in a clear-cut response to the conditioned stimulus and no response to the generalized stimulus we say that the child has learned a *respondent discrimination*.

III. Changes in operant interactions

A. In psychological development, operant behavior, or behavior
sensitive to consequent stimuli, changes systematically in form
(manual, locomotor, and verbal abilities become increasingly
complex) and preceding situations or occasions for their occurrence change in accordance with the maturing biological structure and functioning of the child and the cultural practices of his
family. These changes come about through the actions of
consequent or contingent stimuli, some of which strengthen new
forms of operant behavior or set up new occasions for their
occurrence while others weaken or eliminate old forms of
behaviors and well-established occasions. Two classes of contingent stimuli *strengthen* the form or occasion for operant behavior. One class is called *positive* reinforcers if an organismic,
physical, or social stimulus has been added to the situation. The
second class is called *negative* reinforcers if an organismic,
physical, or social aversive stimulus has been *removed* from the
situation.

Three classes of contingent stimuli weaken the form or the
occasion of operant behavior. The first is the *addition* of aversive
stimuli ("punishment by hurt"); the second is the *removal* of
stimuli with a positive reinforcing function ("punishment by
loss"); and the third involves no change in the situation (the
extinction procedure).

In all strengthening and weakening procedures—whether
deliberate, as in teaching and training, or natural, as in free play,
adventure, and exploration—the functional power of contingent
stimuli for a child changes with the *setting factor* in effect at the
time of the interaction. Food is reinforcing mainly after a period
of having no food (the setting factor of stimulus deprivation);
resting is primarily reinforcing after a period of vigorous or
prolonged activity (the setting factor of fatigue); and praise is
most reinforcing when given by an esteemed person (the setting
factor of a positive social reinforcement history). Thus, the
momentary power of a contingent stimulus is dependent upon
the prevailing setting factor.

B. As noted in IIIA above, during development operant behavior
comes under the control of a succession of preceding situations or
occasions of positive and negative reinforcers. In other words,
preceding situations or aspects of preceding situations, such as

the color or form of an object, come to control a child's operant behavior because they promise various types of reinforcements as consequences. These preceding stimuli, called *discriminative stimuli,* are not elicited as in respondent (reflex) behavior, but they set the occasion for operant behavior, or increase the probability that an operant response of a certain class will occur. Thus an injury to the knee sets the occasion for rubbing it although the child may or may not rub it; a glittering object sets the occasion for approaching and investigating it but the child may or may not choose to do so; and the question "How old are you?" sets the occasion for saying "four" although he may not reply.

Stimuli that resemble a discriminative stimulus for an operant automatically acquire the power to increase the probability of occurrence of that operant class. This is the principle of *operant generalization.* The greater the resemblance between the stimuli the higher the probability of occurrence. Stimuli that acquire discriminative functions for a class of operant behaviors through their resemblance may lose them through differential training, that is, by reinforcing operant behavior to the selected discriminative stimulus and not reinforcing, or punishing, operant behavior to the generalized discriminative stimulus. Thus a young child may say "orange" when he is asked what it is and he may also say "orange" when a red ball is shown to him. If he is reinforced with "Yes, that's right" for his correct response and not reinforced or told "No, that's not an orange" for his incorrect response he will learn to make the proper discrimination.

C. Reinforcing stimuli—those that demonstrate that they strengthen the preceding operant behavior—are grouped into two categories: innate or primary, and acquired or secondary. Innate reinforcers, which are built into the individual as a consequence of his genetic history, may be further subdivided into appetitive (those that maintain the functioning of the body: air, food, water) and ecological (those that stem from interactions with the physical environment or the physical aspects of the social environment, such as movements, sounds, or changes in light intensity). Acquired reinforcers, on the other hand, develop their functional power either through a history of being a discriminative stimulus or a history of conditioning (pairing) with innate reinforcers. Their acquired function can, of course, be eradicated by terminating their discriminative function through nonrein-forcement, or their conditioned function through cessation of pairing with the innate reinforcers.

Reinforcers can be specific or generalized. *Specific* reinforcers acquire their function under only one class of setting factors. For example, coming in out of the rain (operant behavior) is negatively reinforced by the termination of the rain falling on one's head (aversive stimulus). *Generalized* reinforcers, such as money, approval, and attention, acquire their generalized prop-erty through a history involving a variety of setting factors. Money can be used by a hungry person to buy food, by a young man in love to buy flowers for his "date," by a music buff to get a ticket for a concert, or by a teenager to put in the bank toward the purchase of his first car. Most of the response contingencies in human development are generalized reinforcers.

D. The *maintenance* of learned operant behavior depends upon the way it is subsequently reinforced, in other words, on the schedule of reinforcement. Operant behavior reinforced on a *continuous schedule*, meaning every time it occurs, results in a regular pattern of responding. When the learned behavior is no longer reinforced, it weakens relatively quickly although there tend to be irregular, strong recurrences of the response during this extinction process. Operant behavior may also be reinforced on an *intermittent schedule* based either on the amount of response output (*fixed* or *variable ratio* schedules) or time between reinforcements (*fixed* or *variable interval* schedules). In general, fixed schedules tend to slow down responding after a reinforce-ment (referred to as the *post reinforcement pause*) and to accelerate responding prior to reinforcement, while variable schedules tend to generate steady and even performances. Schedules of intermittent reinforcement may be combinations of both ratio and interval schedules, including increasing and decreasing ratios and intervals over the period of training. For example, a teacher may start teaching a child to identify animals by reinforcing every correct response, and as the child pro-gresses, reinforcing, say, every second, fourth, and sixth correct response without disrupting his excellent performance. And finally, operant behavior may be reinforced on a *percentage schedule* consisting of the proportion of contingencies with both acquired and innate reinforcers. Here, a teacher might reinforce

THE BASIC STAGE OF EARLY CHILDHOOD

responses 75 percent of the time with the comment "That's right" and 25 percent of the time with the same comment and simultaneously handing him a sweet. The net result of this arrangement is to increase the power of the acquired reinforcer. From the foregoing account we see that the various schedules of reinforcement not only maintain the learned behavior but also establish individual characteristic ways of responding, often referred to as personality traits.

IV. Development of complex interactions of respondent and operant behaviors

   A. Most human behavior at all developmental stages consists of complex interrelationships of respondent and operant behavior occurring in interactional units linked by stimuli with multiple functions. An operant (opening a box) may produce stimuli with a reinforcing function (the sight of an assortment of candy), a discriminative function (the candy sets the occasion for selecting a piece and putting it in one's mouth), and an eliciting function (salivating). Candy in the mouth is a discriminative stimulus for chewing (operant behavior), for reaching for another piece of candy (operant behavior), and so on. Another example involves social behavior. Saying "Hi" to a friend is a discriminative stimulus for your friend to return the greeting. His response "How are you?" is a reinforcer for your greeting and a discriminative stimulus for your next verbal operant response which might be answering "Fine" or a bit of small talk. If your friend were of the opposite sex and had said "How are you, beautiful (or handsome)?" the reply would not only be a reinforcing stimulus for your greeting and a discriminative stimulus for your next response but perhaps also an eliciting stimulus (blushing) as the embarrassing reaction to the "beautiful" or "handsome" part of the greeting.

   B. Some operant behaviors (drinking cocktails) generate stimuli that have an immediate reinforcing function (feeling good) and a remote aversive function (hangover), and some (taking a cold shower in the morning) are followed by stimuli with the reverse relationship, an immediate aversive effect (cold water on a warm body) and a remote reinforcing effect (feeling fresh, clean, and cool). Situations with such dual response consequences may lead to conflict and conflict resolutions, including the exercise of *self-management* practices. Self-management practices are complex interactions in that the individual takes a hand in arranging part of his internal and external environment to influence his own subsequent behavior in ways he deems desirable. As an example, a man going to a cocktail party on a warm day might drink lots of water beforehand so as to avoid drinking to quench his thirst; on another day he might arrange his work and family obligations so that it will be impossible for him to dally at his favorite cocktail lounge for more than half an hour.

C. Some situations require operant behaviors, usually in the form of an ability or a bit of knowledge, that an individual cannot produce at the moment. He might, then, engage in *problem-solving* behavior to enable him to make the necessary response. This he does by rearranging stimuli in his internal environment, such as tracing back or recalling events that are relevant to the problem, and/or rearranging his external environment, such as transposing the problem into a different context or perspective (e.g., changing a problem from its numerical form to a graphic form). In problem solving (and thinking), as in self-management, the individual uses self-manipulating techniques on his environment to facilitate behaving in a way that is reinforcing to him, in this case, reaching a solution. Problem solving refers to the range of activities extending from simple solutions to everyday routine problems to novel solutions to problems in the arts, sciences, and humanities. Discovering novel solutions is generally called *creative behavior*.

REFERENCES

Baer, D. M. An age-irrelevant concept of development. *Merrill-Palmer Quarterly Journal of Behavior and Development*, 1970, *16*, 238–45.

Bijou, S. W. Ages, stages, and the naturalization of human development. *American Psychologist*, 1968, *23*, 419–47.

Bijou, S. W. & Baer, D. M. *Child Development: A systematic and empirical theory.* Vol. 1. Englewood Cliffs, N.J.: Prentice-Hall, 1961.

Bijou, S. W. & Baer, D. M. *Child Development: Universal stage of infancy.* Vol. 2. Englewood Cliffs, N.J.: Prentice-Hall, 1965.

Freud, S. *Outline of psychoanalysis.* New York: Norton, 1949.

Gesell, A. & Ilg, F. L. *Child Development: An introduction to the study of human growth.* New York: Harper, 1949.

Hurlock, E. B. *Child development.* (5th ed.) New York: McGraw-Hill, 1972.

Kantor, J. R. *A survey of the science of psychology.* Bloomington, Ind.: Principia Press, 1933.

Lipsitt, L. P. "Stages" in developmental psychology. Paper given at the Eastern Psychological Association, Boston, Mass., April 6, 1967.

Piaget, J. Piaget's theory. In P. H. Mussen (Ed.), *Carmichael's manual of child psychology.* Vol. 1. (3rd ed.) New York: John Wiley, 1970. Pp. 703–32.

Skinner, B. F. Current trends in experimental psychology. In W. Dennis (Ed.), *Current trends in psychology.* Pittsburgh: University of Pittsburgh Press, 1947. Pp. 16–49.

Skinner, B. F. *Verbal behavior.* Englewood Cliffs, N.J.: Prentice-Hall, 1957.

Skinner, B. F. *The technology of teaching.* Englewood Cliffs, N.J.: Prentice-Hall, 1968.

2

Exploratory Behavior, Curiosity, and Play

The healthy young child investigates, manipulates, and evaluates objects and events endlessly. Most of this exploratory behavior is called "play." He gets into closets and cupboards, inspects stones, repeats sounds and words, fingers the twitching nose of his pet rabbit, watches his toes disappear in the sand, gazes at his belly as it moves in and out, peers into his sister's nostrils, and on and on. Exploratory behavior has been explained variously as the result of "a natural curiosity," "a love of the natural," "an inherent desire to learn," and "a natural interest in the new and different." Whether or not any of these phrases suggests an adequate explanation of exploratory behavior, the activities all of them attempt to explain are important because they occupy much of a young child's waking behavior and because they seem to be the foundation for a great deal of complex behavior that develops in the later years.

This chapter is divided into two parts: an analysis of exploratory behavior and curiosity and an analysis of play.

EXPLORATORY BEHAVIOR AND CURIOSITY

Exploratory Behavior Viewed as Behavior Motivated by an Emotional State

"The first and simplest emotion which we discover in the human mind is curiosity." So said Edmund Burke over two hundred years ago. Hurlock (1972), and other psychologists as well, still adhere to this notion.

Curiosity is a pleasant emotional state. It provides motivation to explore and to learn new meanings both of which activities are satisfying and conducive to good

14

personal and social adjustment. Curiosity adds a pleasant excitement to life. It acts as a stimulus to physical well-being without disturbing body homeostasis as the unpleasant emotions do (p. 202).

According to this formulation, certain kinds of new and strange situations produce exploratory behavior. (Other kinds of new and strange situations arouse fear.) The young infant expresses exploratory behavior and curiosity by

tensing the face muscles, opening the mouth, stretching out the tongue, and wrinkling the forehead. By the second half of the first year, he stretches his body, leans forward, and grasps the curiosity-provoking object. As soon as he gets it, he begins a more thorough exploration by handling, pulling, sucking, shaking, and rattling it (Hurlock, 1972, p. 203).

In early childhood, curiosity is mainly directed toward the physical world and toward the anatomical differences between boys and girls (Mussen, Conger, & Kagan, 1974, pp. 369–70). Because many kinds of direct exploration are punished, ". . . as soon as the child is able, he asks questions about things that arouse his curiosity. The 'questioning age' begins around the third year and reaches its peak approximately at the sixth year" (Hurlock, 1972, p. 203). These reactive, investigatory, and questioning behaviors, Hurlock goes on to say, must be considered the general behavioral forms of exploratory behaviors, varying among children of the same age. Particularly apparent are differences between boys and girls and among children with contrasting personality patterns (e.g., the outgoing and the withdrawn child).

This notion that exploratory behavior or curiosity is motivated by an emotional state has little scientific promise because the environmental conditions said to arouse it and the behaviors said to manifest it at the various stages of development are far too gross and far too vague to separate them from other kinds of interactions. Furthermore, the successive changes in the forms of exploratory behavior are expressed as age-related norms. Like all norms, they are descriptions of the behavior of groups of children rather than descriptions of the behaviors of an individual child.

Exploratory Behavior Viewed as Behavior Motivated by a Hypothetical Drive

The conception that exploratory behavior is behavior motivated by a particular hypothetical drive is shared by many psychologists (Berlyne,

1960 and 1963; Hunt, 1965; Harlow, Harlow, & Meyer, 1950; and Reese & Lipsitt, 1970). Since Berlyne has developed this view in some detail, we shall focus on his formulation. He states (1963), "Exploratory responses have the function of altering the stimulus field," and then adds, as he rightly should, that "all responses change the stimulus field in some way, and one might very well claim that any one response must have the production of a change in the stimulus field as a part of its function . . ." (p. 287). He goes on to say that, nevertheless, a distinction can be made between exploratory and nonexploratory behavior. ". . . the stimulus changes introduced by non-exploratory behavior are accompanied by biologically important effects on issues other than the sense organs and the nervous system, and this is not true of the changes due to exploration" (p. 287). Thus, he differentiates exploratory behavior from nonexploratory behavior on the basis that the former does not have homeostatic functions; it serves only to change the stimulus field.

Berlyne maintains that the strength and direction of exploratory behavior are influenced by the state of the organism—that is, whether it is in a state of being drugged, fatigued, ill, or healthy—and the properties of external stimuli. The properties of external stimuli may be divided into two classes. One pertains to the properties that are important in other areas of behavior, such as stimulus intensity and stimulus affective value. By stimulus affective value, he means those properties that have evolved from pairings with biologically beneficial (conditioned appetitive stimuli) or aversive stimuli (conditioned aversive stimuli). The other class or properties, called collative properties, depends on information derived from comparing the stimulus in question with others accompanying it, or a present stimulus with stimuli encountered in the past. Included are such properties as novelty, surprise, change, ambiguity, incongruity, blurredness, and the power to induce uncertainty. These properties of stimuli, so Berlyne's theory goes, induce a state of arousal, or a drive state, which naturally leads to *specific* exploratory behavior that lowers this drive state, and in so doing strengthens the antecedent exploratory behavior. This hypothetical sequence of events from arousal to behavior strengthening is a variation of Hull's learning theory, which attempts to explain how reinforcement strengthens operant or instrumental behavior (1943).

Berlyne (1960) and others (Hutt, 1970a) claim that in addition to specific exploratory behavior, there is a category called *diversive* exploratory behavior. Diversive exploratory behavior is motivated by boredom, a hypothetical drive, which leads to a change in the environment. It is as if the individual becomes satiated or "fed up" with the same situation and does things to bring about a change.

Berlyne's analysis of exploratory behavior is questionable in at least three respects. First, the distinction between exploratory and nonexploratory categories on the basis of the occurrence of physiochemical changes (biological functioning) has not as yet been demonstrated and therefore cannot serve as a currently feasible criterion. Second, the claim that specific exploratory behavior is aroused by the stimulus properties of novelty, surprise, change, ambiguity, incongruity, blurredness, and the power to induce uncertainty has not served to delineate the situations in which exploratory behavior actually takes place. For the most part, investigators working in this area concentrate on stimulus complexity and novelty (see Hutt, 1970a), either ignoring the other categories or treating them as part of complexity or novelty. This is not to say, however, that the terms *complexity* and *novelty* themselves are easily definable (Nunnally & Lemond, 1974). The definition of "complexity" is unclear because it may include both the *physical dimensions* of stimuli (the number of distinguishable elements and the extent of the physical dissimilarity among them) and an *individual's* reactions to them (the degree to which the elements in a stimulus pattern are responded to as a unit). Inasmuch as the physical and the functional dimensions of stimuli refer to different phenomena, they should be treated separately. Third, the hypothetical variables and processes, such as arousal, arousal-balance, boredom, and drive reduction, have difficult-to-define, or equivocal meanings. Hutt (1970), for example, states that

. . . any drive is defined by the operations chosen to demonstrate it; the precise relationship between dependent and independent variables is still insufficiently explained to make the term "curiosity" much more than a description of the observed phenomena (p. 71).

Cantor, on the basis of his extensive research with children, has questioned the soundness of the postulated hypothetical internal chains or events (1963), and Cofer and Appley have concluded, after a review of the literature, that the drive-induced concept of exploration is a poor one and a liability to an analysis of exploratory behavior (1964, pp. 814–21).

Exploratory Behavior Viewed as Behavior
Strengthened by Ecological Stimuli

Exploratory behavior, which may be treated functionally as a sequence of operant interactions, is strengthened and maintained by contingent nonappetitive ecological stimuli under specifiable setting factors (Bijou & Baer, 1965, pp. 5–7). To clarify this analysis, we must detail the nature of ecological stimuli and describe the essential setting factors.

Ecological stimuli. Ecological stimuli originate in the child's interactions with (1) physical objects, and (2) the physical dimensions of social and biological stimuli. Included in the first category are interactions with natural objects (stones in a riverbed), and manmade objects (pots in a cupboard). Included in the second category are interactions with the anatomical structures of others and of the individual's own anatomical makeup (the child's loose tooth); his own biological functioning (the changes in his respiration); and his own actions (jumping). As the child interacts with objects, or with the physical aspects of biological and social entities, stimuli are produced. If he were to approach these stimuli and rearrange them, changes would occur in the size, shape, and color; if he were to hit, bend, squeeze, or break them, noises would be emitted; if he were to rub them against his face, they would feel smooth, rough, cold, or wet; if he were to suck, bite, or chew them, they would taste bitter, salty, or sweet, and if he were to put them near his nose, they would smell pleasant or foul.

Kish (1966) calls these *sensory stimuli* and defines their reinforcing property by exclusion:

Until recently, the major classes of events capable of producing reinforcing effects could be categorized as follows: (1) presentation of a substance, such as food, which is related to some organic need condition (primary positive or "organic" reinforcement); (2) removal of such aversive stimulation as bright light, loud sound, and electric shock (primary negative reinforcement); (3) presentation of a stimulus which has had prior association with the conditions of category 1 (secondary positive reinforcement); and (4) removal of a stimulus which has had prior association with the conditions in category 2 (secondary negative reinforcement). It seems reasonable to add tentatively a fifth category to the above group, which we shall call sensory reinforcement. Sensory reinforcement will be used to refer to a primary reinforcement process resulting from the response-contingent presentation or removal of stimuli of moderate intensity which cannot be subsumed under classes 1, 2, 3, and 4. It is unlikely that such a category of reinforcers reflects a basic process difference from the more traditional reinforcers (p. 110).

Designating these stimuli as sensory stimuli creates a problem because all stimuli are sensory stimuli in that they have physical and sensory dimensions; that is, they may be measured in terms of the laws of physics and may be reacted to by an organism. Furthermore, there is no need to define their reinforcing properties by exclusion. We can define them in positive terms by observing the behavior of a child and noting the changes that occur following the introduction of any of these stimuli. If a stimulus in this group strengthens the class of behavior that preceded it, that stimulus has a reinforcing property for that child under the setting factors in effect at that time. We call these stimuli ecological stimuli, and when they have reinforcing properties, *ecological reinforcers.* To distinguish them from appetitive reinforcers, we refer to the behavior they strengthen as exploratory behavior or curiosity.

Animal laboratory research on exploratory behavior concentrates on studying one sensory modality at a time in a variety of species. Thus, research with rats has demonstrated that light increment (Berlyne, Salapatek, Gelman, & Zener, 1964), modification of color and surface texture of the walls of the goal box (Chapman & Levy, 1957), objects to explore in the goal box (Berlyne & Slater, 1957), and luminous patterns (Barnes & Baron, 1961) were all reinforcing. And investigators with monkeys have indicated that complex visual stimulation was also reinforcing (Butler & Harlow, 1954; and Butler & Woolpy, 1963).

Research on exploratory behavior with children is exemplified by the meticulous work of Rheingold and her colleagues (1962 & 1964). In their study on the effects of visual and auditory stimulation on manual responses, Rheingold, Stanley, and Doyle (1964) provided two- to five-year-old children with an opportunity to touch a ball and to discover that it resulted in a 3-second motion picture of brightly colored geometric figures (circles, squares, stars, and crosses of various sizes) moving slowly across a dark field to the accompaniment of a Swiss music box rendition of "Annie Laurie." The experimental question was: Do these visual and auditory stimuli function as reinforcers for this class of operant behavior? Since operant behavior is influenced by schedules of reinforcement (Bijou & Baer, 1961, pp. 58–64), a comparison of children's performances on two schedules of reinforcement yielding different response patterns should supply an answer, or promise of an answer. For example, with established reinforcers, children respond faster with increasing fixed-ratio schedules of reinforcement (schedules in which the reinforcer is delivered following a fixed number of responses). Of the twenty children who were assigned to fixed-ratio schedules, fifteen showed increasing rates of responding with advancing fixed-ratio schedules. On the other hand, none of the five children who were given a continuous-reinforcement schedule (in which each response is followed by the experimental contingency) showed such a progressive increase in rate of responding. The findings strongly suggested that the contingent visual and auditory stimuli used in this study functioned as reinforcers for these young children. The authors concluded that ". . . the present results supply evidence for the reinforcing properties of exteroceptive, rather than primary biologic, or homeostasis-preserving stimuli" (Rheingold, Stanley, & Doyle, 1964, p. 325).

It should be apparent that exploratory behavior cannot be identified on the basis of its form; that is, we cannot say that a child ·is engaging in exploratory behavior when all we see is that he appears to be manipulating objects. In the Rheingold et al. study, ball-touching was exploratory behavior in that it produced moving visual displays and sprightly music. However, ball-touching may not be exploratory behavior, as when a child touches and holds the ball atop the handrail as he assists himself up the stairs. Exploratory behavior must be identified in terms of the functional relationships involved.

In two experimental studies with nursery school children, Antonitis and Barnes (1961) used a bar-pressing response. In the first study, light onset and offset were the contingent stumuli; in the second study, cartoon cutouts and silhouettes were the stimulus events that followed the response. The onset or termination of light ". . . exercised a powerful reinforcing effect on the lever-pressing behavior of the groups, the effects diminishing with successive days. When the pictorial stimuli were added, the results suggested that the onset of light was more reinforcing than termination" (p. 110). In a study by Frey (1960) the children were to press the bar in order to activate one of three different tapes: "That's good," garbled by being played backwards; "That's good"; and "That's bad." All of these consequent stimuli were found to have strong reinforcing effects; that is, the children increased their bar pressing according to the tape they preferred to hear. "That's good" and "That's bad" increased the bar-pressing responses equally; the garbled "That's good" increased the responses somewhat less. Friedlander (1967) used a response requiring pressure on two toys attached to the sides of a playpen to ascertain the preference of babies for different kinds of taped parents' conversations. In two studies on infants by Watson (1969), visual fixation on two blank targets was the response, and visual and auditory stimuli were the reinforcing contingencies. In the first investigation on 14-week-olds, the girls learned under auditory contingencies but not under visual contingencies, while the boys learned under visual but not auditory contingencies. In the second experiment with 10-week-olds, again the girls learned under auditory contingencies, but the boys failed to learn under either auditory, visual, or combined contingencies. Rovee and Rovee (1969) demonstrated that the operant rate of an experimental group of 10-week-old infants tripled within the first six minutes of reinforcement of foot thrusts, whereas the operant rate of the controls, receiving identical but noncontingent visual and somesthetic stimulation was not altered. (Somesthetic stimulation refers to stimulation from bodily movement, in this case, movement of the left leg.) The investigators used a conjugate reinforcement technique which

. . . involves the presentation of a contiguously available event contingent upon a response, such that the event's intensity varies directly and immediately with response rate. The prototype is the handgenerated flashlight in which illumination intensity is controlled directly by the response rate and pressure on a trigger or dynamometer handle (Lipsitt, Pederson, & Delucia, 1966, p. 67).

A study by Friedlander (1966) in a home setting showed that a five-year-old boy continued to manipulate for long periods a toy offering two response options, one with a continuous schedule of reinforcement and the other with a fixed ratio schedule of four responses to one reinforcement, and a wide assortment of light-chime contingencies (steady light in the same place, steady light in different places, and a single stroke of a chime and a series of strokes of a chime). And Hutt (1966), studying exploratory behavior in three- to five-year-old nursery schoolers, exposed each child to a novel object—a red metal box on four legs, with a lever having a blue wooden bell at the end for grasping—and permitted him to manipulate it as he pleased. The directional manipulations of the lever registered on four counters on the surface of the box. Movement of the lever in one of the horizontal directions produced the sound of a bell, while movement in one of the vertical directions resulted in the sound of a buzzer. Four conditions were studied: (1) no sound or vision: the bell and buzzer switched off, and the counters covered up; (2) vision only: noises off, but counters visible; (3) sound only: bell and buzzer on, but counters covered, and (4) sound and vision: noises on, and counters visible. Hutt found that both auditory and visible contingencies were potent in generating and maintaining responses, with the former more so.

Setting factors for exploratory behavior.   An ecological reinforcer, like all reinforcers, is functional *only under certain setting factors.* Investigators report, for example, that infants will, under certain conditions, display exploratory behavior to novelty and complexity. The "certain conditions" necessary for exploratory behavior include: (1) The absence of setting factors that increase the probability of behaviors that are more powerful than exploratory behavior and thereby inhibit it, and (2) the presence of setting factors that increase the reinforcing function of ecological stimuli.

Setting factors that generate behaviors more powerful than exploratory behavior means that a child at the moment is not substantially deprived of homeostatic reinforcers (for instance, he is not hungry or thirsty); he is not fatigued, sleepy, or ill (Piaget [1929], for example, states that exploratory behavior usually takes place in healthy children); he is not responding to strong emotional predispositions (e.g., anger, fear, or joy); he is not responding to strong aversive stimulation (e.g., a wet, cold diaper); and he is not under medication having stimulating or debilitating effects. All of these setting factors generate behaviors that compete against, or override, exploratory behavior, at least during the basic stage of development.

Setting factors that increase the reinforcing function of ecological stimuli include the lack of prior exposure, or the deprivation of opportunities to engage in ecological behavior (Kish, 1966). In everyday language, one might say that not having opportunities to explore "creates in the child a need" for exploratory behavior. It should be noted that deprivation of ecological activity does not mean deprivation of sheer activity, such as running.

Some problems.   Are contingent ecological stimuli natural reinforcers, such as food for a food-deprived person, or are they learned reinforcers acquired through their close relationships with natural reinforcers? The answer is empirical; hence, it must be based on current knowledge. In our first discussion of ecological reinforcers (Bijou & Baer, 1961, pp. 5–7), we stated that in light of the conclusions of a limited number of experimental studies, ecological reinforcers are probably acquired through their close relationships with homeostatic reinforcers. Four years later, in our survey of reinforcers for the neonate (Bijou & Baer, 1965, pp. 99–120), we stated that "stimulus change" and "control of the environment" are probably natural reinforcers in the same way that homeostatic reinforcers are natural. Recent findings seem now to support the latter position. In reviewing the animal literature, Kish (1966) concluded that available data do not lend weight to the view that ecological reinforcers are acquired. Recent research on human infants and young children also indicates that contingent auditory and visual stimuli can, in fact, strengthen operant behavior. Hence, both animal and human laboratory research findings suggest that ecological stimuli are natural (innate) reinforcers: under proper setting conditions, these stimuli strengthen the preceding operant behavior. Furthermore, stimuli discriminative for ecological reinforcers, or stimuli paired with contingent ecological stimuli, acquire conditioned reinforcing properties (Bijou & Baer, 1961, pp. 53–58).

The literature indicates, too, that exploratory behavior strengthened only by ecological reinforcers is weak compared with behavior strengthened by homeostatic reinforcers, or by the withdrawal of strong aversive contingencies. It is apparent, however, that exploratory behavior may be strengthened by the action of these other reinforcers. For example, social reinforcement may be added to ecological reinforcement by members of a child's family and by his preschool and kindergarten teachers, who, believing that exploratory behavior should be encouraged, make a special effort to provide the child with opportunities to engage in this kind of activity. Social reinforcers frequently accompany ecological reinforcers because of the natural coexistence of many social and ecological reinforcers. (Little brother watches big brother's goldfish, not only because of the movement of the goldfish but also because it gives him an opportunity to be near his brother.) Likewise, there are situations in which homeostatic reinforcers augment ecological reinforcers, as in the case of a child examining a bush in the backyard and "discovering" that the pretty red berries also taste sweet. Looked at this way, exploratory behavior contributes substantially to an individual's network of interests, values, and inclinations.

Occurrences of aversive contingencies from physical sources must also be taken into account in understanding the development of exploratory behavior. It is obvious that exploratory behavior in any situation may produce aversive consequences and may thereby reduce or eliminate similar behaviors on future occasions (e.g., a child playing in a pool who falls down and almost drowns may subsequently fear going into the water). To be understood, the effects of an aversive consequence must be viewed functionally, that is to say, in terms of a child's biological makeup and interactional history. We see then that exploratory behavior may be weakened, modified in form, or extinguished completely through the aversive contingencies brought about by exploratory behavior itself.

Aversive contingencies from social sources also affect the development of exploratory repertoires. New and strange situations, per se, are probably not naturally aversive (Rheingold & Eckerman, 1969 and 1973).

However, aversive contingencies can arise from apparent conflicts with moral standards. Many forms of exploratory behavior may be perceived by parents and teachers as immoral (see Chapter 6), and as such, are punished. The best-known example is, of course, a young child's examination of the anatomical differences in a child of the opposite sex. Another source of aversive contingencies is the practices of parents and teachers which restrict exploratory behavior because a child might hurt himself or might inconvenience someone. ("The swing will come back and hit you in the head if you push too hard on it," or "Jane's mother will have to tie up their dog if you go into their yard because he barks and jumps up on people.") Punishment of exploratory behavior for any reason may change the positive reinforcing properties of ecological stimuli to aversive contingencies. When this happens, escape and avoidance behaviors replace exploratory behaviors.

A child's exploratory behavior in relation to physical objects and people may be weak because of their scarcity or because of the overly restrictive practices of his parents. However, it may be strong in relation to stimuli from his own anatomy and physiological functioning because they are always "there." Is this why some grossly underdeveloped children (i.e., those with very limited behavioral repertoires) engage in ritualistic, repetitive, self-stimulating behavior such as rocking? Is this why some therapists attempt to eliminate these behaviors by building strong competitive repertoires? These questions might be considered here by the reader and again in Chapter 7, which deals with child behavior treatment.

Implications. We have examined exploratory behavior as behavior motivated by an emotional state and as behavior "impelled" by a hypothetical exploratory drive, and have presented a case for analyzing it as operant behavior supported by ecological reinforcers in the context of certain setting factors. It follows from the view taken here that exploratory behavior cannot be identified by a special set of response forms, such as seeking, searching, and manipulating. The responses in exploratory behavior can be any response in the child's repertoires: motor, verbal, overt, or covert. It also follows that exploratory behavior cannot be identified by the special properties of antecedent stimuli such as Berlyne's conception of collative properties. The antecedent or discriminative stimulus for exploratory behavior can be any property of physical objects or the physical aspects of the child himself or of others—temporal, spatial, and movement. Whether a given set of physical properties is discriminative for exploratory behavior under the prevailing circumstances depends on whether the child interacts with the stimuli and is reinforced by the consequences, that is, whether the frequency of responding exceeds the operant level.

This analysis points up two interesting characteristics of exploratory behavior. Because ecological stimuli originate in the interaction of a child with physical objects, or in the physical aspects of biological and social stimuli, the reinforcement of exploratory behavior occurs immediately following the response, that is, the interval between the response and the ecological reinforcer is practically zero; consequently that behavior is strengthened quickly. The other characteristic is that reinforcement tends to occur on a continuous reinforcement schedule, suggesting that once acquired, the behavior is relatively easy to extinguish. Hence one would expect that exploratory behavior, observed in laboratory settings, would be strengthened and weakened relatively rapidly (Hutt, 1966). These characteristics hold for objects that behave unpredictably when they are manipulated, like "crazy clay," which bounces a different way each time it is thrown, thus making it consistently interesting to the child.

The most important implication of this analysis of exploratory behavior is that a tremendous amount of a child's behavior repertory is strengthened and maintained by nonappetitive reinforcers. When one thinks of the thousands and thousands of reactions that evolve from a child's interactional history one must remember that the main process involves strengthening through the action of a wide range of conditioned and unconditioned reinforcers, from both appetitive and ecological sources. The fact that so much of the learning seems to come from "trivial" or "unimportant" activities, such as play, should encourage one to study the conditions that produce them and to pinpoint their relationships with other behaviors, especially those considered "important."

PLAY

During the basic stage a child spends more time playing than he does in any other period in his entire life. Not only is more time set aside for play activities but, as Stone and Church (1973) note, the preschool child tends to make everything into a game. In the preceding universal stage, an infant's limited behavioral equipment and the routine activities of living, such as feeding and sleeping, required long periods and afforded him relatively little opportunity for play. In other words, his biological immaturity restricted his range of behavior. In the succeeding societal stage, the time for play is reduced because of family demands and because he embarks upon more formal educational programs that require an increasing share of his time, from preschool to occupational training and activities. Aside from the time devoted to it in the basic stage, play is a fascinating topic, a source of much information about a child's history and personality. Since the history of a preschool child is relatively short, and the interactions occur principally in the family setting, an analysis of his play reveals clearly (1) the forms of behavior that have been strengthened and maintained, and the kinds of stimuli that have acquired discriminative, reinforcing, and emotionalizing functions, that is, the basic behavioral structure of his personality; and (2) his early environment, namely, the practices of his family. Play is also a challenging research subject in its own right because it is generally thought to be good for a child ("All work and no play makes Jack a dull boy.").

Theories of Play

Many theories have been offered to explain why children play. Here are some examples:

1. Surplus-energy theory: Children play because they are so full of animal spirits, so overcharged with muscle energy that they cannot sit still (e.g., Spencer, 1855). Tolman (1932, p. 278) includes a modern version of this theory in his general theory of behavior called purposive behaviorism.

2. Instinct-practice theory: Play is an instinct and a preparation for adult activities (Groos, 1901).

3. Cultural-recapitulation theory: Play is instinctive and determined by heredity. Through play we release the activities of our ancestors and repeat their life work (G. Stanley Hall, 1904).

4. Catharsis theory: Play is a safety valve for pent-up emotions. This theory is associated with Aristotle, Carr, Claparede, Erikson, and Freud.

5. Enjoyment or hedonic theory: Play is *any* activity engaged in for the enjoyment it gives, without consideration of the end result. It is enjoyment of activity for its own sake (Hurlock, 1972; and Sutton-Smith, 1967).

6. Cognitive theory: Play is an aspect of all behavior since all behavior

involves accommodation or bending reality to fit one's existing forms of thought structure. "Play . . . proceeds by relaxation of the effort at adaptation and by maintenance or exercise of activities for the mere pleasure of mastering them and acquiring thereby a feeling of virtuosity or power" (Piaget, 1962, p. 89).

Note that these theories attribute play to an instinct, drive, emotional state, or mental activity, and that one of them (Groos's) also claims that play prepares a child for the future. Attributing play to some internal intangible factor discourages a search for observable determining conditions, thereby delaying our understanding of this behavior. Furthermore, attributing a cause of play to an event that has not yet occurred, such as preparation for some behavior in the future, is inconsistent with the logic of natural science. There is no question that play affects the form and probability of a child's repertories of behavior and hence the way he deals with future encounters; but these are consequences, not causes. Causes are conditions operative at the time an event occurs. Schlosberg (1947) makes this point with an example of the playful behavior of an animal:

A puppy chasing a rolling ball is an excellent example of generalized response to small moving objects. It would seem gratuitous to ask whether or not he is practicing skills necessary for future hunting! Of course such activity *may* develop necessary skills, and it may be worthwhile to investigate the question, but it would seem likely that we would find more about the activity of chasing a ball by studying the conditions which determine the act itself (p. 229).

Another shortcoming of these theories (Piaget's theory is the exception) is the assumption that play is a class of behavior that can be functionally distinguished from other classes of behavior, such as abilities and skills. One can readily show that none of these theories can account for all the instances of play, such as those described by Herron and Sutton-Smith (1971), and that in order to do so, one would have to invoke all the theories listed and perhaps others as well. This simple consideration points out the fact that play is not a unified class of behavior, and theories postulating that play has a unitary cause or set of causes can at best deal only with certain kinds of play.

In our view, play is whatever a child is doing when he, she, or someone else says that he or she is playing. In other words, play is not and cannot be made a useful technical term. Stone and Church (1973) say the same thing but in a little different way:

"Play" is the term we use to describe whatever young children do that cannot be classified as the serious business of life—sleeping, eating, eliminating, getting dressed or undressed, getting washed, going to the doctor, doing small chores (pp. 271–72).

The final point about both classical and contemporary theories of play is that they have produced practically no research on the conditions that strengthen, weaken, extend, or refine play activities (Gilmore, 1966; Herron & Sutton-Smith, 1971). Thus far, studies have done little more than to catalog varieties of play activities on the basis of age, sex, socioeconomic status, and location of residence. Although investigators have used play extensively in research (Levin & Wardwell, 1962) and treatment (Bijou & Sloane, 1966), they have been interested not so much in the conditions that influence play but in the usefulness of play as an investigative and treatment tool. For a review and critique of the major theories of play, see Gilmore (1966), Beach (1945), and Schlosberg (1947); for a comprehensive bibliography on play see Herron and Sutton-Smith (1971).

Functional Analysis of Behaviors Called Play

We restate our position on the nature of play: play is *any* activity of a child when he or someone else says he is playing. It is not a specifiable class of behavior, such as exploratory behavior. It follows from this conception that a thorough analysis of play covers the entire field of human behavior. A given sequence of play might include any of the behavioral repertoires of a child—motor, verbal, overt, covert, and all combinations thereof. One approach to the study of play according to this broad conception (and the one taken here) is to analyze play according to the dominant behavioral process involved, such as the release of emotional reactions. Each sample of play examined would be expected to include other behavioral processes, some occurring simultaneously and some successively. Despite such overlapping, it would be profitable, from an analytical point of view, to concentrate on one dominant mode at a time.

A functional analysis suggests that all play activities can be analyzed in terms of the following categories: (1) orientational-knowledge play, (2) behavior-differentiation play, (3) reinforcement-heightening play, (4) imaginative play, and (5) problem-solving play.

1. Orientational-knowledge play behavior. Often described as exploratory behavior, orientational-knowledge play involves differential behavior, environmental events, and the concepts of generalization and discrimination (Bijou & Baer, 1961, pp. 48–53). It also involves concept formation (abstracting behavior) or differential responding to selected aspects of stimulus classes, such as redness or roundness. The whole area is referred to in the behavior analysis literature as *stimulus control* (Terrace, 1966).

When it is solitary, orientational-knowledge play probably begins with responses to those parts of a baby's body that come into his visual, auditory, and tactual fields (lying in his crib, fingering the suspended colorful string of objects). When the baby acquires body-management, prehensile, and locomotor skills, the range of objects that he contacts is limited only by the materials available and the space for interacting with them. Confined to a playpen, he plays with the objects provided him. Crawling or toddling across a room enables him to look at, touch, feel, mouth, pick up (and drop) any objects in view or within his grasp. Much of this kind of play is supported by ecological, appetitive, and acquired ecological and appetitive reinforcers.

Orientational-knowledge play, like all categories of play, may be social and may include others. This social play results in differential behavior to the biological and social properties of people, after finding out what they are made of and the way they behave. It also results in concept-formation behavior as the participants differentially reinforce a child's responses to selected aspects of physical stimuli ("That's not a dog. It's a cat.").

A child who has had ample opportunities for orientational-knowledge play develops repertories of behavior that are prerequisites for other behaviors, such as preacademic and academic skills, particularly the oral and written responses that describe the physical, social, and organismic worlds. That is to say, if a child has learned to make accurate discriminations and recognize certain relationships between objects, he can more readily learn the name of the objects and describe how they work. In language development, before a child can attach oral labels to the properties of things, he must be able to discriminate their different properties, and the chances are that many of these discriminations are acquired through previous play activities. Furthermore, learning the written equivalents of oral labels is facilitated when the child has made the proper discriminations and has attached to them the proper oral labels. The discriminations he acquired through orientational-knowledge play not only facilitate the acquisition of oral and written labels, but they also provide him with the precursors or preconditions for learning how to describe, in oral and written forms, the properties of things and the way they function. In other words, the products of orientational-knowledge play are among the most important prerequisites for the expansion of knowledge repertories and correspondingly for performance on intelligence tests (see Chapters 4 and 5).

2. *Response differentiation play behavior.* This category of play, often referred to as skill play or practice play, involves the child's interacting with objects in ways that result in successively more effective behavior. In this type of activity the reinforcement is contingent on the *form* or adequacy of the response. If anyone doubts that learning new forms of behavior can be enjoyable and exciting, he has only to observe a young child perfecting any act, from something as simple as putting a spoon into a cup to something as complex as riding a tricycle. Many examples of behavior-differentiation play involving body management, manual dexterity, and locomotion are found in Chapter 7 of Bijou and Baer (1965) and in Chapter 4 of this volume. The reinforcers for differentiation play behavior are primarily intrinsic to the act itself; however, ecological and appetitive reinforcers may also be involved. Behavior-differentiation play, in sum, extends a child's repertory of abilities and skills.

When differentiation play behavior includes others, a great deal of the new behavior acquired is called social play. The social play of preschool children has been described as evolving through four stages: onlooker, parallel, associative, and cooperative (Parten, 1933). In onlooker play, a child watches but does not enter into the play. In parallel play, two or more children play side by side, often with the same playthings, without interacting with each other. In associative play, the children interact with each other and share materials; and in cooperative play, the participants assign and carry out different roles to achieve a common objective. Cooperative play ranges from simple helping behavior to formal activities with rules, such as group games. Hence, playing games with rules falls into this category.

It is possible that onlooker, parallel, and associative play activities contribute to the development of cooperative play, but we cannot be sure since we lack relevant data on these interrelationships. It is clear, however, that learning to play cooperatively is a milestone in a child's development for it provides him with new opportunities to maintain previously learned behavior and to acquire new social as well as other behaviors. It is also clear that verbal behavior facilitates the development of cooperative play since linguistic communication extends the behavioral capacity of the speaker and expands the sensory capacity of the listener (Skinner, 1957). For example, in building a tree house one child may perch himself in a tree and call to his playmate on the ground for boards, nails, etc. Through verbal exchanges and gross motor coordinations, the role of each child is such that the physical power of the child in the tree extends to the pile of boards on the ground, and the visual range of the child on the ground extends to the construction site in the tree. The behavior of each participant is ultimately reinforced by the completion of the house and the activities that ensue. Since the ultimate reinforcer is not effective in the specific acts involved (e.g., handing a board to the child up in the tree), many cooperative ventures during the basic stage of development suffer an early demise.

3. *Reinforcement-heightening play behavior.* This class of play, frequently referred to as repetitious behavior, sense-pleasure play, or exercise play in normal children, and manneristic or self-stimulating behavior in deviant children, increases the intensity or the frequency of reinforcing stimuli. It consists of the repetitious movement of parts of the body (e.g., prolonged turning and twisting of the hands) or of objects (e.g., repeatedly spinning a saucer).

Probably the earliest form of play between a baby and his mother, reinforcement-heightening play is usually stimulated by the mother's pleasant sounds, changes in facial expressions, sudden appearances and disappearances (e.g., peek-a-boo), or patting and jostling. The baby responds with rapt attention, smiles, and gleeful vocalizations. Later, the baby initiates such play by approximating some of the mother's behaviors on the appearance of the mother or on some indication of her imminent appearance (e.g., the sound of footsteps). In the normal course of childrearing, this primitive play extends to modeling behavior, first in simple forms (e.g., saying "mama, mama") and then to more complex patterns (e.g., pat-a-cake, pat-a-cake). Baby-adult play includes, to some extent, respondent components (the happy, joyous, affective part) but mainly if it is operant behavior supported primarily by social reinforcers, and secondarily, by ecological and mildly aversive and nonsocial conditioned reinforcers.

4. *Imaginative play behavior.* Imaginative play, fantasy play, symbolic play or make-believe play may or may not involve objects and people. When it does, it is known as dramatic play; when it does not, as

daydreaming. This type of play is employed extensively in child psychoanalytic therapies (Bijou & Sloane, 1966) because it is said to uncover clues as to the child's motivations and his acting-out repertories.

Two behavioral concepts are central in imaginative play: (1) weak stimulus control, where the child's behavior is only partially controlled by antecedent conditions, as in seeing a horse and pretending that it is a zebra, and (2) strong emotional-motivational setting factors, especially those arising from frustration (nonreinforcement), conflict (vacillation), conditioned aversive stimulation (anxiety), and rapturous delight or joy. Imaginative play is reinforced by some of the conditioned reinforcers that are produced by the activity in the "real" stimuli, for example, a boy pretending to be a pilot. It also permits a child to engage in reinforceable behavior that is punished in actual situations (e.g., pretending to gobble up the cake prepared for Sunday's picnic). Finally, it provides a child with opportunities to be negatively reinforced by engaging in behaviors that reduce aversive-emotional and conditioned aversive-emotional states, as in reenacting a frightening experience such as survivng a car accident, or play-acting a pending, unavoidable, aversive situation, such as going to the dentist.

5. *Problem-solving play behavior.* Play of this sort, sometimes referred to as constructive play (Hurlock, 1972, pp. 327–28), is characterized by behavior in relation to a problem situation for which a child has no ready response that is likely to be reinforced. In the early stages of development, the sequence is loose, sometimes terminating in a solution, sometimes in a partial solution, and sometimes in no solution at all. Experimentation, or doing something and watching to see what happens, is a dominant activity in this kind of play. The range of manipulations can be extensive or limited, depending on the repertories acquired in previous situations.

In solitary problem-solving play the activities consist principally of making things from available materials (sand, water, boards, boxes, blocks, clay, paper, paste). Examples include how to make a sand castle stand (add water to the sand) or how to keep the tide from washing over the sand castle (build walls). The solutions to problems encountered in this kind of play add to the child's repertory of abilities as well as his repertory of knowledge, as discussed in Chapters 3 and 4.

Problem-solving play that includes other individuals invariably requires cooperative behavior. In the early stages such behavior consists of a set of social abilities or techniques. This type of play is generally evidenced later on—at the end of the basic stage or the beginning of the societal stage of middle childhood—because it depends heavily on the participants' facile use of language and their ability to withstand some delays in reinforcement and the support given by adults (Hart, Reynolds, Baer, Brawley & Harris, 1968).

Problem-solving play and problem solving, discussed in Chapter 4, may, for all practical purposes, be one and the same thing, and both may be viewed as related to creative behavior, or the production of novel responses. A painter solving a problem of "perspective" or a child solving a problem of "perspective" may be engaging in similar interactions. In both instances they are confronted with a situation for which they have no immediate response and they cope with it by rearranging conditions, explicit and implicit, until they arrive at a response that they accept as the solution. The production of novel responses in relation to a specific situation and to the child's own history may be enhanced by the appropriate use of response contingencies (Goetz & Baer, 1973).

Free Play Versus Structured Play

Discussions of play often center around the question of whether it is free or structured and quickly a value judgment is usually attached to each: free play is deemed desirable; structured play, undesirable. Viewing play in terms of this dichotomy creates the impression that free play gives vent to a natural impulse or instinct while structured play serves to hamper these natural inclinations. Both free play and structured play, like all behavior, have their particular determining conditions and both can be studied by the experimental procedures of the natural sciences (Steinman, 1970).

Structured play is the behavior a child engages in when he is presented with a situation in which space, materials, sometimes other children, and explicit or implicit instructions and guidance are provided in order for him to achieve some objective. A mother saying, "Here are some blocks. I'd like to see you make a beautiful house with them," is structuring the play. On the other hand, free or unstructured play is the behavior a child engages in when he is similarly presented with a comparable situation and is merely told to play. ("You can take your blocks on the patio and play with your friends now.") The conditions determining the form of his play activities are a function of the situation in the form of materials (Quilitch & Risley, 1973), the setting, the behavior of the participants, and the consequences of a child's history, both genetic and personal. Free play is rarely pure. When it moves in directions that threaten the child's health or welfare or the moral standards of the immediate group, the person in charge promptly intervenes and redirects the situation. Both structured and free play, properly arranged and supervised, contribute mightily to the development of a child. Neither form does this automatically.

Implications of a Functional Analysis of Behavior Called Play

A functional analysis of play suggests that play is an activity that increases all of a child's repertories (some considered desirable and some undesirable), influences his motivational structures, and provides invaluable opportunities for enhancing adjustment. Because play has varied functions for each individual, it is essential that those interested in enlightened childrearing practices and improved preschool education should understand the processes underlying the different kinds of play and the procedures for strengthening, weakening, and maintaining each. The practical applications of a functional analysis of play will be discussed further in Chapter 8, which deals with preschool education.

REFERENCES

Antonitis, J. J. & Barnes, G. W. Group operant behavior: An extension of individual research methodology to a real-life situation. *Journal of Genetic Psychology*, 1961, *98*, 95–111.

Barnes, G. W. & Baron, A. Stimulus complexity and sensory reinforcement. *Journal of Comparative and Physiological Psychology*, 1961, *54*, 466–69.

Beach, F. A. Current concepts of play in animals. *The American Naturalist*, 1945, *79*, 523–41.

Berlyne, D. E. *Conflict, arousal, and curiosity.* New York: McGraw-Hill, 1960.

Berlyne, D. E. Motivational problems raised by exploratory and epistemic behavior. In S. Koch (Ed.), *Psychology: A study of science.* Vol. 5. New York: McGraw-Hill, 1963. Pp. 284–364.

Berlyne, D. E., Salapatek, P. H., Gelman, R. S., & Zener, S. L. Is light increment really rewarding to the rat? *Journal of Comparative and Physiological Psychology*, 1964, *58*, 148–51.

Berlyne, D. E. & Slater, J. Perceptual curiosity, exploratory behavior, and maze learning. *Journal of Comparative and Physiological Psychology*, 1957, *50*, 228–32.

Bijou, S. W. & Baer, D. M. *Child Development: A systematic and empirical theory.* Vol. 1. Englewood Cliffs, N.J.: Prentice-Hall, 1961.

Bijou, S. W. & Baer, D. M. *Child Development: Universal stage of infancy.* Vol. 2. Englewood Cliffs, N.J.: Prentice-Hall, 1965.

Bijou, S. W. & Sloane, H. N. Therapeutic techniques with children. In L. A. Pennington & I. A. Berg (Eds.), *An introduction to clinical psychology.* (3rd rev.) New York: Ronald Press, 1966.

Butler, R. A. & Harlow, H. F. Persistence of visual exploration in monkeys. *Journal of Comparative and Physiological Psychology,* 1954, *47,* 258–63.

Butler, R. A. & Woolpy, J. H. Visual attention in the rhesus monkey. *Journal of Comparative and Physiological Psychology,* 1963, *56,* 324–28.

Cantor, G. N. Responses of infants and children to complex and novel stimulation. In L. P. Lipsitt & C. C. Spiker (Eds.), *Advances in child development and behavior.* New York: Academic Press, 1963.

Chapman, R. M. & Levy, N. Hunger drive and reinforcing effect of novel stimuli. *Journal of Comparative and Physiological Psychology,* 1957, *50,* 233–38.

Cofer, C. M. & Appley, M. H. *Motivation: Theory and research.* New York: Wiley, 1964.

Frey, R. B. The effects of verbal reinforcers on group operant behavior. Master's thesis, University of Maine, 1960.

Friedlander, B. Z. Effects of stimulus variation, ratio contingency, and intermittent extinction on a child's incidental play for perceptual reinforcement. *Journal of Experimental Child Psychology,* 1966, *4,* 257–65.

Friedlander, B. Z. The effect of speaker identity, voice inflection, vocabulary, and message redundancy on infants' selection of vocabulary reinforcement. Paper presented at biennial meeting of Society for Research in Child Development, New York, 1967.

Gilmore, B. Play: A special behavior. In R. N. Haber (Ed.), *Current research in motivation.* New York: Holt, Rinehart, 1966. Pp. 311–25.

Goetz, E. M. & Baer, D. M. Social control of form diversity and the emergence of new forms of children's block building. *Journal of Applied Behavior Analysis,* 1973, *6,* 209–17.

Groos, K. *The play of man,* trans. by E. L. Baldwin. New York: Appleton, 1901.

Hall, G. S. *Adolescence.* New York: Appleton, 1904.

Harlow, H. K., Harlow. M. K., & Meyer, D. R. Learning motivated by a manipulation drive. *Journal of Experimental Psychology,* 1950, *40,* 228–34.

Hart, B. M., Reynolds, N. J., Baer, D. M., Brawley, E. R., & Harris, F. R. Effect of contingent and non-contingent social reinforcement on the comparative play of a preschool child. *Journal of Applied Behavior Analysis,* 1968, *1,* 73–76.

Herron, R. E. & Sutton-Smith, B. *Child's play.* New York: John Wiley, 1971.

Honig, W. K. (Ed.) *Operant behavior: Areas of research and application.* Englewood Cliffs, N.J.: Prentice-Hall, 1966.

Hull, C. L. *Principles of behavior: An introduction to behavior therapy.* New York: Appleton-Century-Crofts, 1943.

Hunt, J. McV. Intrinsic motivation and its role in development. *Nebraska Symposium on Motivation,* 1965, *13,* 198–274.

Hurlock, E. H. *Child development.* (5th ed.) New York: McGraw-Hill, 1972.

Hutt, C. Exploration and play in children. In P. A. Jewell & C. Loizos (Eds.), *Play, exploration, and territory in mammals.* London: Academic Press, 1966.

Hutt, C. Specific and diversive exploration. In H. W. Reese & L. P. Lipsitt (Eds.), *Advances in child development and behavior.* Vol. 5. New York: Academic Press, 1970a. Pp. 119–80.

Hutt, C. Curiosity in young children. *Science,* 1970b, *6,* 68–71.

Kish, G. B. Studies in sensory reinforcement. In W. K. Honig (Ed.), *Operant behavior: Areas of research and application.* Englewood Cliffs, N.J.: Prentice-Hall, 1966.

Levin, H. & Wardwell, E. The research uses of doll play. *Psychological Review,* 1962, *59,* 27–56.

Lipsitt, L. P., Pederson, L. J., & Delucia, C. A. Conjugate reinforcement of operant responding in infants. *Psychonomic Science,* 1966, *4,* 67–68.

Mussen, P. H., Conger, J. J., & Kagan, J. *Child development and personality.* (4th ed.) New York: Harper & Row, 1974.

Nunnally, J. C. & Lemond, L. C. Exploratory behavior and human development. In H. W. Reese (Ed.), *Advances in child behavior and development,* 1974, *8,* 59–109.

Parten, M. B. Social play among preschool children. *Journal of Abnormal and Social Psychology,* 1933, *28,* 136–47.

Piaget, J. *The child's conception of the world.* New York: Harcourt Brace, 1929.

Piaget, J. *Play, dreams, and imitation in childhood.* New York: Norton, 1962.

Quilitch, H. R. & Risley, T. R. The effects of play materials on social play. *Journal of Applied Behavior Analysis,* 1973 *6,* 573–78.

Reese, H. W. & Lipsitt, L. P. *Experimental child psychology.* New York: Academic Press, 1970. Pp. 355–62.

Rheingold, H. L. & Eckerman, C. O. The infant's free entry into a new environment. *Journal of Experimental Child Psychology,* 1969, *8,* 271–83.

Rheingold, H. L. & Eckerman, C. O. Fear of the stranger: A critical examination. In H. W. Reese (Ed.), *Advances in Child Development and Behavior,* 1973, *8,* 185–222.

Rheingold, H. L., Stanley, W. C., & Cooley, J. A. A method for studying exploratory behavior in infants. *Science,* 1962, *136,* 1054–55.

Rheingold, H. L., Stanley, W. C., & Doyle, G. A. Visual and auditory reinforcement of a manipulatory response in the young child. *Journal of Experimental Child Psychology*, 1964, *1*, 316–26.

Rovee, C. K. & Rovee, D. T. Conjugate reinforcement of infant exploratory behavior. *Journal of Experimental Child Psychology*, 1969, *8*, 33–39.

Schlosberg, H. The concept of play. *Psychological Review*, 1947, *54*, 229–31.

Skinner, B. F. *Verbal behavior.* Englewood Cliffs, N.J.: Prentice-Hall, 1957.

Spencer, H. *Principles of psychology.* London: Longmans, Green, 1855.

Steinman, W. M. Is free play free? *Educational Product Report*, 1970, *3*, 6–8.

Stone, L. J. & Church, J. *Childhood and adolescence.* (3rd ed.) New York: Random House, 1973.

Sutton-Smith, B. The role of play in cognitive development. In W. W. Hartup & N. L. Smothergill (Eds.), *The young child.* Washington, D.C.: National Association for the Education of Young Children, 1967.

Terrace, H. S. Stimulus control. In W. K. Honig (Ed.), *Operant behavior: Areas of research and application.* Englewood Cliffs, N.J.: Prentice-Hall, 1966.

Tolman, E. C. *Purposive behavior in animals and men.* New York: Century, 1932.

Watson, J. S. Operant conditioning of visual fixation in infants under visual and auditory reinforcement. *Developmental Psychology*, 1969, *1*, 508–516.

3

Cognitive Behavior: Abilities

The locomotor, manual, and verbal skills that a baby acquires during the universal stage of development, together with his increased strength and energy, enable him to interact more extensively with his environment during the basic stage of development. Consequently, the number and complexity of the behaviors acquired increase rapidly during this stage. These early childhood activities have been classified in various ways. In the 1940s, Gesell and Ilg (1949) categorized them into sensorimotor (locomotor and prehensive), verbal, and personal-social and adaptive skills, and established age norms for each. Now, in the mid 1970s, child psychologists more typically group a young child's behavior repertoires into sensorimotor, cognitive, and social, with sensorimotor abilities viewed as antecedents to cognitive behavior. Although we shall also consider these behaviors as cognitive, we shall not follow the current practice of viewing social behavior as a separate category.

COGNITIVE BEHAVIOR AND ABILITIES

An understanding of cognitive development requires a clarification of the meaning of cognition. Kagan and Kogan (1970) whose explanation is typical of those found in the child development literature state that

. . . cognition stands for those hypothetical psychological processes invoked to explain overt verbal and motor behavior as well as certain physiological reactions. Cognitive process is a superordinate term, subsuming the more familiar titles of imagery, perception, free association, thought, mediation, proliferation of hypotheses, reasoning, reflection, and problem solving. All verbal behavior must be a product of cognitive processes, as are dreams and intelligence test performances.

But skeletal muscle movements of visceral reactions are not necessarily linked to cognition (p. 1275).

This treatment of cognition as "hypothetical psychological processes invoked to explain overt verbal and motor behavior as well as certain physiological reactions" cannot be incorporated into behavior analysis because it stresses unobservable mental activities rather than observable functional relationships. A more useful meaning of the term cognition is suggested by the *Random House Dictionary of the English Language* (1971): "Cognition refers to the act or process of knowing," which can quite reasonably mean: (1) *knowing how to do things*, and (2) *knowing about things* (Skinner, 1968).

The first category, knowing how to do things, usually refers to *abilities*. Functionally speaking, an ability refers to the probability of occurrence of a class of operant behavior with a certain *form* that is specified by the situation. A form of behavior may be said to be specified by a situation in the sense that a certain form of behavior has in the past been reinforced in that situation. When a parent says, "Debbie can ride a tricycle," she means that Debbie has the ability to ride a tricycle, and that it is highly probable that when she is presented with a tricycle she will sit on it, pedal it, and steer it. In addition to the characteristic form of an ability, three other conditions must be taken into account in a functional analysis: (1) the antecedent stimulus condition or the occasion for the act, (2) the consequent stimulus event or response contingency, and (3) the setting event or the context of the interaction. For example, a twisting movement of a child's hand on a doorknob may open a door and enable him to get out of a rainstorm (escape from an aversive condition). The same twisting movement, in contact with a friend's nose, may produce screaming and escape behavior (removal of an acquired aversive social condition for the friend) and the magical appearance of a menacing adult (an acquired aversive social condition for the child).

The abilities of a preschool child may be classified on the basis of the response topography to antecedent stimuli grouped as follows:

1. The anatomy and physiology of the child's own body, or the organismic environment (antecedent stimulus: hurt to the left toe; ability response: hopping on the right foot)

2. Physical objects, or the physical environment (antecedent stimuli: scissors and paper; ability response: cutting paper with scissors)

3. People, or the social environment (antecedent stimuli: two children playing a picture matching game; ability response: participating as the third player)

The second category of knowing behavior, knowing about things, may be referred to as *knowledge* and is functionally defined as the probability of occurrence of a class of reinforceable operant behavior *on a specified occasion*. In other words, knowledge is analyzed here as *discriminative operant behavior* (see Bijou & Baer, 1961, pp. 48–53) which, of course, may be verbal or nonverbal or a combination of both. Knowledge may be divided into the following categories:

1. Simple choice behavior (taking orange juice when given a choice between orange juice and tomato juice)
2. Conceptual or abstract behavior (collecting only round flat stones along the seashore without regard to size and color)
3. Describing past events (the details of one's birthday party)
4. Describing how things work (that a ball will roll down an inclined board)

To cover the full range of behaviors included under cognitive, we must consider one more class of behavior: *problem solving*. Problem solving might well be treated as another category under abilities for it fits our definition of an ability. To do so, however, creates complications because problem solving—changing the situation in ways that alter one's own behavior—may involve any and all of the behavioral repertories in *both* the abilities and the knowledge categories described above. "Since there is probably no behavioral process which is not relevant to the solving of some problem, an exhaustive analysis of techniques would coincide with an analysis of behavior as a whole" (Skinner, 1969, p. 133). We therefore treat problem solving as a category unto itself and emphasize that it is characterized by the interactions (problem-solving techniques) that *precede* the final or solution response.

The subdivisions of cognitive behavior are presented in Table 3.1. It is important to note that the categories are not simple stimulus and response relationships but are *complex interactions*. Abilities entail a three-component sequence: attending, perceiving and effecting, and an ability response. Knowledge also consists of a three-unit sequence with a knowledge response in place of an ability response, i.e., attending, perceiving and

Table 3.1   Categories of Cognitive Behavior

I	II
Abilities	*Knowledge*

Three-component sequences of four-term contingencies with emphasis on the *response topography* in relation to the antecedent, environmental condition.

1. The organismic environment: behavior in relation to body management and locomotion.
2. The physical environment: behavior in relation to objects.
3. The social environment: behavior in relation to adults and peers.

Three-component sequences of four-term contingencies with emphasis on the *antecedent stimulus.*

1. Simple discriminative behavior
2. Conceptual or abstract behavior
3. Verbal behavior about current and past events
4. Behavior about the way things work (cause and effect relations)

III

Problem Solving

Four-component sequences of four-term contingencies with emphasis on the interactions *preceding* the final response (solution).

(Problem solving may be subdivided in a variety of ways, one of which, for example, is the locus of the problem— the person himself, the physical environment, and the social environment.)

effecting, and a knowledge response. Problem solving, on the other hand, consists of a four-component sequence: attending, perceiving and effecting, altering (rearranging overt and covert conditions to produce responses), and a solution response. Furthermore, each component in all four sequences is made up of a four-term contingency with (1) an antecedent discriminative stimulus function, or the occasion for the behavior, (2) an operant response function, (3) a consequence stimulus function, and (4) a setting event or factor. Each of these terms will be defined and illustrated later.

Up to this point we have presented an overview of a functional analysis of cognitive behavior and have given an example of how a category is analyzed. In the remainder of this chapter, we shall elaborate on the development of abilities while Chapter 4 will contain an extended account of knowledge and problem solving. Chapter 5 will deal with the relationship between the development of cognitive repertoires and performance on tests.

ABILITIES

The concept of ability pervades all areas of psychology and, most particularly, psychological measurement. Ability is typically defined as a hypothetical construct that determines the level or quality of performance or adjustment, for instance, a good "sense" of balance, rhythm, and coordination. (For a further discussion of the meanings of abilities, see Anastasi, 1968 and Cronbach, 1970.) Ability as a hypothetical construct is avoided here because the characteristics attributed to it are inferred entirely from the performance of an individual or from the mean performance of a group of individuals. That is to say, the definition of ability as a hypothetical construct is circular. Attending a concert where a young child is faultlessly performing Chopin's *Polonaise*, we remark that she plays so well because she has a natural talent. By our observation, we are (1) describing what we see and hear—she plays so well—and (2) attributing the performance to a hypothetical construct within the child—her natural talent. The ability observed defines both the ability and its cause.

Ability, it will be recalled, is here defined as the probability of the occurrence of a class of operant behavior of a certain form in relation to a situation. Let us suppose that a preschool teacher, on the school playground with her class, says to one of the girls, "Becky, can you swing?" Becky turns, glances at the teacher and the swing, says "Yes," and walks to the swing. She exhibits her ability: She sits on the seat, grasps the ropes, pushes herself back with her feet, swings forward, pumps back, pumps forward, and in a little while, swings effortlessly. The teacher smiles and says, "Becky, you certainly can swing."

Figure 3-1 is a diagram of the sequence showing the attending, perceiving (including perceptual reaction), and effecting phases, and the analysis of each into discriminative function (SF^D), operant function (RF), reinforcing function (SF^R), and setting event or factors (SE). The symbol meanings in Figure 3-1 are:

SE   The setting event or factor, or the circumstances prevailing over the entire sequence: A preschool teacher with her class on the preschool playground.

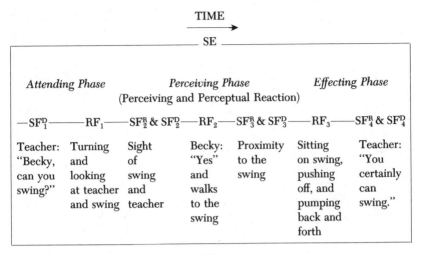

TIME

SE

Attending Phase	Perceiving Phase (Perceiving and Perceptual Reaction)		Effecting Phase

$-SF^D_1$———RF_1———SF^R_2 & SF^D_2———RF_2———SF^R_3 & SF^D_3———RF_3———SF^R_4 & SF^D_4

Teacher: "Becky, can you swing?"	Turning and looking at teacher and swing	Sight of swing and teacher	Becky: "Yes" and walks to the swing	Proximity to the swing	Sitting on swing, pushing off, and pumping back and forth	Teacher: "You certainly can swing."

Figure 3-1. Functional analysis of an ability sequence

Attending Phase

SF^D_1 A verbal stimulus by the teacher with a discriminative function (SF^D_1): "Becky, can you swing?"

RF_1 Becky makes an attending response (RF_1) to the teacher: She turns, glances at the teacher and the swing.

SF^R_2 The stimulus with a reinforcing function (SF^R_2) for the attending response (RF_1) has two components: (1) the sight of the teacher and (2) the discriminative reaction to the swing.

Perceiving Phase

SF^D_2 The sight of the teacher and the swing.

RF_2 Perceiving response: Becky says, "Yes," and walks to the swing.

SF^R_3 The reinforcer (SF^R_3) has two components: (1) the teacher's continued attention, and (2) Becky's proximity to the swing.

Effecting Phase

SF^D_3 The teacher's attention and Becky's proximity to the swing.

RF_3 The effecting response is an ability response, or a response with a specific form: Becky sits on the swing's seat, grasps the ropes, pushes herself back with her feet, swings forward, pumps back, pumps forth, etc.

SF^R_4 The reinforcer function of the stimulus (SF^R_4) has two components: (1) the
& teacher's smile and comment, "You certainly can swing," and (2)
SF^D_4 swinging movement back and forth through the air. The discriminative

stimulus function of the stimulus (SF_4^D) sets the occasion for continued swinging.

According to this conception, the definition and analysis of an ability change with development. When we say that Henry has the ability to open and close a door, we mean that he probably has all the behaviors necessary to open and close doors (that is, turn a knob or a latch, push or pull the door to move it, etc.). However, he may be unable to cope with a garage door that rolls upward. After he learns how to open such a door, our definition of Henry's ability to open and close a door is extended. Also according to this definition, the cause of an ability (the probability of occurrence of a response of a given form on a specific occasion) is expressed in terms of the antecedent situation (or the occasion for the act), the consequent stimulus event (or the response contingency), and the setting factor (or context of the interaction).

The difference between an ability and a skill should be mentioned. Ability refers to the performance of an act, and skill is descriptive of performance with a high degree of proficiency (Adams, 1969; Fitts, 1964). Where the line is drawn is arbitrary. If we compare the behavior of a young girl who swims for recreation with that of a girl who is practicing for the Olympics, we would characterize the former as having the ability to swim and the latter as having the ability to swim with great skill and proficiency. Psychologists doing research on abilities generally concern themselves with the conditions that transform behavior to some acceptable criterion; research on skills aims to determine the conditions that bring behavior to a high level of precision. According to this distinction, most of the behaviors acquired in the basic stage are abilities but they are frequently referred to as skills.

It might also be noted that activities requiring a preschool child to achieve a high level of performance, such as playing the violin, may produce a musical genius who is developmentally retarded in other areas of activity. The time required to perfect one particular skill may, if carried to extremes, deprive a child of opportunities for contacts with his peers, adults, and playtime activities in general.

In the discussion of abilities, we shall refer occasionally to the age norms of development (average age for the performance of tasks, such as walking, talking, and eating with a spoon). It is therefore well that we point out the similarities and differences between a normative and a functional analysis. Both types of analyses are alike in that they can be objective and can refer to observable behavior. They are different in that a normative analysis is concerned with the *average topography of a class of behavior for a group* of children of similar ages while a functional analysis deals with the *relationship between a class of behavior of an individual child and its determining conditions*, conceptualized as the four-term contingency: the antecedent stimulus function, response function, consequent stimulus function, and setting factor.

Norms of development are used to compare children in the subdivisions of a culture stratified on the basis of socioeconomic status, educational attainment, and the like or they may be used to compare children in different cultures. They also serve to compare the performance of an individual child with the average performance of the group of children on which the norms are based (the standardization population). When related to some practical criterion, such as school achievement or adjustment level, they may be used to select and classify children for grade placement, therapy group placement, and the like. Norms are used also as a source of information based on group probabilities and predictions: the chances are such and such that a given child with a given normative rating, or score, will succeed in performing a given task, such as the work of his grade placement or a therapy program.

A functional analysis is used to describe the behavioral repertory of an individual child—the things he can do and the things he knows about (he can stack ten blocks, recite the letters of the alphabet, etc.)—as a consequence of his past interactional history (Ferster & Perrott, 1968, p. 530). Inventories that assess such repertories are known as *criterion-referenced tests* (see Chapter 5). Information from criterion-referenced tests is used to understand (identify) the conditions that maintain a child's behavior and to plan educational and treatment programs specifically for him.

1. Abilities in relation to the organismic environment: refinements and elaborations of body management and locomotion. The forms of a child's response in relation to his own anatomy and physiology, his abilities in relation to his organismic environment, consist primarily of body management and locomotion behaviors. In the universal stage of development, the infant's management of parts of the body and movement in space result from differential contingencies from organismic, physical, and social sources. The organismic contingencies are more dominant than the physical and social contingencies because the young infant must be biologically capable of making a response (lifting and turning his head in the prone position) before that response can become a part of his behavior repertory through the influence of physical and social contingencies (raising and turning his head enables him to get a horizontal view of the room and to see the social activities going on).

In the early basic stage of development, progress in body management and locomotor abilities is also a function of organismic, physical, and social contingencies, with organismic contingencies being the most influential. Moreover, in this stage, the organismic conditions change in ways that *facilitate* the acquisition of motor skills (Eichorn, 1970; Tanner, 1970). Specifically, these physiological changes consist of (1) a shift in the proportions of the parts of the body, with relatively slow head growth and fast limb growth; (2) increases in strength of the skeletal system as cartilage is replaced by bone, (3) rapid development of muscles; and (4) deeper and slower respiration, stabilization of heart rate, and increases in blood pressure (Thompson, 1954).

Thus, biological maturation during early childhood produces conditions that (1) improve the baby's response potentialities: greater muscle and bone strength contribute to better body balance; (2) expand his opportunities for contacts: stronger bones and muscles promote more effective manipulation of objects; and (3) provide him with facilitating setting factors: more stable internal functioning, higher energy levels, greater endurance, and good health all serve to improve attending behavior and to extend the length of interactional sequences (Eichorn, 1970; Tanner, 1970). The high correlation between changes in biological maturation (measured by age) and advances in gross motor abilities is shown in the following samples from normative studies: at 2 to 3 years, walks on tiptoe, runs about ten steps, and sits on chair; at age 3 to 4 years, walks up stairs, stands on one foot, and swings and slides; and at age 4 to 5 years, hops, jumps, skips, and somersaults.

Because of the close relationships between biological maturation and increases in the gross motor abilities in infancy and early childhood, it is tempting to theorize that abilities evolve like biological phenomena. In fact, Gesell (1954), a maturational theorist, claimed that motor abilities, as well as adaptive, linguistic, and personal-social abilities, unfold like embryological structures. This conception, although intriguing, contributes little to an understanding of psychological development (Dennis, 1941 & 1960) because it does not take into account that many skills must be learned in sequence, the more basic ones being prerequisite for the more advanced ones (Bijou & Baer, 1965, pp. 108–21); nor does it take into account that physical and social variables play increasingly important roles in the more advanced stages of development.

2. *Abilities in relation to the physical environment: refinements and elaborations of manual dexterity.* In a consideration of abilities in relation to the physical environment, there are two topics of concern: the refinements and elaborations of manual dexterity, and their subsequent extension into self-care abilities.

Manual abilities. Manual abilities, like body management and locomotor abilities, develop as a result of a child's interactional history. In other words, the kinds of manual acts performed and their rate of acquisition by an infant, baby, and young child depend upon maturational level, organismic makeup, setting factors, opportunities to interact with physical objects and events, and contingencies of reinforcement. The reinforcers for the development of manual abilities during this stage are the same as those that are effective for the development of motor skills, with ecological reinforcers playing an increasingly dominant role. Ecological reinforcers, it will be recalled, are stimuli generated by operant behavior in relation to the physical environment (Bijou & Baer, 1965, pp. 116–18; Chapter 2 of this volume). And an important set of conditions necessary for ecological or exploratory behavior is the biological maturation of the child which permits increasingly diverse interactions.

A young infant's biological immaturity, an organismic component of causal conditions, retards the rate of his manual development (Bijou & Baer, 1965, pp. 108–21). In the toddler and preschooler, the dramatic advances in biological maturation have the opposite effect: they accelerate the rate and increase the range of potential manual operants and thereby expand the opportunities for contacts with the physical environment. The rapid progression in the development of manual abilities is shown by the following items from standardized normative tests: age 2 to 3 years: unscrews lids from bottles and jars, turns the leaves of a book, builds a tower of four or five blocks, imitates marks with pencil or crayon, smears paint; age 3 to 4 years: cuts with scissors, throws and catches a ball, and copies a circle and a cross on paper; age 4 to 5 years: folds a triangle from square paper in imitation of a model, copies a square, builds a pyramid with blocks by imitation, draws a recognizable picture of a man, and bounces a ball.

Because hand preference generally stabilizes during the preschool period (Belmont & Birch, 1963), speculation on the conditions that determine handedness is of interest. Like so many other psychological interactions, hand preference is attributed to heredity by some investigators and to the environment by others. The evidence for either position is not particularly convincing; probably hand dominance results from the interaction of both hereditary and environmental conditions. A tenable statistical hypothesis is that "sidedness," or laterality, tendencies are distributed on a normal curve. According to this view, a small percentage of neonates have high left-sided operant levels, a very large percentage have mixed-sided operant levels, and a small percentage have high right-sided operant levels. As a consequence of childrearing practices in a typically right-handed society, these percentages shift during infancy and the early preschool years and stabilize near the end of the basic stage. In a population of five-year-olds, for example, one finds a small percentage of the children with a high left-sided operant level, a small percentage with a mixed-sided operant level, and a large percentage with a high right-sided operant level. In this markedly skewed distribution, the dominant left-sided and ambidextrous children were, as infants, high in the left-sided operant level frequencies and the right-sided children, were, as infants, with mixed-sided operant and high right-sided level frequencies. The exact percentages of children in each category at a given age level depend on the community's specific childrearing practices with respect to sidedness and on the method of measurement. The side dominance of a particular child depends on his biological makeup and on the particular sidedness practices of his mother and other members of the family.

The decision to change a child's left-handed way of doing something to a right-handed performance is often complicated by the belief that interfering with a child's natural tendencies will cause serious emotional problems, including stuttering (Hildreth, 1949 & 1950). Any emotional problems that might arise in the course of changing handedness is likely to come not from the frustrations but from the aversive contingencies used in the training. Changing a child from left- to right-hand dominance, like the establishment and maintenance of any ability, requires effective instructional programming; that is, arranging positive response contingencies for more frequent use of the right hand in specific tasks (Ames & Ilg, 1964).

Newly acquired motor and manual skills bring a child into contact with situations that expand his behavioral repertoire; they also expose him to conditions that may harm him and restrict his rate of development. As the result of a child's encounters with aversive contingencies (1) he may avoid situations that have immediate aversive consequences (keep away from a stove), (2) the parent may change or eliminate dangerous areas or objects (put a training gate in front of a stairwell or remove a heavy, valuable piece of metal sculpture from a low table), or (3) the parent may restrict the range of the child's activities (keep him in a playpen).

Manual abilities in relation to self-care. Self-care abilities are considered a class of manual dexterity, the class that is related to the biological and behavioral self. As the infant becomes more biologically mature and acquires abilities in body control, locomotion, prehension, and verbal behavior, the parents and other members of the family encourage self-care behaviors by presenting opportunities for self-help and by instructing, prompting, modeling (reinforced imitation), and reinforcing successive approximations to acts of self-care. They put a spoon with food into his hand and guide his hand to his mouth; they smile and say "All gone" and "Good girl" or "Good boy" when all the food has been eaten. On the other hand, they also begin to ignore and disapprove of the child's continuing unnecessary dependent behavior, like "Carry me" after he is well able to walk. Such training in self-care abilities, which includes eating, dressing, toileting, and performing ablutions, is usually informal and is integrated into the everyday routines. The changes that occur are indicated by the following normative findings: *Eating*, at age 2 to 3 years: begins to use fork, gets drink without help, and pours from a small pitcher; at age 4 to 5 years: uses knife for spreading and cutting, and serves self. *Dressing*, at age 2 to 3 years; puts on shoes and boots with help, dresses and undresses self with help; at age 4 to 5 years; puts on shoes and boots without help, dresses self completely, zips and buttons, and makes imperfect knot. *Toileting*, at age 2 to 3 years: asks to go to the bathroom during the day (often too late), and uses bathroom for bowel movements; at age 4 to 5 years; bladder control at night and general independence in toileting. *Ablutions*, at age 2 to 3 years; dries hands without help, washes face and hands with help, using soap, and helps while being bathed; at age 4 to 5 years: washes face and hands and brushes teeth without help, and bathes self with supervision.

Formal training in self-help abilities, if it occurs at all, takes place when the mother decides that her child should begin to do more things for himself, notably those skills that he has not learned in the context of everyday living (Hall, Axelrod, Tyler, Grief, Jones, & Robertson, 1972). Perhaps because so much learning takes place informally, the current literature on training a normal child in self-care is sparse, although one can find hints and suggestions in general how-to-do-it childrearing books, such as those by Becker (1971), McIntire (1970), and Patterson and Gullion (1968). It may be that the trend will be to concentrate more on specific training to overcome problem behaviors in normal children. An example of such a book is Azrin and Foxx's (1974) volume on toilet training the normal child.

On the other hand, the literature on self-care training of the retarded and handicapped child is substantial, as the *Publication List* of the National Association for Retarded Citizens indicates (1974). Additional references on behavioral procedures for self-care training of the retarded child include publications by Bensberg (1965), Bensberg, Colwell, and Cassell (1965), Foxx and Azrin (1974), Mahoney, Van Wagenen, and Meyerson (1971), O'Brien, Bugle, and Azrin (1972).

3. *Social abilities: refinements and elaborations of behavior toward adults and peers.* Social abilities refer to a child's knowing how to respond to adults and peers. What he does in relation to adults and peers, when he does it, and how he does it depend on the social practices of his family, his immediate social group. In other words, the occasion (discriminative stimulus) on which a young child responds and the forms his social responses take are a result of the contingencies family members have provided in the course of family living, with operant modeling playing a major role. A child's ability in relation to the physical environment is established according to the same kind of dynamics: his jumping over a foot-high pile of building blocks (the form of the response for that physical object) is largely dependent on the properties of the blocks, such as their height or bulk, and his past interactions with similar obstacles. If he clears the hurdle, his jumping behavior in relation to those blocks and similar objects is reinforced; if he lands among the blocks and hurts himself, he is punished by the natural consequences and his behavior on future similar occasions is altered.

When a young child has opportunities to play with children approximately his own age, the social abilities he acquires depend upon his history with members of his family, the contingencies provided by his peers (Charlesworth & Hartup, 1967), and the practices, including social standards and values, of the supervising adults: parents, relatives, teachers, friends, and babysitters (Hart, Reynolds, Baer, Browley, & Harris, 1968).

The acquisition of social abilities together with the acquisition of self-care behaviors described above, often referred to as the development of autonomy and independency (Gewirtz, 1972; and Maccoby & Masters, 1970), tend to generate what adults consider to be problem behaviors. Normative studies, for example, show that three-year-olds "want" to be independent of adult assistance and become difficult to handle, and that four- and five-year-olds gradually become more friendly and cooperative and try to avoid social disapproval (Bossard & Boll, 1960). The development of initial independent behaviors is probably slow and erratic not because of its inherent complexities, as might be said of learning to read, but because (1) the antecedent social stimuli (a word, a smile, a frown from a parent) and the setting factors (a period of family grief because of the death of a relative) are typically subtle and thus are not always attended or responded to, (2) the response topographies vary widely in similar functional situations as in the several different prescribed ways of greeting an adult, and (3) the response contingencies are frequently absent or long delayed.

Social abilities in relation to adults.   Social abilities in relation to adults may be divided into two kinds: (1) behaving in ways to obtain reinforcers through the behavior of others (response differentiation), and (2) following instructions (stimulus control).

Behaving in ways to obtain reinforcers through the activities of others pertains to the acquisition of socially acceptable requesting behavior: getting others to do things for you in ways that are mutually reinforcing (Bijou & Baer, 1965; and Skinner, 1957). While some classes of such behavior may originate in respondent behavior, such as crying because of stomach pains, they may soon acquire operant properties starting with "spoiled" crying, proceeding to sounds ("eh-eh-eh"), and then to words and gestures. After the young child masters one-word sentences, short phrases, and short sentences, additional contingencies are imposed to encourage him to make his requests in words consistent with the family's concept of courtesy and good manners. Often he is instructed, and sometimes reinforced, for qualifying his requests with words like "Please," "Thank you," or "Excuse me."

Following instructions may be defined as one's ability to make the appropriate response to a verbal request or command (Striefel & Wetherby, 1973). It consists of doing something for others and thereby provide them with reinforcers. Following instructions ranges from a child's attending responses ("Look at me while I'm talking to you") to carrying out complex instructions such as borrowing a cup of sugar from the next door neighbor, or putting things away and getting ready to go out to the schoolyard for a play period. Many of these behaviors are established and maintained through modeling, others through response contingencies alone, and still others through a combination of instructions and response contingencies.

Although few studies have been conducted on the functional relationship between instructions and the formation of appropriate responses in the homes of normal children, at least one study has been carried out in a preschool (Schutte & Hopkins, 1970). Here it was demonstrated that teacher attention contingent upon the child's following instructions was a necessary condition for strengthening and maintaining that class of behavior. However, there have been several studies done in the home and preschool on emotionally disturbed (e.g., Sloane, Johnston, & Bijou, 1967; Wahler, 1969; and Zeilberger, Sampsen, & Sloane, 1968) and developmentally retarded children (e.g., Striefel & Wetherby, 1973; and Whiteman, Zakaras, & Chardos, 1971). In all instances the investigators were concerned with evaluating the conditions that made following instructions functional for these two classes of deviant children. In a sense, these investigators were contributing to the literature on child behavior therapy.

Social abilities in relation to peers. In the American culture, the development of peer social abilities comes after the child has developed a social repertory in relation to adults. Therefore, the social abilities of a child in relation to peers are a function of his history with members of his family, his interactions with peers, and the practices of supervising adults. Because a young child's initial opportunities to learn these behaviors usually take place in play settings, a taxonomy of peer social abilities would greatly overlap with the classification of play discussed in Chapter 2. Nevertheless a few comments might be made about peer social abilities.

Social abilities in relation to peers involve treating a peer not as a structural and dynamic physical object but as a biological and behaving person. Examples of such behavior include touching each other's face and body, listening and explaining, taking turns in the use of equipment and materials, and sharing possessions (Stone & Church, 1973).

The transition from responses to peer-as-object to peer-as-person is usually gradual and erratic requiring considerable adult supervision because the child is required to learn acceptable ways of managing the emotional behavior that generates from chain breaking or frustration.

SUMMARY

A well-known characteristic of the basic stage of early development is the rapid increase in the number of things a child learns to do in relation to his environment. These performances, which are mostly refinements and elaborations of abilities acquired in the basic stage, are conceptualized here as a category of cognitive behavior.

An ability is viewed here not as a capacity or "a possession" but rather as the probability of occurrence of an operant in an operant class (a family of operants which performs the same function, e.g., the various ways a child may hold a pencil in drawing a house) with a form or topography that has been reinforced in a given situation. This definition of an ability could easily mislead one into believing that it is a simple stimulus-response relationship or "habit." It is in fact a complex interaction consisting of three phases: (1) attending (paying attention to the situation), (2) perceiving (categorizing the situation), and (3) effecting (responding in a form that was previously reinforced in that situation). Further, each phase in the interactional sequence is analyzed into four components: (1) discriminative stimulus or occasion, (2) operant response, (3) reinforcing stimulus, and (4) setting event (See Figure 3-1, page 43).

The large number of abilities acquired in the basic stage may be divided conveniently on the basis of the situations in which they occur, viz: (1) body management and locomotion skills in relation to the organismic environment (a child's own biological structure functioning), (2) manual performances in relation to the physical environment, and (3) verbal behavior (with a high saturation of "manners") in relation to the social environment.

The development of abilities in relation to both the organismic and physical environments increases rapidly during most of the basic stage compared to the rate of development of abilities in relation to the social environment. However, they slow down relative to this point of reference near the end of this period. These shifts in the relative rates of development may be attributed in large measure to changes in organismic factors (biological maturation) in the early part of the basic stage and to changes in social factors in the later part of this period.

REFERENCES

Adams, J. A. Motor behavior. In M. H. Marx (Ed.), *Learning: Processes*. Toronto, Ont.: Macmillan, 1969. Pp. 481–507.

Ames, L. B. & Ilg, F. L. The developmental point of view with special reference to the principle of reciprocal neuromotor intervening. *Journal of Genetic Psychology*, 1964, *105*, 195–209.

Anastasi, A. *Psychological testing*. (3rd ed.) New York: Macmillan, 1968.

Azrin, N. H. & Foxx, R. M. *Toilet training in less than a day: How to do it*. New York: Simon & Schuster, 1974.

Becker, W. C. *Parents are teachers.* Champaign, Ill.: Research Press, 1971.

Belmont, L. & Birch, H. G. Lateral dominance and right-left awareness in normal children. *Child Development*, 1963, *34*, 257–70.

Bensberg, G. J. (Ed.) *Teaching the mentally retarded: A handbook for ward personnel.* Atlanta, Ga.: Southern Regional Education Board, 1965.

Bensberg, G. J., Colwell, C. N., & Cassell, R. H. Teaching the profoundly retarded self-help activities by behavior shaping techniques. *American Journal of Mental Deficiency*, 1965, *69*, 674–79.

Bijou, S. W. & Baer, D. M. *Child development I: A systematic and empirical theory.* Englewood Cliffs, N.J.: Prentice-Hall, 1961.

Bijou, S. W. & Baer, D. M. *Child development II: Universal stage of infancy.* Englewood Cliffs, N.J.: Prentice-Hall, 1965.

Bossard, J. H. S. & Boll, E. S. *The sociology of child development.* (3rd ed.) New York: Harper & Row, 1960.

Charlesworth, R. & Hartup, W. W. Positive social reinforcement in nursery school peer groups. *Child Development*, 1967, *38*, 993–1002.

Cronbach, L. J. *Essentials of psychological testing.* (3rd ed.) New York: Harper & Row, 1970.

Dennis, W. Infant development under conditions of restricted practice and of minimum social stimulation. *Genetic Psychology Monographs*, 1941, *23*, 143–89.

Dennis, W. Causes of retardation among institutional children: Iran. *The Journal of Genetic Psychology*, 1960, *96*, 47–59.

Eichorn, D. Physiological development. In P. H. Mussen (Ed.), *Carmichael's manual of child psychology.* New York: John Wiley, 1970. Pp. 157–283.

Ferster, C. B. & Perrott, M. C. *Behavior principles.* Englewood Cliffs, N.J.: Prentice-Hall, 1968.

Fitts, P. M. Perceptual-motor skill learning. In A. W. Melton (Ed.), *Categories of human learning.* New York: Academic Press, 1964. Pp. 224–86.

Foxx, R. M. & Azrin, N. H. *Toilet training the retarded.* Champaign, Ill.: Research Press, 1974.

Gesell, A. The ontogenesis of infant behavior. In L. Carmichael (Ed.), *Manual of child psychology.* (2nd ed.) New York: John Wiley, 1954. Pp. 335–73.

Gesell, A. & Ilg, F. L. *Child development: An introduction to human growth.* New York: Harper & Row, 1949.

Gewirtz, J. L. *Attachment and dependency.* New York: Winston, 1972.

Hall, R. V., Axelrod, S., Tyler, L., Grief, E., Jones, F. C., & Robertson, R. Modification of behavior problems in the home with a parent as observer and experimenter. *Journal of Applied Behavior Analysis*, 1972, *5*, 53–64.

Hart, B. M., Reynolds, N. J., Baer, D. M., Brawley, E. R., & Harris, F. R. Effect on contingent and non-contingent social reinforcement on the cooperative play of a preschool child. *Journal of Applied Behavior Analysis*, 1968, *1*, 73–76.

Hildreth, G. The development and training of hand dominance: I. Characteristics of handedness. *The Journal of Genetic Psychology*, 1949, 75, 197–220.

Hildreth, G. The development and training of hand dominance: IV. The development of problems associated with handedness. *The Journal of Genetic Psychology*, 1950, 76, 39–100.

Kagan, J. & Kogan, N. Individual variation in cognitive processes. In P. H. Mussen (Ed.), *Carmichael's manual of child psychology*. New York: John Wiley, 1970. P. 1275.

Lipsitt, L. P., Pederson, L. J., & Delucia, C. A. Conjugate reinforcement of operant responding in infants. *Psychonomic Science*, 1966, *4*, 67–68.

McIntire, R. W. *For love of children*. Del Mar, Calif.: CRM Books, 1970.

Maccoby, E. E. & Masters, J. Attachment and dependency. In P. H. Mussen (Ed.), *Carmichael's manual of child psychology*. Vol. 2. (3rd ed.) New York: John Wiley, 1970. Pp. 73–158.

Mahoney, K., Van Wagenen, R. K., & Meyerson, L. Toilet training of normal and retarded children. *Journal of Applied Behavior Analysis*, 1971, *4*, 173–81.

National Association for Retarded Citizens. *Publication List*. Arlington, Texas: Author, 1974. [*Address:* 2709 Avenue E East]

O'Brien, F., Bugle, C., & Azrin, N. H. Training and maintaining a retarded child's proper eating. *Journal of Applied Behavior Analysis*, 1972, *5*, 67–72.

Patterson, G. R. & Gullion, M. E. *Living with children*. Champaign, Ill.: Research Press, 1968.

Schutte, R. C. & Hopkins, B. L. The effects of teacher attention on following instructions in a kindergarten class. *Journal of Experimental Analysis of Behavior*, 1970, *8*, 117–22.

Skinner, B. F. *Verbal behavior*. Englewood Cliffs, N.J.: Prentice-Hall, 1957.

Skinner, B. F. *The technology of teaching*. Englewood Cliffs, N.J.: Prentice-Hall, 1968.

Skinner, B. F. *Contingencies of reinforcement: A theoretical analysis*. Englewood Cliffs, N.J.: Prentice-Hall, 1969.

Sloane, H. N., Johnston, M. G., & Bijou, S. W. Successive modification of aggressive behavior and aggressive fantasy play by management of contingencies. *Journal of Child Psychology & Psychiatry*, 1967, *8*, 217–26.

Stone, L. J. & Church, J. *Childhood and adolescence*. (3rd ed.) New York: Random House, 1973.

Striefel, S. & Wetherby, B. Instruction-following behavior of a retarded child and its controlling stimuli. *Journal of Applied Behavior Analysis*, 1973, *6*, 663–70.

Tanner, J. M. Physical growth. In P. H. Mussen (Ed.), *Carmichael's manual of child psychology*. New York: John Wiley, 1970. Pp. 77–155.

Thompson, H. Physical growth. In L. Carmichael (Ed.), *Manual of child psychology.* (2nd ed.) New York: John Wiley, 1954. Pp. 292–334.

Wahler, R. G. Oppositional children: A quest for parental reinforcement control. *Journal of Applied Behavior Analysis,* 1969, *2,* 159–70.

Whitman, T. L., Zakaras, M., & Chardos, S. Effects of reinforcement and guidance procedures on instruction-following behavior on severely retarded children. *Journal of Applied Behavior Analysis,* 1971, *4,* 283–90.

Zeilberger, J., Sampsen, S. E., & Sloane, H. N., Jr. Modification of a child's problem behaviors in the home with the mother as therapist. *Journal of Applied Behavior Analysis,* 1968, *1,* 47–53.

4

Cognitive Behavior:
Knowledge and Problem Solving

Traditionally, knowledge is treated as a "thing" acquired, stored, and brought forth as needed. The information theory of behavior, for example, unflatteringly likens the human being to a computer that receives stimuli (input), processes them through mental operations, stores them in a "memory bank" (throughput), and retrieves them on demand (output). The Piaget theory of development also treats knowledge as an entity: "Knowledge does not merely derive from the taking in of external data; the organism in interacting with the environment transforms or constructs external reality into an object of knowledge" (Furth, 1971, p. 295). In contrast, we define knowledge here as learned behavior controlled by antecedent stimuli. In the jargon of behavior analysis, knowledge is *stimulus control* (Terrace, 1966) and consists of a series of interactions with an attending phase, a perceiving phase (including perceptual reaction), and a doing-something-about-it, or affecting, phase (see Chapter 3). To ask where knowledge is when one is not using it is like asking where one's lap is when one is standing.

The following is an example of a knowledge sequence. You are sitting at a picnic table in a park talking with friends. Someone taps you on the back. You stop talking and turn around and look (an attending response) and "see" that it is a boy (a perceiving response) and you behave accordingly (an effecting response), "Hello. What can I do for you?" Your attention and question prompt (set the occasion for) the boy to talk to you. He asks, "Did you see a little brown and black dog?" Your reply is a category of knowledge (verbal behavior about current and past events), "Yes, I saw a little brown and black dog running in that direction." The child says, "Thanks" and runs off in the indicated direction.

Figure 4-1 is a diagram of the sequence showing the attending, perceiving (including perceptual reaction), and effecting phases, and the

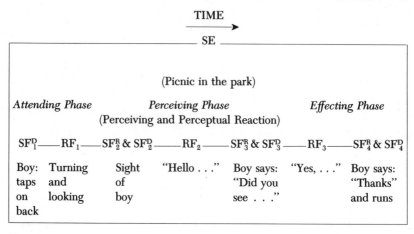

Figure 4-1. Functional analysis of a knowledge response

analysis of each into discriminative stimulus function (SF^D), operant behavior function (RF), reinforcing function (SF^R), and setting factors (SF). The symbol meanings in Figure 4-1 are:

SE   The setting event or factor or the circumstances prevailing over the entire interactional sequence: You are talking with a friend sitting at a picnic table in the park.

Attending Phase

SF^D_1 A tactual stimulus: Tap on your back.

RF_1 You make an attending response to the tap: You turn around, look in the direction of the source of stimulation, and see a boy (presumably the one who tapped you).

SF^R_2 The sight of the boy (stimulus) has a reinforcing function in that turning around and looking (RF_1) clarifies the stimulus (Lipsitt, Pederson, & Delucia, 1966).

Perceiving Phase (Including Perceptual Reaction)

SF^D_2 The sight of the boy also has a discriminative function, that is to say, it sets the occasion for you to interpret what you perceive or see (RF_2).

RF_2 You say to yourself something like, "It's a boy who wants to talk to me" and you respond on that interpretation (i.e., make a perceptual reaction) by saying aloud: "Hello. What can I do for you?"

SF^R_3 The boy says, "Did you see a little brown and black dog?" This reply is a stimulus with a reinforcing function for your greeting and inquiry (RF_2).

Effecting Phase

SF_3^D The boy's question is also a discriminative stimulus for your next response (RF_3).

RF_3 You make an effecting response, and in this case it is a knowledge response: "Yes, I saw a little brown and black dog running in that direction."

SF_4^R Your words produce a reinforcing stimulus (SF_4^R): "Thanks" and a discrimi-
&   native stimulus (SF_5^D) for the boy's next response: Running in the direction
SF_5^D indicated.

Knowledge subsumes a wide range of activities: (1) simple discriminative behavior (putting edible rather than nonedible things in the mouth); (2) conceptual or abstract behavior (sorting blocks according to color); (3) verbal behavior in relation to current and past events (describing what you saw on the way to school); and (4) behavior in relation to the way things work (heating water to make it bubble and steam).

Two features of this classification scheme should be noted. First, the interactions in these categories are by no means independent of one another. Not only are they interrelated, but they are ordered roughly in their degree of complexity: simple discriminative behavior, conceptual behavior, behavior in relation to current and past events, and behavior in relation to how things work (cause-and-effect relationships). Second, included in each category are interactions in relation to one's own biological structure (discriminating one part of one's anatomy from another), physiological functioning (certain foods give you indigestion), and behavior (what you did, what you are doing, or what you plan to do).

CATEGORIES OF KNOWLEDGE

Simple Discriminative Behavior

Simple discriminative behavior may involve nonverbal responses (on entering a school building a child turns to the right to go to her classroom), or verbal responses (when asked whether the color on the left or right is darker, she says "The color on the left"), and it may be in relation to nonverbal situations (the corridors of a school building) or verbal situations (a child is asked, "Should you use the word *good* or *well* in describing Herbie's skill on the jungle gym?"). In addition, simple discriminations may be made between two objects or situations, as in the above examples, or discriminations may be made between doing something or not doing something. Whether a child responds or does not respond to a class of stimuli depends on his reinforcement history with such stimuli and with others similar to them. For example, a child may underestimate the distance between himself and the ground and jump off a high box. Besides hurting himself, his mother reprimands him for not "using his head." These aversive consequences will decrease the probability of that behavior occurring in that situation, at least for a while. This example also illustrates that "judgment" is differential behavior in relation to environmental events. In this case the events are in relation to the physical world. Differential behavior may occur in relation to the organismic world (differentiating between hunger pains and a stomach ache), and to the social world (differentiating between a moral and an immoral act, as discussed in Chapter 6).

A neonate shows differential respondent and operant behavior to a variety of stimuli under controlled laboratory conditions. Through his interactions with objects and the consequences of these interactions he begins to respond differentially to patterns of physical properties. Responses to people are made on the basis of a constellation of physical, social, and biological characteristics (size, dress, tone of voice, or vigor of movement). These discriminations generalize and serve him well. Through continued acculturation a young child makes finer and finer distinctions; for example, he makes social distinctions between parents and siblings, physical distinctions between wet and dry things, and organismic distinctions between his own biological makeup and the biological makeup of others.

Simple discriminative behavior, imitation, and modeling. In most instances of discriminative behavior, the discriminative stimulus and the operant behavior have *different forms.* When the nursery school teacher says, "Now, it's time for painting, Henry," the discriminative stimulus is her instruction to Henry; the operant is Henry's going to an easel, picking up a brush, and painting a house. In imitative behavior or modeling (note that we treat these terms as synonyms), the discriminative stimulus and the operant have *similar forms.* The similarity may be in the *structures* of the discriminative stimulus and the operant response. The discriminative stimulus may be the model's clapping his hands and instruction to "Do this," and the operant response, the child clapping his hands. The similarity may also be in the *products* of the behavior. The discriminative stimulus may be the presentation of a drawing of a circle, with the instruction "Make one like this," and the child produces a circle drawn on paper. The model's behavior is reinforced by the child's imitative response; the child's behavior is reinforced by the model's response ("That's right") and sometimes by natural reinforcers (looking to the top of a tree in imitation of a model's behavior and catching sight of a ripe peach).

An adequate analysis of imitative behavior includes an account of the child's social history conceptualized as an interrelated succession of discriminative stimuli, response functions, reinforcing stimuli, and setting factors (Baer & Sherman, 1964; Gewirtz, 1971; and Steinman, 1970a). Early in life a baby discovers that matching his behavior, even crudely, with that of others tends to be reinforced, and that not matching (or doing the opposite) is generally ignored or gently reprimanded. Initial matching behavior involves vocal and verbal responses; later, when a baby is able to approximate the motor responses of others, eager elders engage him in matching play (patty-cake, patty-cake, bye-bye, etc.). Such play is highly reinforcing, and as a result, the responses readily take new forms and the stimuli acquire new discriminative and reinforcing functions (Brigham & Sherman, 1968 and Burgess, Burgess, & Esveldt, 1970). Because of a history with intermittent reinforcement and with social setting factors, an average six-month-old infant has a strong tendency to imitate others, even without explicit instructions to do so (Steinman, 1970b). The probability of imitative behavior is increased further when the model possesses discriminating and reinforcing characteristics similar to those of individuals the child has imitated in the past, that is, the child tends to imitate another adult or his preschool teacher (Wilson, 1958). Furthermore, the greater the similarity between a mother and a teacher in physical and social characteristics, the more the child tends to imitate the teacher and to identify her with the mother (Bandura & Huston, 1961; Bandura, Ross, & Ross, 1963; and Mussen & Parker, 1965).

Conceptual or Abstract Behavior

Most of the child development literature treats *concept* as a mental entity, that is, as something formed by mentally combining the characteristics or particulars of a class of objects or events (Flavell, 1970). Kagan (1966), for example, views a concept as a fundamental agent of intellectual work, its structure changing with development. In contrast, a concept is treated here as discriminated behavior in relation to aspects of stimuli. Mechner (1965) and others have pointed out that in simple discriminative behavior, a child responds to differences between stimulus classes (building materials as opposed to fabrics) whereas in conceptual behavior, he responds to common aspects of stimuli *within* stimulus classes (classifying building materials on the basis of substance—wood, metal, or plastic—and fabrics on the basis of the texture—wool, cotton, or rayon).

Glaser (1968) points out some of the salient characteristics of conceptualizing behavior:

The formation of concepts and the process of abstraction are probably never complete. Perhaps as the child grows up, the concept of river and the concept of redness become reasonably stable, but in the course of living, a challenging instance usually waits around the bend. In school such concepts as subtraction, a grammatical class like prepositions, longitude in geography, and mass and weight in physics, constantly grow and change so that response of the individual is probably never quite restricted to a specific collection of properties, although for many "practical" purposes a particular set of properties will dictate the student's behavior. The dimensions by which concepts are abstracted and classified may be obvious, such as particular colors and shapes; or more subtle, such as those which define Mozart's music and the paintings of the Dutch masters; or extremely subtle, such as the properties that define instances of justice and freedom. Concept dimensions can be direct perceptual experiences such as light and sound, or they can be indirect, that is, experienced through words and symbols. Concepts also have different structures, depending upon how their dimensions are combined to form the concept. They may be additive or conjunctive, such as orange and round, or they can be relational, like the concept of time (pp. 2–3).

A child's conceptual repertories play a critical role in his social and intellectual interactions. In fact, a child's score on an intelligence test is closely related to the extent of his conceptual repertory. The vocabulary score of an intelligence test such as the Stanford-Binet Intelligence Scale (Terman & Merrill, 1960) correlates very high with the total test score. Therefore, knowing a child's score on the vocabulary test enables one to estimate with fair accuracy his total test score. Furthermore, responses to the vocabulary part of an intelligence test such as the Wechsler-Bellevue Scales of Intelligence (Wechsler, 1967) are often scored on the basis of quality, with concrete definitions (in terms of the use of an object) given a lower score than abstract definitions (in terms of classification or attributes). For example, young children tend to define an orange as "You eat it" or "It tastes good" whereas older children more often define it as "a fruit" or "a round, orange-colored citrus fruit that tastes sweet." A cognitive approach to child development would attribute the qualitative differences in conceptual responses to differences in cognitive structures.

An alternative interpretation is that these differences are a function of differences in past interactions a child has had with these stimuli. In other words, a child may not give the required level of conceptual response because he has not had the kind of interactional history that would enable him to acquire such a refined concept; or perhaps he did have a history that did allow him to develop such a concept but it did not include positive contingencies for more elaborate descriptive statements. In any event, the child's response is a description of his interactions with the object (e.g., "An orange is to eat" or "You eat it. It tastes good"). The conditions that control different responses during intelligence testing may be revealed by further analysis and assessment. For example, we may survey the objects that are likely to evoke the word "orange" from children at two different age levels. In so doing we would find (1) children who say "orange" only when shown an orange, and not in response to any other object including a lemon and a grapefruit, (2) children who say "orange" in response to all citrus fruits, (3) children who say "orange" in response to all small round objects including fruits, and (4) children who do not say "orange" to any of the objects presented including oranges and other citrus fruits. We would also find that older children typically respond in categories 1 and 2, and younger children in categories 3 and 4. This type of investigative procedure shows "where each child is" with respect to the concept "orange." Other relationships between repertories of cognitive behavior and scores on intelligence tests, as well as the results of competence tests, will be discussed in the next chapter.

Since isolated properties of objects do not occur in nature, people must arrange relevant discriminative stimuli and contingencies of reinforcement in order for a child to learn concepts. A mother who in the normal course of family living names things ("That's a horse."), points out the critical features of similar objects ("A tricycle has three wheels."), draws out conceptual behavior ("What do you call that?"), encourages and confirms an appropriate response ("Yes, that's a car."), and gently corrects misconceptions ("That's not a pony; it's a big dog.") provides a positive, stimulating home situation which, among other things, is conducive to learning concepts. It should be apparent that mere exposure to a variety of interesting objects and events—conditions that correlate highly with the socioeconomic status of the family—does not guarantee that a child will acquire the essential concepts of his society. Exposure to objects and events must be accompanied by people who are willing and able to help a child learn to respond differentially between and within stimulus classes, as prescribed by society.

One of the goals of preschool education is to help a child acquire new concepts. It becomes abundantly clear that such learning is slow and difficult when one approaches this teaching task carefully and systematically through programmed instructional techniques. For example, Etzel and her students studied the procedures for teaching three basic academic concepts to preschool children. One investigation by Bybel and Etzel (1973) dealt with helping a child to make a left-right visual discrimination between the letters *b* and *d*. A child was pretrained by teaching him to make the proper phonetic responses to two characters in an illustrated story: "Boughty Bee," a line drawing of a mother and baby kangaroo, and "Mother Duh," a line drawing of an elf sitting in front of a pole. Embedded in the "Boughty Bee" picture was the letter *b*, and in the "Mother Duh" picture, the letter *d*. Teaching involved fading-out the irrelevant cues (all of the picture except the letter *b* or *d*) and fading-in the criterion cues (making the letters stand out more and more boldly until each became the only figure on the page) so that, at the end of training, a child called the letter *b*, "Boughty Bee," and the letter *d*, "Mother Duh." Mastery of these verbal responses enabled a child to make the required left-right visual discrimination. Another study by Dixon, Spradlin, and Etzel (1973) was concerned with teaching the concept of "in front of" in spatial relationships to children with poor articulation. The program consisted of pictures in which a ball, leaf, heart, or tree was over, under, behind, or in front of a child, bear, duck, or chicken. In the training, the distractors (the objects over, under, or behind) were faded out and the relevant cues were faded in (the objects in front of the central figure were made more dominant). In addition, the child was instructed to move his finger from the central figure to the object. That requirement was discontinued (faded out) as training progressed. The findings showed that the addition of a motor response (movement of finger from central figure to object) to a pointing response facilitated acquisition and retention of the concept. A third study by Schilmoeller and Etzel (1973) dealt with the role of discriminative stimuli in preparing material for teaching the concepts of color, "sun," "man," and "tree" so that the child commits few or no errors. The investigation demonstrated the effects that criterion-related and non-criterion-related discriminative stimuli can have upon concept learning and how discriminative stimuli should be designed to make them functional.

A concept, then, is an interaction in which operant behavior is controlled by a property, or a combination of properties, of an object or event in the physical world which includes signs (e.g., words and numbers) and symbols (e.g., pictures and diagrams), and the physical aspects of biological phenomena (e.g., the body as a thing) and social phenomena (e.g., the physical characteristics of one person bowing to another). The dimensions of objects that control a child's behavior can be determined by observing what the child does in various situations. In watching a child who was asked to pick out the knives from a collection of miscellaneous objects, we note that the child picks only those items with a cutting edge despite their differences in material, size, color, and form. We may rightly conclude that the child "knows" the concept of knife.

Glaser's description of conceptualizing behavior (1968) serves well as a summary:

. . . in our rich, challenging, multi-stimulational environment, concepts provide a kind of stability, and concept learning is a process of constant revision to maintain this stability. The concept we call "river" can be applied to a single object or instance, like the Monongahela River, but is not properly restricted to the one instance; it applies to a class of instances with properties and dimensions in common. The child who applies the term "river" to only a single object of his experience has an incomplete concept. It will take some time, learning time, for him to use the concept in a way that is socially standardized, so that he can share the concept with his fellows but also can use it inventively and metaphorically to talk about a "river of fear" or a "river of generosity" (Brownell & Hendrickson, 1950). In learning to do this, he will make some errors and have some difficulties in applying the concept of river when contrasted to a stream or a creek (pp. 1–2).

Self-concepts and self-reactions. Just as a child develops concepts about objects, symbols, and the physical dimensions of the biological and social worlds, so does he acquire concepts about his own biological and behavioral makeup. He classifies his physique as long and lean, or short and fat; his biological functioning as high energy or low energy; his social behaviors as shy and withdrawn, or outgoing and gregarious; and his intellectual ability as inferior, average, or superior. These self-reactions, sometimes referred to as attitudes toward self, produce stimuli that have discriminative and setting properties that play a part in determining behavior in many social situations. How a child solves an arithmetic problem at the blackboard and describes his solution to the class will depend on (1) his history with arithmetic problems and in talking to groups, (2) setting factors (a bad cold), (3) his reactions to his own behavior and to the behavior of the particular teacher and the children in the class. A self-concept, like all conceptual behavior, is established and modified by interactions with people, or the social environment.

In some theories of child development (Jersild, 1960), the self-concept is treated as the key process governing behavior. In these approaches, the term is usually defined phenomenologically. For example, Wylie (1961) defines the self-concept as "the subject's conscious perceptions of his environment and of his self as he sees it in relation to that environment." Since the subject's conscious perceptions of the environment and how he perceives his self in relation to it can be known to another person only by the verbal account of the subject, such a definition involves correlated rather than functional relationships. That is to say, it involves relationships between two response classes: a person's actions and his verbal responses to these actions. For example, in a nursery school, one might say to a child who is playing alone, "I see you're playing by yourself, and not with the other children," to which the child might answer, "They play rough and they could hurt me." Phenomenologically, this response would be taken to indicate that the child perceives the social situation as being hostile and he perceives himself as being readily hurt if he were to participate. The child's comment about his behavior is interpreted as revealing his perceptions that are the causes of his nonparticipation. From a functional point of view, the same response would be interpreted as suggesting that the social situation might be aversive to the child and that certain probes (e.g., presenting him with test situations, or observing him in other social situations) are necessary to determine whether this is in fact the case and/or whether other nonaversive conditions (e.g., the strength of the intrinsic reinforcers in the current activity) play a part.

The self-concept as a vaguely defined attitude toward oneself, or as an inaccessible hypothetical process governing behavior, has led to theoretical confusion and requires a thorough reevaluation (Coller, 1971; and Wylie, 1961). On the other hand, the self-concept as an interaction under the control of one's own biological and behavioral characteristics has an important place in a functional analysis of human development. Among other things, it is related to self knowledge, discussed in the next section.

Verbal Behavior in Relation to Current and Past Events

When we say that a child knows what is happening or what happened sometime in the past, we are usually referring to his probable responses to questions about his reactions to (1) his own behavior or self knowledge ("I think I'm big enough to go to school.") or to ongoing external events ("The men are putting out the fire."), (2) past events pertaining to his own behavior or the behavior of others that he had observed ("My stomach feels funny when I ride on a roller coaster." "My mother had fried eggs for breakfast."), and (3) past events he has not observed but which have been acquired through contact with the verbal behavior of others, as well as his contact with pictures, printed materials, and the electronic media ("Abraham Lincoln was a brave man because he freed the slaves.").

A young child's accounts of what he is doing, what he has done, or what he has observed—categories (1) and (2) above—are only as accurate and complete as those around him require. If parents, siblings, and nursery school teachers regularly ask a child what he is doing, thinking, planning, and feeling or what he did while playing, visiting, or at school, and differentially reinforce his responses, he develops verbal skills in relating self-reactions and interactions. On the other hand, a child whose parents, siblings, and teachers rarely ask such questions has little opportunity to develop refined self-accounting and reporting repertories. An informal study at the University of Illinois Child Behavior Preschool revealed that developmentally accelerated four-year-old children could describe little of their past behavior even immediately following the completion of an activity. With training in verbalizing about events as they occurred—saying what they were doing at the time they were doing it—and reinforcement for accurate recall, the children's reports improved markedly. Risley and Hart (1968) made the same observation with four-year-old disadvantaged black children and also demonstrated that the nonverbal behavior of these children could be altered by reinforcing the related verbal behavior. Childrearing practices and early educational procedures that reinforce recall strengthen a child's knowledge of present and past events and also help him to discriminate between describing and interpreting events, and between fantasy and reality (interactions with external events).

In order to be able to describe the activities of contemporary and historical figures and significant cultural and physical events that he does not directly observe—category (3) above—the preschool child must have opportunities to describe what he sees in representative forms, such as in pictures, films, TV, etc. and to paraphrase what he hears. These efforts must be systematically reinforced. The ability of a young child to respond to his own verbal behavior helps him build a verbal repertory about his society, that is, he comes to know the "story of his society" as it has been interpreted by the community.

Training a child to observe and report on his own and others' behavior and to paraphrase the verbal behavior of others expands his repertory of knowledge about past events and also improves his ability as a problem-solver, in that the range of his responses for altering problem situations is increased.

Behavior in Relation to the Way Things Work

A person's knowledge about how things work is judged by his answers to questions about cause-and-effect relationships and/or his behavior in actual situations (letting some air out of a balloon to make it smaller, or calling someone's name to get him to look in your direction). The preschool child's knowledge of cause-and-effect relationships is variable; some of his notions are completely faulty, being illogical, distorted, and magical in content; some are partially faulty; and some are correct (Hurlock, 1972). Cognitive theory attempts to account for this kind of mixture in terms of (1) the way the child perceives the environment (this is known as the phenomenological environment), and (2) the hypothetical status of his thought processes on a scale of centricity ranging from self-centered (egocentric) to society-centered (sociocentric). On the other hand, behavior theory seeks answers for these variations through an analysis of the meaning of certain stimuli to the child (their stimulus functions deter-mined by probes or tests) and his interactional history with cause-and-effect relationships.

Clearly, then, the preschool child's interactional history with cause-and-effect relationships is made up of the direct and indirect contacts (through the verbal and nonverbal behavior of others) he has had with actual events. The number of direct contacts is limited not only by his brief history but also by the restrictions imposed by biological immaturity, the economic resources of his family, and the protective practices of his parents. His indirect contacts, consisting of what he hears, sees, and is told by members of his family and the mass media are also limited, and at times, distorted. If the parents provide inaccurate information either because they do not know the correct answers or because they are reluctant to "tell the truth," particularly in relation to sexual matters, the child acquires a faulty knowledge of causal relationships. And if TV and radio programs and movies provide explanations in terms of superstitions, accidental happen-ings, and magic, the child is apt to acquire misconceptions (Maccoby & Wilson, 1957; and Thayer & Pronko, 1958). It is apparent, then, that knowledge about cause-and-effect relationships is more closely related to a child's interactional history than to his age or his intelligence test score, and that the best developed and most accurate knowledge of causal relationships is a result of a child's interactional history of direct contacts.

Some psychologists claim that children under seven or eight years do not truly understand cause-and-effect relationships. For these theorists, knowledge of causal relationships refers to the developmental status of hypothetical cognitive processes. However, when knowledge of cause-and-effect relationships is defined either as stating a rule or as demonstrating a functional relationship, knowledge of cause-and-effect relationships is observed in young children even at the time they first engage in exploratory behavior.

There are at least two ways of studying a child's repertory of cause-and-effect relationships. One consists of presenting him with the phenomenon and asking him to show how it works or to predict what will happen when some change occurs. Ausubel and Schiff (1954) used this method in studying a child's understanding of the law of gravity. Kindergarten, third- and sixth-grade children were presented with a lever and fulcrum problem with a red wooden block on one arm and an identical size green block on the other, the task being to predict which arm would fall when the support was released. Each child was given two series of trials, given in a counter-balanced order. In the "relevant" series, the longer arm with a same-sized block (with reference to the fulcrum) always fell as one would expect according to the law of gravity. In the "irrelevant" series, the arm (regardless of its length with reference to the fulcrum) which held the red block regularly fell for no explicable reason. The findings were that older children had more difficulty in dealing with the "irrelevant" series than did the younger children, evidently because they knew more about the law of gravity. This type of procedure for the study of a child's knowledge of cause-and-effect relationships is, of course, limited to the study of a child's reactions to phenomena that can be readily demonstrated and varied.

Another way of studying a child's knowledge about how things work is by interviewing him. An advantage of this method is that it can be used to investigate knowledge of *any* causal relationship; a disadvantage is that the findings may be affected by the relationship between the interviewer and the interviewee. The appearance, manner, and procedure of the interviewer create discriminative stimuli that tend to increase the probability of certain classes of responses (e.g., saying "Yes" or saying "No"). Under such "pressure" to deliver answers, a child may produce a mix of distortions and knowledge in his responses (Skinner, 1957).

PROBLEM SOLVING

A mildly hungry young child eyeing a glass cookie jar on a high kitchen shelf faces a problem if he cannot figure out how to reach that shelf and get a cookie. He looks around the room, sees a chair, moves it beneath the shelf, stands on it, reaches the jar, opens it, gets a cookie, and eats it. A functional analysis of this sequence of events, diagrammed in Figure 4-2, specifies the setting event or factor (SE), which is twofold: the child is alone in the kitchen and has had no food during the past two hours. Figure 4-2 also shows that the analysis consists of four phases: attending, perceiving, altering, and effecting. A detailed account of the sequence reads as follows: An object on the shelf (SF_1^D) attracts the child's attention and he makes visual contact with it (RF_1). His attending behavior clarifies the stimulus (glass jar), which has both a reinforcing function (SF_1^R) for the attending response, and a discriminative function (SF_2^D) for the perceiving response (RF_2): "That jar has cookies in it." The glass cookie jar has a conditioned reinforcing function (SF_2^R) by virtue of the fact that the sight of cookies has been paired with eating cookies. Its location on a high shelf (SF_3^D) sets up the problem of how to reach it. The child surveys the kitchen situation, sees a chair, moves it beneath the shelf, and stands on it (SF_3). This maneuver brings him into close proximity to the jar, which is a stimulus with a reinforcing function (SF_3^R). It also sets the occasion (SF_4^D) for reaching for the jar, opening it, taking a cookie, and putting it into his mouth (RF_4).

A generalized functional definition of problem solving takes this form: Problem solving refers to interactions in which a person cannot respond immediately either to reduce ongoing deprivation of reinforcing stimuli, or to escape or avoid aversive stimuli and therefore sets about to alter the situation so that he can make a reinforceable response. The behaviors in problem solving may involve manipulating (1) physical objects and events, as in the example of the boy moving a chair and standing on it to get a cookie; (2) social conditions (putting words and sentences together in a way to convey "bad" news to someone without arousing a strong emotional reaction); (3) personal conditions (to lose weight, restricting eating to three small meals a day and no snacks); or (4) abstract conditions (transposing numbers and signs to solve an arithmetic problem). The problem-solving behaviors that lead to the solution must be in the child's repertoire; if his learning history has not included situations that developed the required responses, the problem is insoluble for him. The child in our example must be able to conceive (conceptualize) the chair as an object to

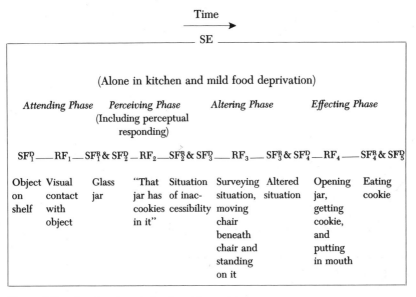

Time

SE

(Alone in kitchen and mild food deprivation)

Attending Phase	Perceiving Phase (Including perceptual responding)		Altering Phase		Effecting Phase	

SF_1^D —— RF_1 —— SF_1^R & SF_2^D — RF_2 —SF_2^R & SF_3^D —— RF_3 —— SF_3^R & SF_4^D — RF_4 —— SF_4^R & SF_5^D

Object on shelf	Visual contact with object	Glass jar	"That jar has cookies in it"	Situation of inac- cessibility	Surveying situation, moving chair beneath chair and standing on it	Altered situation	Opening jar, getting cookie, and putting in mouth	Eating cookie

Figure 4-2. Functional analysis of problem solving

stand on in order to extend his reach, and he must be able to move the chair beneath the shelf and stand on it to solve the problem, at least in that way. He may, however, have the required repertory to solve it in a different way. For example, he may slide the jar off of the shelf with a broom handle and, if he is lucky, catch it before it lands on the floor.

Problem solving should not be confused with trial-and-error learning. In problem solving an individual engages in a succession of activities that have some probability of altering the situation to enable him to make a solution response; in trial-and-error learning the individual tries one thing after another until he hits upon a solution.

Problem-solving behavior may range on a scale from "practically all overt" to "practically all covert." In our example, problem solving was near the "practically all overt" end of the scale (looking around the room, seeing the chair, pushing it into place, etc.). A different situation might produce some problem-solving behavior that would be near the "practically all covert" end of the scale. If there were no objects in the kitchen on which the child could stand to reach the cookie jar, he might *recall* where he last saw a suitable object and bring it into the kitchen. When most of the problem-solving activity is near the "practically all covert" end of the scale, it is generally called productive thinking. This kind of covert problem-solving behavior is not prevalent among children of preschool age nor are preschoolers often able to describe how they arrive at their solutions (Elkind, 1967).

Some may take issue with the statement that young children do not often engage in covert problem-solving behavior and claim that the incessant questioning typical of young children—the "whys" with which they plague their parents—is a manifestation of covert problem solving or thinking. That may be so, but there are other ways of interpreting the "why" behavior of preschoolers. Gesell and Ilg (1949) say simply that it is an inborn tendency.

Whence this Why? which becomes particularly insistent at the ages of four, five and six. It is an untaught tendency of his growing mind. It is as instinctive as his play and phantasy. It resembles a startle response evoked by new or strange situations, and is based on the inborn capacity to wonder (p. 435).

Another possibility is that this "why" behavior has a variety of social functions for the young child. He may ask a question to attract the attention of a listener (in which case any answer might do), to initiate and maintain conversation with a listener (in which case, too, any answer might do), to describe the environment (He may ask, "Why is water coming out of the dog's mouth?" instead of saying, "Water is coming out of the dog's mouth."), or to guide his own behavior (He may ask, "Why is the room dark?" instead of saying, "How do I turn on the light?"). These alternative explanations suggest that we look to research carried on in natural settings to find the various meanings (functions) that repetitive inquiries may have for a young child before jumping to the conclusion that it manifests mental problem solving or an "inborn capacity to wonder." Unfortunately this kind of research, although not complicated, has yet to be accomplished. A simple study might involve (1) taking a baseline measure of the child's asking behavior in a given situation, (2) varying the answers to his questions, and (3) determining the classes of answers that are functional for that child in that situation. The same procedure would be repeated with the same child in other situations and with different children in similar situations.

The inclusion of covert events in problem-solving behavior may seem to be inconsistent with the behavioristic assumption that psychology deals exclusively with the observable interactions between a total functioning biological individual and environmental events. But it is not inconsistent so long as the covert part of problem-solving behavior is inferred from observable events and conditions. The procedure involved is very much like that of a detective who must solve a murder. Direct knowledge of the perpetrator of the criminal act is not accessible to him because the event has already occurred. All he sees is the end-product: a dead body at the scene of the crime. He pieces together available clues, draws inferences about who might have committed the crime, and then looks for collaborative evidence, including a creditable confession from the suspect. In the same way, the psychologist cannot have direct knowledge of the cause of a solution response because the determining conditions were inaccessible to him; they occurred at a covert level within the problem solver. His job is to piece together the clues, to draw inferences about the events that occurred, and to produce data that can be used to evaluate his inferences. If the data are supportive, he has confidence that he now has some knowledge of the events that preceded problem solving. If they are not supportive, he must reexamine and reevaluate his clues, draw another set of inferences, and evaluate them on the basis of further findings.

Research on a functional analysis of problem solving by young children makes certain assumptions about the nature of the covert behavior: namely, (1) that they are verbal, nonverbal, or a combination of both; (2) that they have the same physical and functional properties as overt interactions; (3) that they have evolved from the individual's genetic and personal history; and (4) that they are a part of a sequence that is maintained ultimately by external stimuli with reinforcing properties.

A study by Parsons (1973) exemplifies such research. Preschool children were given problems that required them to count the number of figures drawn at the left side of a rectangular box and then to mark a corresponding number of dissimilar objects in a larger series at the right. Thus, a problem might consist of counting the eight stick figures on the left and then counting off and circling eight of the eleven stars displayed on the right. Children who could not do this task were systematically prompted and reinforced for counting aloud and for circling the correct number of items on the right side of the rectangular box. As training progressed, the frequency of reinforcement for mediating responses was reduced to zero, and finally, counting aloud was prohibited. Upon completion of the training, the children were able to solve the problems without resorting to overt counting. Parsons concluded, "Once developed, the mediating behaviors were maintained in the chain by the terminal, solution contingent reinforcer" (p. 84).

Parsons's findings highlight another characteristic of problem solving. An individual who has solved a problem would probably not engage in problem-solving behavior on similar occasions but would, instead, be more likely to display a smooth sequence of responses that would be described as an ability. The next time the child in our example sees the out-of-reach cookie jar, he would in all probability immediately push the kitchen chair to the shelf, stand on it, reach for the jar, open it, get a cookie, and start to munch on it. Furthermore, any other attractive objects on a high shelf would also be expected to generate similar behavior. This would be an example of stimulus generalization.

We conclude our discussion of problem solving by speculating on the conditions that make for effectiveness in this activity. One condition certainly is the extensiveness of a child's abilities and knowledge repertories and this, in large measure, is related to the opportunities and contingencies that have constituted his play history. Another condition is his ability to manipulate problem situations. Competence of this sort is enhanced by providing the child with opportunities and guidance in contrived problem situations (such as, "This picture shows a chicken in a yard with a dog. See whether you can help the chicken find its way out of the yard.") and also by situations with response contingencies that strengthen the child's ability to describe his own behavior, as discussed in the section on verbal behavior about current and past events. The third and final condition that bears on problem-solving competence relates to a child's reinforcement history for solving problems in natural settings.

Creativity, Creative Behavior, and Problem Solving

Creativity is an honorific word in our society (Wallach, 1970, p. 1211). It refers to something that is said to be beneficial to the individual, the society, and even the race (Hurlock, 1972, pp. 319–20). From time to time the term has been associated with other concepts that enjoy high esteem, namely: intelligence, talent, giftedness, intuition, invention, discovery, and originality. Recently, Skinner (1974, pp. 113–15) drew a parallel between creative thinking in human behavior and the production of "mutations" in natural selections. The rather substantial psychological literature on creativity, primarily about adults, is, in the main, devoted to (1) the products of creative behavior, such as paintings, music compositions, and scientific laws, (2) the intellectual and personality characteristics of "creative" people, and (3) the hypothetical or actual processes involved in creative behavior. Those studies concerned with creative processes, which are of central interest here because of their quest for cause-and-effect relationships, have approached the problem from the point of view of psychometric correlational analyses (Guilford, 1956; and Torrance, 1962), cognitive theory (Wallach & Kogan, 1965), and learning theory (Maltzman, 1960). Only lately has the behavior analysis approach entered into the picture through the research of Baer and his colleagues (Goetz & Baer, 1973; Goetz & Salmonson, 1972; and Holman, Goetz, & Baer, in press).

In the study of creativity, the question of definition is particularly important because many parents, teachers, and psychologists assume that "everybody" knows what it is. Since this is not so, it is essential that we ask the critical question: What is creative behavior and what are the conditions and processes that establish and maintain such behavior? We define creative behavior as a special case of problem solving. From our previous discussion of problem solving, it should be obvious that problem-solving *situations* range from trivial to momentous; problem-solving *behaviors*, from quick and easy to prolonged and deliberate; and *solutions* to problems, from ordinary to original. Creative behavior is the term applied to a problem-solving solution that is considered original. An original solution may be defined with reference to its rare occurrence in a group, as in normative or actuarial studies. When a five-year-old child arrives at an unusual solution for his age, we say he is clever; when he produces a unique solution for his age, we say he is creative. Or an original solution may refer to its rare occurrence in the history of a particular person in a single problem-solving setting, or in reference to all previous problem-solving settings. In research, all of the problem-solving episodes must be observed to ensure that the solution is in fact novel or original for a person.

Since creative behavior is not viewed here as an expression of a creative faculty but, instead, as the behavior of an individual in relation to specific environmental events, all references to this problem-solving ability must be in specific terms. Thus it is not meaningful to speak of a child as being creative; we must specify the area of his creative behavior—in music, painting, social affairs, science, mechanical technology, and so on.

According to this analysis, creative behavior can be taught. That is to say, a teacher or parent or the child himself can identify and arrange conditions and contingencies to increase the probability of producing original solutions. While applied behavior research has not yet developed the details of the most expeditious procedures for teaching creative behavior in specific subject areas, it seems clear from behavior analysis (Skinner, 1968, pp. 115–44) that such instruction should (1) help a child build extensive repertoires of abilities and knowledge; (2) provide him with opportunities, or all sorts of unusual situations, to engage in problem-solving behavior; (3) give him guidance and support in approaching new problems, and (4) withdraw assistance in such a way that the reinforcing contingencies become a part of the problem-solving behavior itself.

The research by Baer and his colleagues mentioned above aims to develop an approach to teaching creative behavior to preschool children. We shall therefore describe their work in some detail. In the first study, by Goetz and Baer (1971 & 1973), the blockbuilding behavior of three preschool girls was analyzed according to the forms produced in completed block constructions. Praise and descriptive comments about the forms produced were given contingent on the child's producing any form she had not previously constructed during the current session (but not on subsequent appearances of that form within that session). This procedure increased the number of different forms built per session. In addition, new forms (forms never seen in any of the child's blockbuilding sessions) emerged at higher rates during the period of reinforcement of first appearances of different forms than during baseline periods or during periods of reinforcement of same forms on their subsequent appearances.

In a second study on three preschool girls Goetz and Salmonson (1972) studied the separate effects of praise and descriptive reinforcement in terms of increases in new forms in easel painting. When using praise reinforcement, the teacher acknowledged a painting form as being "good" but no specific aspect was singled out for comment ("Isn't that nice," or "See what you have here."). In descriptive reinforcement, she described the specific form painted ("That's a very straight line you've painted across the paper," or "Now you're doing a zigzag back and forth."). Descriptive reinforcement was found to be more effective than praise in the production of new forms in easel painting.

In the third investigation by Holman, Goetz, and Baer (in press) two experiments were conducted, both on the problem of generalization of creative behavior. The first was concerned with the generalization of form diversity from easel painting to blockbuilding. The two preschool boys who served as subjects were socially reinforced—a combination of praise and descriptive reinforcement—for each new painting form in a session but were never reinforced for new forms in blockbuilding. For both children, reinforcement for each new painting form resulted in substantial increases in painting form diversity, which is a finding substantiating the results of the Goetz and Baer study (1971 & 1973). However, this increase was not associated with systematic changes in the children's rates of inventing new forms in blockbuilding. The authors postulated that generalization across tasks did not occur because the two activities were too dissimilar.

In the second experiment, this interpretation was put to test. The three preschool boys who served as subjects were invited to come to the laboratory twice a day, on the first occasion to do two building tasks (first with blocks, then with Lego), and on the second occasion, two art tasks (first felt-tip pen drawing, then painting). Each child was reinforced with tokens, praise, and descriptive comments for the first production of any pen-drawing form during a session. A form that may have appeared in any previous day's session was also reinforced in the current session. One child was also reinforced for new Lego constructions following reinforcement training for new pen-drawing forms. The directly treated activity, pen drawing, showed an increase in form diversity and in rate of new forms over sessions, and the child who was also reinforced for new Lego construction forms showed an increase in form diversity and cumulative new forms in that activity. Some generalization occurred from pen-drawing to painting, the topographically similar tasks. However, none was shown for blockbuilding or Lego construction, the topographically dissimilar tasks. Postchecks two months after completion of training showed maintenance of the directly reinforced activity and its topographically related activity only for the two boys who had received more extended training.

These studies indicate that reinforcement of form diversity in such play activities as blockbuilding, easel painting, pen drawing, and Lego construction increases the rate of form diversity and new forms. Generalization of creative behavior to other tasks was quite variable, somewhat inconsistent, and usually of limited magnitude (Holman, Goetz, & Baer, in press). It is clear that future research on young children that deals with creative behavior with art media will have to be concerned with conditions and procedures that expedite generalization in topographically similar and dissimilar tasks. Positive findings from such efforts would most certainly enhance the whole preschool teaching enterprise.

REFERENCES

Ausubel, D. P. & Schiff, H. M. The effect of incidental and experimentally induced experience in the learning of relevant and irrelevant causal relationships by children. *Journal of Genetic Psychology*, 1954, *84*, 109–23.

Baer, D. M. & Sherman, J. A. Reinforcement control of generalized imitation in young children. *Journal of Experimental Child Psychology*, 1964, *1*, 37–49.

Bandura, A. & Huston, A. C. Identification as a process of incidental learning. *Journal of Abnormal and Social Psychology*, 1961, *63*, 311–18.

Bandura, A., Ross, D., & Ross, S. A. Vicarious reinforcement and imitative learning. *Journal of Abnormal and Social Psychology*, 1963, *67*, 601–7.

Brigham, T. A. & Sherman, J. A. An experimental analysis of verbal imitation in preschool children. *Journal of Applied Behavior Analysis*, 1968, *1*, 151–58.

Brownell, W. A. & Hendrickson, G. How child learns information, concepts, and generalizations. In N. B. Henry (Ed.), *Learning and instruction*. Yearbook for the National Society of the Study of Education, 1950, *49*, Part I. Pp. 92–128.

Burgess, R. L., Burgess, J. M., & Esveldt, K. C. An analysis of generalized imitation. *Journal of Applied Behavior Analysis*, 1970, *3*, 39–49.

Bybel, N. W. & Etzel, B. C. A study of pretraining procedures for establishing cue relevance in the subsequent programming of a conceptual skill. Paper presented at the biennial meeting of the Society for Research in Child Development, Philadelphia, Pa., 1973.

Coller, A. R. *The assessment of "self-concept" in early childhood education.* Urbana, Ill.: ERIC Clearinghouse on Early Childhood Education, 1971.

Dixon, L. S., Spradlin, J. E., & Etzel, B. C. A study in stimulus control procedures to teach an "in-front" spatial discrimination. Paper presented at the biennial meeting of the Society for Research in Child Development, Philadelphia, Pa., 1973.

Elkind, D. Cognition in infancy and early childhood. In Y. Brackbill (Ed.), *Infancy and early childhood*. New York: Free Press, 1967.

Flavell, J. H. Concept development. In P. H. Mussen (Ed.), *Carmichael's manual of child psychology*. Vol. 1. (3rd ed.) New York: John Wiley, 1970. Pp. 983–1060.

Furth, H. G. Piaget's theory of knowledge: The nature of representation and interiorization. In J. Eliot (Ed.), *Human development and cognitive processes*. New York: Holt, Rinehart & Winston, 1971.

Gesell, A. & Ilg, F. L. *Child study: An introduction to the study of human growth.* New York: Harper & Row, 1949.

Gewirtz, J. L. Conditional responding as a paradigm for observational imitative learning and vicarious reinforcement. In H. W. Reese (Ed.), *Advances in child development and behavior*. Vol. 6. New York: Academic Press, 1971. Pp. 273–304.

Glaser, R. Concept learning and concept teaching. In R. M. Gagne & W. J. Gephart (Eds.), *Learning and school subjects*. Itasco, Ill.: F. E. Peacock Publishers, 1968. Pp. 1–36.

Goetz, E. M. & Baer, D. M. Social reinforcement of "creative" blockbuilding in young children. In E. A. Ramp & B. L. Hopkins (Eds.), *A new direction for education: Behavior analysis—1971.* Lawrence, Kansas: The University of Kansas Support and Developmental Center for Follow Through, 1971.

Goetz, E. M. & Baer, D.M. Social control of form diversity and the emergence of new forms in children's blockbuilding. *Journal of Applied Behavior Analysis,* 1973, 2, 209–17.

Goetz, E. M. & Salmonson, M. M. The effects of general and descriptive reinforcement on "creativity" in easel painting. In G. Semb (Ed.), *Behavior analysis and education—1972.* Lawrence: University of Kansas, Department of Human Development, 1972.

Guilford, J. P. The structure of the intellect. *Psychological Bulletin,* 1956, 53, 267–93.

Holman, J., Goetz, E. M., & Baer, D. M. The training of creativity as an operant and an examination of its generalization characteristics. In B. C. Etzel, J. M. LeBlanc, & D. M. Baer (Eds.), *Contributions to behavioral research: Festschrift in honor of Sidney W. Bijou,* in press.

Hurlock, E. H. *Child development.* (5th ed.) New York: McGraw-Hill, 1972.

Jersild, A. T. *Child psychology.* (5th ed.) Englewood Cliffs, N.J.: Prentice-Hall, 1960.

Kagan, J. The developmental approach to conceptual growth. In J. J. Klausmeir & C. W. Harris (Eds.), *Analysis of concept learning.* New York: Academic Press, 1966. Pp. 97–115.

Lipsitt, L. P., Pederson, L. J., and Delucia, L.A. Conjugate reinforcement of operant responding in infants. *Psychonomic Science,* 1966, 4, 67–68.

Maccoby, E. E. & Wilson, W. C. Identification and observational learning from films. *Journal of Abnormal and Social Psychology,* 1957, 55, 76–87.

Maltzman, I. On the training of originality. *Psychological Review,* 1960, 67, 229–42.

Mechner, F. Science education and the behavioral technology. In R. Glaser (Ed.), *Teaching machines and programed learning II. Data and directions.* Washington, D.C.: National Education Association, 1965. Pp. 441–507.

Mussen, P. H. & Parker, A. L. Mother nurturance and girls' incidental imitation learning. *Journal of Personality and Social Psychology,* 1965, 2, 94–97.

Parsons, J. A. Development and maintenance of arithmetic problem-solving behavior in preschool children. Doctoral dissertation, University of Illinois at Urbana-Champaign, 1973.

Risley, T. R. & Hart, B. Developing correspondence between non-verbal and verbal behavior of preschool children. *Journal of Applied Behavior Analysis,* 1968, 1, 267–81.

Schilmoeller, K. J. & Etzel, B. C. An experimental demonstration of some variables involved in establishing functional cues in "errorless" stimulus control procedures. Paper presented at the biennial meeting of the Society for Research in Child Development, Philadelphia, Pa., 1973.

Skinner, B. F. *Verbal behavior.* Englewood Cliffs, N.J.: Prentice-Hall, 1957.

Skinner, B. F. *The technology of teaching.* Englewood Cliffs, N.J.: Prentice-Hall, 1968.

Skinner, B. F. *About behaviorism.* New York: Knopf, 1974.

Steinman, W. M. Generalized imitation and the discrimination hypothesis. *Journal of Experimental Child Psychology,* 1970, *10,* 79–99. (a)

Steinman, W. M. The social control of generalized imitation. *Journal of Applied Behavior Analysis,* 1970, *3,* 159–67. (b)

Terman, L. M. & Merrill, M. *Stanford-Binet Intelligence Scale. Manual for the third revision: Form L-M.* Boston: Houghton Mifflin, 1960.

Terrace, H. S. Stimulus control. In W. K. Honig, *Operant behavior: Areas of research and application.* Englewood Cliffs, N.J.: Prentice-Hall, 1966. Pp. 271–344.

Thayer, L. O. & Pronko, N. H. Some psychological factors in the reading of fiction. *Journal of Genetic Psychology,* 1958, *93,* 113–17.

Torrance, E. P. *Guiding creative talent.* Englewood Cliffs, N.J.: Prentice-Hall, 1962.

Wallach, M. A. Creativity. In P. H. Mussen (Ed.), *Carmichael's manual of child psychology.* (3rd ed.) New York: John Wiley, 1970. Pp. 1211–72.

Wallach, M. A. & Kogan, N. *Modes of thinking in young children: A study of the creativity-intelligence distinction.* New York: Holt, Rinehart & Winston, 1965.

Wechsler, D. *Wechsler preschool and primary scale of intelligence manual.* New York: Psychological Corp., 1967.

Wilson, W. C. Imitation and the learning of incidental cues by preschool children. *Child Development,* 1958, *29,* 393–97.

Wylie, R. C. *The self-concept.* Lincoln: University of Nebraska Press, 1961.

5

Assessment of Cognitive Repertories: Intelligence and Competence

A child's cognitive repertories—his abilities, knowledge, and problem-solving skills—are assessed for different reasons. A researcher might assess the cognitive repertories of a group of children to evaluate a preschool curriculum for the underprivileged, whereas a clinical or educational psychologist might direct his assessment toward determining the general level of development in order to prevent subnormal development (as in monitoring the progress of "high risk" children), or planning an educational program (as in evaluating a child's "readiness" to enter the first grade).

There are two main measurement strategies for assessing cognitive repertories: *norm-referenced* testing and *criterion-referenced* testing. Norm-referenced testing involves obtaining responses to items, carefully selected by means of statistical sampling, that make up a standardized test such as the Stanford-Binet Intelligence Scale (Terman & Merrill, 1960) and the Wechsler Preschool and Primary Scale of Intelligence (Wechsler, 1967). A child's test results, expressed as an IQ score, are designated as high, medium, or low in comparison with the results of a group of same-age children (Popham, 1971). Norm-referenced testing is associated with the statistical theory of intelligence.

In contrast, assessment by criterion-referenced testing aims to obtain an inventory of a child's cognitive repertories, such as comprehending instructions, playing cooperatively, writing words, or solving simple arithmetic problems *without comparison* with the performance of others. The results from such testing indicate the degree of mastery of a specified task (Glaser & Nitko, 1971) and give the parent, teacher, therapist, or researcher a starting point for instruction, treatment, or experimental study. This psychometric technique is associated with the behavior analysis approach to measuring a child's competence.

In this chapter we shall discuss the meaning of scores on norm-referenced intelligence tests from two points of view: the statistical theory of intelligence and behavior analysis. We shall also discuss the major misinterpretations of such scores in educational and clinical practice. And finally we shall discuss the behavioristic concept of competence as measured by criterion-referenced tests and we shall comment on the proper use of norm-referenced and criterion-referenced tests.

THE STATISTICAL THEORY OF INTELLIGENCE

The statistical theory of intelligence measured by a norm-referenced test is presented diagramatically in Figure 5-1. Intelligence, the central term in the figure, is a hypothetical mental concept. According to this theory, the amount of intelligence an individual has is the main determiner of his performance (responses) on a standardized intelligence test, represented at the right side of the figure. Performance on a test is summarized by a score that indicates the relative place of an individual among those in his normative, or standardization, group. Percentile ranks, age equivalents (mental age scores [MAs] related to chronological ages, expressed as IQs), standard scores, and stanines are among the techniques used for this purpose. A child's score on an intelligence test depends largely on the specific items in the test. These items have been included because they are cognitive, correlate with school achievement, and discriminate among children of different ages. For example, in the construction of a mental-age test of intelligence, an item is placed at the four-year-old level if it is failed by most children three years or younger and is passed by most children five years or older. A well standardized intelligence test for preschool children, therefore, is one that yields progressively higher scores for progressively older children.

Figure 5-1 Statistical Theory of Intelligence: Analysis of Performance on a Norm-Referenced Test

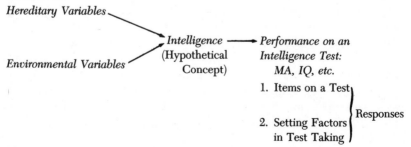

Here are some examples of test items from the Stanford-Binet Intelligence Scale (Terman & Merrill, 1960): At two years the average child is expected to discriminate geometric figures (circle, square, and triangle), identify by pointing to parts of the body of a paper doll, identify by name pictures of familiar objects, and build a tower of four or more blocks from a model. At five years the average child is expected to choose between two pictures on the basis of which is prettier, define words such as stove, ball, and bat in terms of use, count four objects, and solve a two-piece jigsaw puzzle.

Performance on an intelligence scale is influenced not only by the test items themselves, but also by setting factors in the test situation: the presence of others and their effect on the child, the health of the child, or the manner in which the tests are presented, etc. For example, the test administrator's statement that "It is important to try very hard to do the best you can," might hinder one child's performance by increasing his distractible behavior, whereas it might improve another child's performance by mobilizing more effective self-management behavior.

The amount of a child's intelligence, according to the statistical theory of intelligence, is generated from hereditary and environmental variables, represented at the left side of Figure 5-1 with arrows to indicate that they are the antecedents to intelligence. The contribution of hereditary variables is inferred from research on (1) the performance of children reared together or apart and differing in their genetic relatedness: identical twins, fraternal twins, and siblings (Jensen, 1970), and (2) the performance of children of retarded parents reared in families with average or above average socioeconomic status (Skodak & Skeels, 1949). This concept of heredity, which is based on correlations among intelligence tests, differs sharply from the genetic concept of heredity. In cellular genetics, heredity refers to the relationships among (1) identifiable genetic substances in the sex cells of the parents, (2) biological reproduction under controlled conditions, and (3) identifiable characteristics in the anatomical structure and physiological functioning of the progeny (Hirsch, 1971).

In the statistical theory of intelligence, the environmental variables are sociological constructs, such as socioeconomic status of the family, father's occupation, or educational attainment of parents. The influence of those variables is inferred from correlations between scores on intelligence tests and sociological measures. Such correlations, like all correlations, provide us with some information about the strength of relationships *but provide no information whatsoever about causes*. A high correlation between a father's occupation and his offspring's IQs does not necessarily mean that the first variable causes the second; certainly one cannot conclude that as a father moves into higher-level occupations the IQs of his children will increase: it may very well be that a father's occupation and his children's IQs vary correspondingly because of some other condition. For example, money, prestige, power, and social position, the reinforcing contingencies that strengthen the father's behaviors in moving to a higher occupational classification, may be the same ones that strengthen his children's behavior in increasing their school achievement.

Although the statistical theory of intelligence is easy to understand because of its compatibility with cultural beliefs about ability (if you can do something, it's because you have something to do it with as a tool or instrument), it has nevertheless led to disagreements about the nature of intelligence, and the relative importance of heredity and environment in determining it.

(1) There was disagreement over whether intelligence is a general unitary function on the one hand or a composite of several of many more or less independent abilities on the other. (2) There was disagreement over whether intelligence is innate, and grows in a child in somewhat the same way as he grows in stature, or whether mental abilities are learned and thus increased or decreased in accord with the degree of enrichment or impoverishment of a child's environment (Bayley, 1970, p. 1163).

Controversy over whether intelligence is best characterized as a unitary entity, as general intelligence, or a composite of several elements, such as verbal intelligence, social intelligence, and mechanical intelligence, is associated with factor-analytic research. Factor-analytic research on intelligence typically consists of (1) administering batteries of tests, (2) correlating their relationships, and (3) analyzing the correlations to determine the ways in which the tests group themselves (Do tests involving spatial relationships correlate highly with tests involving memory for sentences?). The findings in such studies are a function of the tests, the population tested, and the specific factor-analytical technique employed. The clusters of correlated relationships revealed in the analysis are given names—verbal meaning, reasoning, memory, etc.—and these names are used to describe the structure of intelligence that is presumably responsible for the way the children performed on the tests. This procedure commits what has been called the nominal fallacy: it assigns a name to a class of observed behavior and postulates that the name refers to an entity that causes the behavior. For example, a child who does extremely well on all the verbal items of a test is described as verbally adept because he has high verbal intelligence.

Not all factor-analytic studies are devoted to inquiring into the hypothetical nature of intelligence; some are concerned with analyzing the behavioral requirements of intelligence tests (Cronbach, 1970). Thurstone and Thurstone (1941), for example, administered twenty-one tests to a large number of schoolchildren and found through factor analysis seven clusters of correlations on which they based a series of workbooks to train preschool children in each of the seven areas. Used in this way, factor-analytic studies provide information on some of the requirements for success in school performance and thereby contribute to curriculum planning and task analysis.

The hypothetical nature of intelligence is not always inferred from correlations among tests; sometimes it is simply proclaimed by the test constructor. Thus Wechsler (1952), author of one of the most popular individually administered tests of children's intelligence asserts rather expansively: "Intelligence is the aggregate or global capacity of the individual to act purposefully, to think rationally, and to deal effectively with the environment" (p. 3). Regardless of what an author of intelligence tests thinks about the nature of intelligence, the test he constructs measures a child's responses to the tests' items that are selected for inclusion because they have cognitive characteristics, correlate highly with school achievement, and discriminate among successive age groups of children.

Some psychologists are not content to speculate on intelligence as a hypothetical capacity or an ability; they prefer to conjecture about the physiological structure and process involved, despite the fact that their investigations in no way deal with an individual's physiological makeup. A practice current among many investigators is to relate intelligence to some aspect of the brain or the central nervous system. Thus, Hunt (1961) argues that ". . . intelligence should be conceived as intellectual capacity based on central processes hierarchically arranged within the intrinsic portions of the cerebrum" (p. 362).

Whether viewed as a hypothetical capacity or as the functioning of some aspect of the neurological system, the statistical concept of intelligence, because of its circularity, fails to offer even some explanation of the differences in performance on intelligence tests. To illustrate: (1) A child is given the task of putting together a four-piece puzzle that supposedly measures problem-solving ability; (2) his behavior is observed and described (he looks at the pieces momentarily and then puts them together correctly); (3) his good performance is attributed to his good problem-solving ability. Not only is the explanation of the child's good performance circular, but it unfortunately leads many investigators to seek answers to psychological problems in terms of physiology and biochemistry, and it erroneously conveys the impression that the behavioral and biological branches of science are so well developed that they can be coordinated with a high degree of precision.

We turn now to the second disagreement over the statistical theory of intelligence noted by Bayley (1970): the relative importance of heredity and environment in determining level of intelligence. This question arose many years ago when we had only a limited knowledge of genetics and when it was easy to think of causal conditions as things that could be possessed in varying amounts, like property. However, advances in genetics, psychology, and the philosophy of science have made the issue a pseudo-problem. The contemporary view is that *both* hereditary and environmental variables are important in determining *any* biological trait or psychological characteristic. Neither hereditary nor environmental influences can exist without the other; both are essential components interacting continuously and therefore exerting influence from the moment of conception. There is no organism without genotypes (the genetic constitution of an organism or group of organisms) and there are no genotypes without an environment. The heredity-environment question is comparable to asking a racing car owner, "Which is more important, the car or the driver?"

BEHAVIOR ANALYSIS OF NORM-REFERENCED INTELLIGENCE TESTS

Performance on a norm-referenced intelligence test, according to a behavior analysis, is a function of the test situation and an individual's interactional history. Figure 5-2 illustrates the relationship.

The behavior analysis of intelligence test performance and the statistical theory formulation are the same in one respect, namely, that performance on an intelligence test is, in part, a function of the specific items and the setting factors in a test situation. However, they differ markedly in their conception of the antecedent of the performance. The statistical theorists believe that it is hypothetical intelligence determined by hereditary and environmental variables; the behavior analysts believe it is a child's interactional history, especially that part which generates his cognitive repertories. The psychological history of a child (represented on the left side of Figure 5-2) begins prenatally at the time of viability, the time that all the biological systems (nervous, circulatory, digestive, endocrine, etc.)

Figure 5-2 Behavioral Concept of Intelligence: Analysis of Performance on a Norm-Referenced Test

Interactional History ⟶ *Performance on a Test of Intelligence:*
                                                                Summarized as MA, IQ, etc.

Prenatal—from Viability
to Birth: 1. Items on a Test ⎫

Behavior of an ⟶ Environmental   ⎬ Responses
Integral   Variables from   2. Setting Factors ⎭
Organism   Organismic, Physical,   in Test Taking
                      and Biological
                      Sources

Postnatal—From Birth to
Assessment Time:

Behavior of an ⟶ Environmental
Integral   Variables from
Organism   Organismic,
(Biological   Physical, and
phenotype)   Social Sources

begin to interact with one another to form a new unified organism (Bijou & Baer, 1965). During prenatal development, the observable biological characteristics, or the biological phenotype, of the fetus interact with environmental stimuli from three sources: (1) its interoceptors, or stimuli from its own internal functioning, (2) the surrounding physical conditions, namely the uterus and the amniotic sac, and (3) the appetitional reinforcers supplied biologically through the mother, such as nutrition and oxygen. These interactions result in the anatomy and physiology (the individual's biological phenotype) that are present at birth. Immediately after birth, the biological processes that provided the fetus with the appetitional reinforcers are replaced by physical and social processes: hence, from birth on, an infant's biological phenotype (his organismic characteristics) interacts with the physical and social conditions that comprise the environment, resulting in a wide range of behavior repertories.

The Interaction of Hereditary and Environmental Variables

The interaction of hereditary and environmental variables in producing a child's biological and psychological characteristics may be best understood when thought of as a two-phase process. In phase one, fertilization to birth, the interaction produces the unique anatomy and physiology of the individual, including his species characteristics (those features that define him as a *homo sapiens*). Thus, the biological characteristics (developed and potential) of the neonate are a function of the interaction of variables in the sex cells of the parents with the prenatal environment. In phase two, birth to the end of the life cycle, the interaction of hereditary and environmental variables produces both the maturational (or biological growth) characteristics and the unique organization of behavior repertories of the individual. Of particular interest here is how a child's biological characteristics influence the development of his cognitive repertories. Our position is that a child's biological characteristics influence the acquisition of cognitive repertories by providing one of the sources of *opportunities* for the development of such behavior.

This is accomplished in at least three ways. *First,* his biological characteristics are among the conditions that determine the range of responses he is likely to develop. Certain responses may not develop at all (locomotion in the grossly retarded); others may develop in partial or distorted forms (spastic speech); and still others may develop fully, though relatively late in the biological development cycle. *Second,* an individual's biological characteristics may restrict his range of responses to the environment. For example, he may have a propensity for certain diseases or physiological malfunctioning such as cardiac arrhythmia, or cyclical deficiencies, such as rapid fatigability. *Third,* an individual's normal or deviant anatomy and physiology may serve as stimuli that influence his social interactions. If dark skin color or a disfiguring birthmark, almond-shaped or cross eyes, and spasticity or pigeon-toes are discriminative stimuli for others' aggression, avoidance, or escape, a child with such biological features may be disadvantaged in developing many behavior repertories, cognitive or otherwise. If, on the other hand, a child's physical characteristics are either within the range of, or slightly above, the acceptable social norms, chances are that he will have an average frequency of social contacts and will probably develop extensive behavioral repertories. In other words, an individual's organismic characteristics may hinder or enhance the development of cognitive repertories, depending upon the social contingencies in effect.

From the foregoing analysis, it should be evident that the *relationship* between a child's performance on an intelligence test and his hereditary characteristics *is indirect.* Cognitive repertories sampled on an intelligence test are not related to genetic variables in a simple one-to-one relationship;

there are no genes that can be directly traced to abilities, knowledge, and problem-solving skills. The cognitive concepts discussed in Chapters 3 and 4 refer to classes of behavior that have evolved through the *cumulative* interactions between a child's unique biological makeup and the sequence of environmental events that constitute his developmental history.

If society should ever sanction experimental research in human genetics, biological psychologists would undoubtedly study the relationships between genetic substances in the sex cells of parents and the behavior of the offspring. Obviously, research on these relationships would be complicated and difficult, considering that some would have to be studied before birth, and some after birth in order to determine the influence of genetics over the individual's entire history of stimulating conditions. The information resulting from an experimental analysis of the relationships between genetic variables and behavior would be comparable to that now being reported on the relationship between drug and surgical interventions, on the one hand, and changes in behavior, on the other.

Let us now reexamine the concept of environment. In the statistical theory of intelligence, environmental variables include the socioeconomic status of the family, father's occupation, and parents' educational attainment. These variables are described as sociological because they are derived from *group* performance and because their relationships are summarized by statements, such as "On the average, children from high socioeconomic families have higher intelligence test scores than children of comparable age from low socioeconomic families," and "On the average, first-borns score higher on tests than do subsequent siblings."

In contrast, a behavioral analysis of intelligence considers environmental variables—those observable events with which a child has been in actual contact. The environment is not something "out there" which a child moves into or out of at will. Rather, the environment includes every person, every place, every happening, every thing that the child *interacts with at the moment*. Hence, throughout life, the individual is interacting with environmental events. Every stimulus class has physical dimensions, and after one or more interactions with an individual, it also usually takes on functional (meaningful) dimensions for him. The physical dimensions of a stimulus class are measured solely in terms of space and time; its functional dimensions are measured solely in terms of a child's behavior (Bijou & Baer, 1961). Since children in a particular culture are exposed to similar objects and events with similar contingencies, a stimulus class develops comparable functions for most children of that culture. Because each child's history is unique, however, some objects or events have unique meanings for an individual. Since most children in our culture like candy, we assume that candy is reinforcing; yet this may not be true for a child who is allergic to chocolate, or who has been taught that candy decays his teeth. Consequently, observation may reveal that candy given to a child contingent upon a desired response does not increase the strength of that response. Obviously then, candy does not have a reinforcing function for him. The only sure way to determine what functions a stimulus class has for a child is to observe his behavior in relation to that stimulus class.

As a child interacts with his environment, his behavior is altered—sometimes impressively or trivially, sometimes immediately or remotely. So, too, is his environment altered—significantly, immediately, or remotely. Environmental changes, in particular, have a significant implication for a behavior analytical conception of a child: a child's behavior changes the environment in ways that influence the behavior of others and of himself as well. This dual influence is exemplified by the child who, accompanying his mother on a shopping trip to a department store, persists in making a nuisance of himself by whining and complaining about being tired. As they pass the candy counter, he spies a display of lollipops and he asks his mother to buy him a bag, which she promptly does. (His request and her compliance change his environment: he now has a bag of lollipops.) He eats one, then glances at his mother struggling with her parcels, remarks that she has lots of things to carry, and asks whether he can help carry some. (His behavior toward his mother has changed from grumbling accompanier to accommodating helper.) As a consequence of the constant interaction between a child and his environment, the various aspects of the environment continuously acquire different "meanings" for him. A chair starts out as an object a baby can hold on to so that he can pull himself erect; through further interactions, it becomes an object that helps him support himself while he remains erect; then it becomes an object to sit on; and later, an object to stand on to extend his reach. When changes in interactions are progressive, we refer to them collectively as development (Bijou & Baer, 1961).

This analysis of the interlocking relationship between a child and his environment renders meaningless the shopworn question as to whether a child is passive and at the mercy of the environment (the conception that the child "does nothing" until the environment presents appropriate stimuli), or whether he initiates activity and the environment accedes to his demands (the notion that the child "seeks" stimulation). Changes in the environment, including those initiated by the child, produce stimulations; the child responds to those environmental stimulations in ways that have been shaped by his genetic and personal history. In behavior analysis the relationship between a child and his environment is not seen as a struggle between opposing forces, as psychoanalysis would have it; rather it is seen as a natural, interdependent, interactional system, and like all interactional systems, its degree of balance varies from time to time.

Before concluding this section on the relationships among heredity, environment and scores on an intelligence test, we should briefly consider the current discussions of the relationship between race and IQ. The question is worth noting because the answer may affect public policy on the preschool education of children, particularly from minority racial groups. For example, if there is evidence that black Americans have lower IQ scores than white Americans because of hereditary factors, one might conclude that preschool programs such as Head Start have failed because blacks do not have the intellectual potential to profit from "enriched" early education. On the other hand, if there is evidence that black Americans make lower IQ scores than white Americans because of environmental factors (or if the issue, upon critical examination, is a false problem [Kamin, 1973]), one might conclude that compensatory preschool programs have failed because the programs themselves are inadequate, especially in their follow-through educational procedures.

Ever since World War I, when psychological tests were used on large segments of the population, psychometric studies have shown that blacks score an average of 15 points lower on intelligence tests than whites. Some investigators believe that this difference is due to hereditary racial differences—in other words, that the intellectual potential of black Americans is lower than that of white Americans. This view has long attracted a fair amount of attention, but when Jensen (1969) cast the issue in terms of the educational potential of black American children, it generated an acrimonious controversy.

Jensen's conclusion, based primarily on correlational data from a variety of identical twin and adoption studies, has been seriously questioned both on the basis of the adequacy of the data (e.g., Kamin, 1973), and the fallaciousness of his assumptions (e.g., Hirsch, 1971). Included among the fallacies are (1) equating the genetic concept of hereditability with aptitude for learning, (2) generalizing about individuals from group data, (3) inferring quality of the nervous system of groups of individuals from correlations among tests, and (4) generalizing from limited samples to entire populations.

Our own conclusion about the relationship between race and intelligence test scores is expressed succinctly and forcibly by Schoenfeld (1974):

When I try to summarize what I have been saying, it all seems to me to reduce to the simple statement that the idea of "race differences in intelligence" is nonsense. Nonsense in the framing of the question, nonsense in the populations tested, nonsense in the instrument used, nonsense in the "intelligence" that is postulated . . . Surely that bit of psychological nonsense may be put aside so we can get on with the real problems of race in our contemporary world (p. 32).

Constancy of the IQ and Mental Growth Curves

In the 1930s and 1940s, heated debate raged between faculty members of the University of Iowa and Stanford University over the constancy of the IQ obtained from the Stanford-Binet Intelligence Scale. The Iowa group, looking at changes in the IQ scores of children of retarded parents reared in average and above-average family environments, espoused IQ variability. The Stanford group, focusing on the shortcomings of the statistical and research design in the Iowa studies, championed IQ constancy. Several decades later, the issue is still alive, and according to some, still unresolved.

Will an understanding of the question of IQ constancy lead to some acceptable answers? We know that group data from intelligence tests administered yearly to the same groups show that, on the average, IQ scores remain constant. This means that children who score above the mean on the first test tend, on the average, to score above the mean on subsequent testing, while children who score below the mean on the first test tend, on the average, to score below the mean on subsequent testings. This finding confirms the notion that IQ scores are relatively constant for groups of children and supports the practice of predicting academic performance of groups of children from intelligence test scores. On that basis one may say that IQs on groups of children are constant in the sense that intelligence tests can predict, on an actuarial basis, the school performance of a group of children. A prediction of academic performance typically takes this form: based on past performances of comparable children, the chances are 80 to 20 that a child in a group with an IQ of 120 will be successful in schoolwork.

Granted the statistical constancy of the IQ for groups, what about an individual child? On successive administrations of an intelligence test, will Jenny's IQ remain about the same? Data show that some children make increasingly higher scores, some increasingly lower scores, some fluctuate in an irregular pattern, and that the IQ of a normal young child may fluctuate as many as 25 points (Sontag, Baker, & Nelson, 1958).

A comprehensive review of the literature on the IQ constancy of individual children led Reese and Lipsitt (1970) to conclude:

In summary, study of individual growth curves, test-retest correlations, and absolute score changes demonstrates conclusively that the IQ is not constant. While most children do not show gross changes in relative placement after the preschool years, smaller changes are the rule rather than the exception. An IQ is not a fixed attribute of an individual in the way that blood type is (p. 539).

We may say, then, that for groups of children, IQs are constant in the statistical sense; for an individual child, IQs tend to be variable, depending on the specific interactions in his history.

Closely related to the question of IQ constancy is the assumption that intelligence as measured on tests grows in some natural characteristic way. Since the early days of mental testing, psychologists have been trying to find *the* mental growth function with the hope that it would turn out to be something like the height and the weight curves for boys and girls. Thus far success has eluded them. Intelligence test data from studies spanning many years show similarities and differences in intelligence "growth" curves depending on the age-span covered, the kind of intelligence tests used, the particular population sampled, and the method of analyzing the data. As a result, many investigators have reluctantly come to the conclusion that there is no such thing as *the* mental growth function, that there are only curves that show the performance of specific groups of children on successive administrations of *specific* intelligence tests.

The Meanings of a Score on an Intelligence Test

In sum, an intelligence test score may be said to have two meanings, one normative, associated with a statistical theory of intelligence, and one functional, associated with a behavioral analysis of intelligence. Normatively, the score is an indicator of the probability of school success. This follows from the fact, described previously, that a test score is meaningful when it is compared with scores of children of the same age, and that items on the intelligence test have been selected because they are judged to be cognitive in nature, discriminate well between successive age groups, and correlate highly (average correlation is about .55) with some measure of schoolwork, i.e., grades, teachers' estimates of ability, or scores on school achievement tests. So if five-year-old Billy scores above the mean of his age peers, say IQ 130, his chances for doing well in school are favorable. If, on the other hand, five-year-old Freddy scores below the mean of his age group, say IQ 65, his chances for doing well in school are unfavorable. The probabilities of success in school are estimated on the percentage of children in the standardization group with IQ scores about 130 and about 65 who have done well in schoolwork. Therefore, one of the meanings of a child's performance on an intelligence test is his *aptitude for schoolwork* in the schools as they are organized and operated in our society today (Anastasi, 1968; Glaser, 1963; Humphreys, 1971; Reese & Lipsitt, 1970; and Thorndike & Hagen, 1969).

The functional meaning of an intelligence test score diverges from the above view and relates instead to a child's interactional history. A child who makes a low score is regarded as one who probably has had limited opportunities to develop cognitive repertories. This disadvantage may be the direct result of abnormal anatomical structure and physiological functioning (mentioned previously), inadequate reinforcement and discrimination programming, excessive aversive contingencies, reinforcement of aversive behaviors, or deficiencies in social reinforcement (Bijou, 1966). On the other hand, a child whose intelligence test score is high is apt to have had a history conducive to the development of extensive cognitive repertories. The chances are he has had good physical health, many opportunities to interact with cognitive objects and events and with parents and other adults who value educational achievement and who tend to use positive procedures for establishing and maintaining cognitive behaviors (Terman, 1925).

MISINTERPRETATIONS OF AN INTELLIGENCE TEST SCORE IN EDUCATIONAL AND CLINICAL PRACTICE

Misunderstanding of the meaning of a child's intelligence test score has led to questionable practices with respect to (1) predicting potentiality for training and education, (2) determining the causes of deviant development, and (3) using a "profile" of mental abilities to plan an instructional program.

Potentiality for Training and Education

In flies, as well as in men, the genetic endowment determines the entire range of reactions, realized and unrealized, of the developing organism in all possible environments. A much less happy formulation, often met with in the literature, is that the genotype determines the limits, the upper and the lower extremes, which a character, say a geotactic response, or stature, or IQ, can reach. This would make sense only if we were able to test the reactions of a genotype in all possible environments. Environments are infinitely variable, however, and new ones are constantly invented and added . . . It would require not a scientific but something like a divine knowledge to predict how much the stature, or IQ, or mathematical ability of any individual or population could be raised by environmental or educational modifications or improvements (Dobzhansky, 1972, p. 530).

Let us say that a young child from an average, or above average, socioeconomic home makes an IQ of 80 on an intelligence test. Reviewing the child's achievement and family background, the examiner concludes that the child is functioning at about his intellectual ability (sometimes referred to as "native intelligence") and recommends an educational program that will presumably enable him to progress at his current slow developmental rate. Now let us suppose that another young child, this one from a below-average socioeconomic status, also makes an IQ of 80 on the same test, whereupon the examiner reports that the child, because of various deprivations due to his family's status, is functioning below his intellectual capacity. She therefore recommends a remedial educational program that will presumably accelerate his rate of academic achievement. Because intelligence, as measured by the test, and environment, as estimated by the examiner, are conceived of as opposing forces, the first child is said to be working at the upper range, and the second child at the lower range, of his intellectual capacity. However, there is no empirical justification for following such a model. Let us elaborate.

We do know that conditions in a person's life can change so radically that his cognitive repertory is reduced to that of an infant, as in the case of a severely regressed psychotic patient in the back ward of a psychiatric hospital. But what do we know about teaching procedures that accelerate cognitive development? The practice of predicting the limits of a child's cognitive development from an intelligence test is not only based on a fallacious assumption about what is measured but also discourages research aimed at improving educational procedures. As we stated earlier, a child's IQ is not a measure of his potential for learning, that is, his future behavior; IQ measures the consequences of his interactional history up to the time of the test. If, between testings, his educational environment is favorably altered, he should perform at higher test levels; if it is downgraded, he should perform at lower test levels; and if it remains approximately the same, he should score fairly consistently at about the same test level.

Determining Causes of Deviant Development

Performance on intelligence tests is often used to determine the causes of deviant behavior. On the basis of differential performances on selected items (memory for digits versus general information) referred to as "clinical signs," children are diagnosed "minimal brain damage," "learning disability," "dyslexia," "perceptual confusion," and the like. This is a most unfortunate practice, for (1) it invariably attributes the problem to something hypothetical in the child's biological structure rather than to the possibility of observable deviant biological, physical, and social conditions in his actual interactional history; (2) it groundlessly assumes that for each diagnostic label there is an appropriate treatment program, an assumption that usually leads first to a frantic search for the treatment program and then to a conviction that the child is incapable of learning or adjusting; and (3) it assumes that an intelligence test is an instrument that differentiates among clinical categories. It is essential to remember that an intelligence test is constructed to differentiate between successive age groups on cognitive tasks and to correlate significantly with academic achievement in the public schools, and not to establish differences in diagnostic categories.

Using Mental Abilities Profiles for Instructional Planning

Intelligence test results are frequently used to obtain "a picture" of a child's mental abilities (his performance on several different tests of intelligence or on the subtests), plotted as a profile that might read, "Verbal ability is high, memory span is average, arithmetical ability is low." The profile is usually discussed with a parent or a teacher to help her understand the child's mental makeup and to prepare a training or teaching program which would take into account his strengths and weaknesses. On the face of it, this practice has some appeal but little serviceability, mainly because it is not supported with facts. First, intelligence tests are not constructed to yield this kind of information. Clusters of responses to intelligence-test items are not reliable indicators of mental traits. Second, a profile tacitly suggests that a child's strengths and weaknesses are a fixed part of the child's intellectual structure. Instead, the properties of the categories in a profile are hypothetical and are inferred from test performance, as they are in the statistical theory of intelligence. Third, the categories in a profile consist of clusters of test-item scores and not of components of abilities related to real-life situations. A psychological report stating that five-year-old Janet has high verbal fluency, average numerical ability, low spatial ability, and low rote memory for digits does not provide a parent or a teacher with information that can be used to prepare an effective reading readiness program for her. That kind of information is best obtained by a criterion-referenced test, the topic that we shall now consider.

THE BEHAVIORAL CONCEPT OF COMPETENCE AND CRITERION-REFERENCED TESTS

Criterion-referenced tests, as we said earlier, aim to *inventory* a child's cognitive repertories, *without* comparison with the performances of other children. When criterion-referenced tests are administered before instruction or treatment takes place, the results define a child's competence in a particular task or area—his baseline performance. A comparison of the results of tests administered before and after a unit of instruction or treatment defines his achievement or gain in that domain. In essence, a criterion-referenced test is a refinement of the old-fashioned, schoolteacher method of finding out through informal testing or probing how much a child knows about a subject. For example, before beginning a unit on making change, a teacher should find out what a child knows about money; she first asks him to name the coins and give the value of each; then to give her change for a dime, then a quarter; to give her change from fifty cents after buying toothpaste for thirty cents. When she has finished, she may note in the record book that the child knows all the coins except the fifty-cent piece and can make correct change up to twenty-five cents. Appropriate teaching starts at that point.

Glaser (1971) gives a precise definition of a criterion-referenced test:

A criterion-referenced test is one that is deliberately constructed to yield measurements that are directly interpretable in terms of specified performance standards. Performance standards are generally specified by defining a class or domain of tasks that should be performed by the individual. Measurements are taken as representative samples of tasks drawn from this domain and such measurements are referenced directly to this domain for each individual measured (p. 41).

Performance on a criterion-referenced test, from the behavior analysis point of view, is a function of the immediate test situation and the previous interactions that comprise the history of the child. This formulation is shown diagramatically in Figure 5-3. Responses to the items on a criterion-referenced test, represented on the right side of the figure, are related to (1) the nature of the test items and (2) the setting factors in taking the test. The items on this type of test come from an analysis of a criterion task (the procedure is often referred to in educational circles as *task analysis*) and are selected for inclusion in the test because of their sensitivity to increases in the proportion of children passing from a pre- to a post-treatment.

Figure 5-3 Behavioral Concept of Competence: Analysis of Performance on a Criterion-Referenced Test

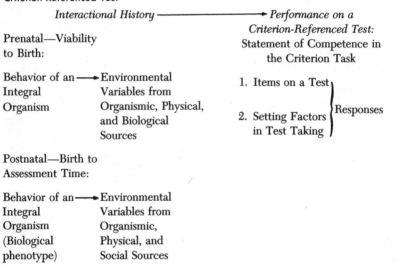

How a child performs on the items of a criterion-referenced test depends upon the specific relevant events in his particular interactional history, shown on the left side of Figure 5-3. This part of the analysis—the remote causal conditions—it will be recalled, is exactly the same as the behavioral concept of intelligence, shown diagramatically in Figure 5-2 (see p. 87). In other words, from the point of view of behavior analysis, a child's performance on both a norm-referenced intelligence test and a criterion-referenced competence test is a function of his interactional history.

Applications

Criterion-referenced tests are used in educational and clinical service for three purposes: (1) to diagnose problem behavior, (2) to monitor learning, and (3) to assess readiness for placement in a prescribed educational program, such as the first grade. Clinically, they are used as an aid in arriving at a behavioral diagnosis by inventorying the child's repertoires that bear on the problem and then recommending procedures that would probably remediate the problem. That is to say, they identify the child's strengths and suggest procedures that might capitalize on the strengths (Bijou & Redd, 1975). A behavioral diagnosis does not aim to place a child in a psychiatric category ("This is an autistic child."), or in an educational pigeonhole ("This is a trainable retarded child."), nor does it result in speculations about a child's current living conditions ("He has a rejecting mother."), or his past interactions ("He comes from a deprived home background."), or the hypothetical underlying causes, neurological ("He is a brain-damaged child."), or otherwise. What is of concern in a behavioral diagnosis is the observable behavior of the child and the conditions and procedures that can be used here and now to reduce or eliminate the problem.

In monitoring learning, criterion-referenced testing is used primarily in individualized programs in which the materials are graded in difficulty and in which the teaching procedures are modified on the basis of observations or findings from systematic evaluations of the child's responses. Thus, in using remedial writing programmed instructional material, the teacher tests the child at the beginning of each unit to see whether he has the prerequisite behavior to succeed in that unit (Can he discriminate the numbers from one to six?), and again at the end of each unit to see whether he has achieved all the objectives in that unit (Can he name the numbers and recite them in serial order?). Testing for monitoring purposes may proceed along the lines of the instructional plan. In a remedial writing program for handicapped young children (Bijou, 1972), the testing evaluated progress on four types of simultaneous progressions: (1) from writing on wide-lined, wide-spaced paper to writing on finer-lined, standard primary paper; (2) from copying letters or words from a model to writing from dictation; (3) from writing single letters to writing words, phrases, and sentences; and (4) from printing to writing in script.

Lastly, criterion-referenced testing is used to assess progress in developing readiness for a prescribed educational program. A procedure of this sort was used by Hunt and Kirk (1974) to prepare socioeconomically disadvantaged children for enrollment in the first grade. Instruction, which centered on the critical skills needed in grade one included (1) identification of color (red, orange, yellow, blue, brown, and green), (2) position (in, on, under, in-front-of, between, and in-back-of), (3) shape (square, round, star, oval, cross, and trapezoid), (4) number identification (from 1 to 6) and (5) child-child communication (expressing simple needs and wants directly and through someone else). The children were systematically evaluated at the beginning of training and periodically during training to determine their degree of mastery of each of these skills in terms of (1) perceptual identification, (2) spoken identification, (3) listening identification, and (4) communication between pairs of children.

By way of summary, we wish to point out that the recent trend toward increased use of criterion-referenced tests (Popham, 1971) reflects the need for information from tests that describes an individual child's abilities and knowledge in relation to real-life situations and to changes in real-life situations. This observation does not forecast the eventual elimination of norm-referenced tests; they will continue to be needed for the purpose for which they were designed. In the light of the accumulated data on psychometric tests, it should now be clearer than ever before that the results of norm-referenced intelligence tests should be interpreted as measuring children's aptitude for schoolwork in the public schools as they now exist, and as such, are helpful in making administrative decisions about the selection, classification, and prediction of *groups* of children. In contrast, the results of criterion-referenced tests should be interpreted as measuring an individual child's competence in particular subjects, and as such, aid in making pedagogical decisions about training, educational, or treatment programs for him.

The use of criterion-referenced tests in child therapy and early childhood education will be discussed further in Chapters 7 and 8.

REFERENCES

Anastasi, A. *Psychological testing.* (3rd ed.) New York: Macmillan, 1968.

Bayley, N. Development of mental abilities. In P. H. Mussen (Ed.), *Carmichael's manual of child psychology.* Vol. 1. (3rd ed.) New York: John Wiley, 1970. Pp. 1163–1210.

Bijou, S. W. A functional analysis of retarded development. In N. Ellis (Ed.),

International review of research in mental retardation. Vol. 1. New York: Academic Press, 1966. Pp. 1–19.

Bijou, S. W. The technology of teaching young handicapped children. In S. W. Bijou & E. Ribes-Inesta (Eds.), *Behavior Modification: Issues and extensions.* New York: Academic Press, 1972. Pp. 27–42.

Bijou, S. W. & Baer, D. M. *Child Development: A systematic and empirical theory.* Vol. 1. Englewood Cliffs, N.J.: Prentice-Hall, 1961.

Bijou, S. W. & Baer, D. M. *Child Development: Universal stage of infancy.* Vol. 2. Englewood Cliffs, N.J.: Prentice-Hall, 1965.

Bijou, S. W. & Redd, W. H. Child behavior therapy. *American Handbook of Psychiatry.* New York: Basic Books, 1975.

Cronbach, L. J. *Essentials of psychological testing.* (3rd ed.) New York: Harper & Row, 1970.

Dobzhansky, T. Genetics and the diversity of behavior. *American Psychologist,* 1972, *26,* 523–30.

Glaser, R. Instructional technology and the measurement of learning outcomes: Some questions. *American Psychologist,* 1963, *18,* 519–21.

Glaser, R. A criterion-referenced test. In W. J. Popham (Ed.), *Criterion-referenced measurement: An introduction.* Englewood Cliffs, N.J.: Educational Technology Publications, 1971.

Glaser, R. & Nitko, A. J. Measurement in learning and instruction. In R. L. Thorndike (Ed.), *Educational measurement.* (2nd ed.) Washington, D.C.: American Council on Education, 1971. Pp. 625–70.

Hirsch, J. Behavior-genetic analysis and its biological consequences. In R. Cancro (Ed.), *Contributions to intelligence.* New York: Grune & Stratton, 1971. Pp. 88–106.

Humphreys, L. G. Theory of intelligence. In R. Cancro (Ed.), *Intelligence: Genetic and environmental influences.* New York: Grune & Stratton, 1971. Pp. 31–42.

Hunt, J. McV. *Intelligence and experience.* New York: Ronald Press, 1961.

Hunt, J. McV. & Kirk, G. Criterion-referenced tests of semantic mastery in school readiness: A paradigm with illustrations. *Genetic Psychology Monographs,* 1974, *90,* 143–82.

Jensen, A. R. How much can we boost IQ and scholastic achievement? *Harvard Educational Review,* 1969, *39,* 1–123.

Jensen, A. R. IQ's of identical twins reared apart. *Behavior Genetics,* 1970, *1,* 133–46.

Kamin, L. J. Heredity, intelligence, politics, and psychology. Address given at the Eastern Psychological Association Meeting. Washington, D.C., May, 1973.

Popham, W. J. (Ed.) *Criterion-referenced measurement: An introduction.* Englewood Cliffs, N.J.: Educational Technology Publications, 1971.

Reese, H. W. & Lipsitt, L. P. *Experimental child psychology.* New York: Academic Press, 1970.

Schoenfeld, W. N. Notes on a bit of psychological nonsense: "Race differences in intelligence." *The Psychological Record,* 1974, *24,* 17–32.

Skodak, M. & Skeels, H. M. A final follow-up study of one hundred adopted children. *Journal of Genetic Psychology,* 1949, *75,* 85–125.

Sontag, L. W., Baker, C. T., & Nelson, V. L. Mental growth and personality development: A longitudinal study. *Monograph for the Society of Research in Child Development,* 1958, *23,* No. 2.

Terman, L. M. *Genetic studies of genius.* Vol. 1. Palo Alto, Calif.: Stanford University Press, 1925.

Terman, L. M. & Merrill, M. A. *Stanford-Binet Intelligence Scale: Manual for the third revision, Form L-M.* Boston: Houghton Mifflin, 1960.

Thorndike, R. L. & Hagen, E. *Measurement and evaluation in psychology and education.* (3rd ed.) New York: John Wiley, 1969.

Thurstone, L. L. & Thurstone, T. G. Factorial studies of intelligence. *Psychometric Monographs,* 1941, No. 2.

Wechsler, D. *The measurement of adult intelligence.* (3rd ed.) Baltimore, Md.: Williams & Wilkins, 1952.

Wechsler, D. *Wechsler preschool and primary scale of intelligence manual.* New York: Psychological Corp., 1967.

6

Roots of Moral Behavior

In Chapters 3 and 4, we were concerned with how a young child acquires abilities, knowledge, and problem-solving skills in relation to objects in his physical world, people in his social world, and himself as a biological and psychological (behavioral) individual. These behaviors, under certain circumstances, are considered appropriate; under certain other circumstances, they are considered inappropriate because they conflict with the rules of conduct or moral standards established by the members of his family, particularly his parents.

In this chapter we focus on how the child learns to comply with these rules. In situations where there is a supervising adult, the child's adherence to the group's moral practices is ordinarily attributed to his reinforcement history with that adult or others like him. A child's moral behavior under adult "policing" is clearly a case of discriminative operant behavior. When there is no supervising adult, however, his adherence to moral practices is generally attributed to the "internalization" of external standards reified in something like "conscience." This kind of explanation has run into numerous theoretical difficulties (Aronfreed, 1969). Such questions have arisen as "What process accounts for the transfer from external controls to internal controls?" "What is the nature of the internal agent?" "What changes its power?" Hence, one of the central challenges in an analysis of early moral behavior is an alternate formulation of how a child comes to cope with the moral standards of his family when he is on his own.

This chapter (1) presents an outline of the general moral code of western industrial societies, together with an elaboration of the general code for children between four and six years old, (2) examines the three major contemporary theories of moral behavior and development, (3) presents a behavior analysis of early moral development, (4) analyzes the well-known facts of moral training practices in terms of behavioral concepts and principles, (5) describes a behavioral approach to initial moral training, (6) presents a detailed example of moral training based primarily on positive contingencies, and (7) comments on the status of research and application.

Throughout the chapter we refer frequently to moral, unmoral, and immoral behavior. It may be helpful to explain at the outset the meanings of each of these terms. Moral behavior supports the moral code in effect for a child. Unmoral behavior, contrary to the moral code, is displayed by a child who has not yet had ample opportunities to learn how to comply. Immoral behavior, also contrary to the moral code, is displayed by a child who has had sufficient opportunities to learn how to comply.

THE GENERAL MORAL CODE
OF WESTERN INDUSTRIALIZED SOCIETIES

A family's rules and regulations about moral behavior constitute its moral code. Although there are as many moral codes as there are families, family codes revolve around the society's general code or social norms. Because the general code of a society, as it might be studied by a sociologist or an anthropologist, provides a reference for comparisons of family practices within and between societies, we should know something about its composition.

The moral code of a modern western industrialized society is anything but a neat package. It consists of a set of rules—laws, manners, customs, traditions, and folkways—that must be followed if one is to be an accepted member of that society. The moral code prescribes the behavior expected of an individual on the main occasions of living: birth, education, leisure activity, earning a livelihood, courtship, marriage, establishing a family, worshiping, and death. The moral code also assigns, in a gross way, the penalties for violations, many of which—ostracization, name-calling, ridicule, and even death—are imposed subtly and without formal decree. In addition to the changes in the code which occur constantly as the result of continual changes in the society itself, there are internal variations related to age, sex, socioeconomic status, occupation, or geographical location. Inasmuch as the differences in the moral code on the basis of age, or stage of development, are particularly relevant here, we shall detail their characteristics relative to four age groups.

Ages 4 to 6. Children in these later years of the basic stage are expected to conform to a simple moral code that pertains principally to how they are to behave toward adults, peers, and property. Training in and maintenance of the behavior are mainly the task of parents, older siblings, and preschool or kindergarten teachers. At the end of the basic stage, youngsters who do not conform are generally described as retarded, dependent, immature, or unmoral.

Ages 7 to 12. In middle childhood—phase I of the societal stage—children are expected to comply with, and to be able to understand and discuss, the standards of behavior toward adults, peers, and property. Some of the rules of this code are refinements and extensions of the basic-stage code; others are first approximations of the code for children in the next stage of development. Parents, peers, teachers, and community leaders all contribute to the training and maintenance of moral behavior during this phase. Those children who do not conform by the end of middle childhood are designated as retarded, emotionally disturbed, or predelinquent, depending on their social histories and the nature and severity of their infractions.

Ages 13 to 20. In adolescence—phase II of the societal stage—individuals are expected to adhere to and describe a set of standards that, again, are refinements and extensions of the previous code, plus first approximations of the adult code. Although parents, teachers, and others still have a role, the training and maintenance of behavior in compliance with this moral code are more often in the hands of social agency representatives, such as the school and the juvenile court, athletic coaches, special teachers, job supervisors, and peer groups. Nonconforming individuals are now viewed as immoral, alienated, abnormal, psychopathic, delinquent, or criminal, depending on the infractions and the setting factors.

Ages 21 and above. In adulthood—phase III of the societal stage—individuals are expected to understand and abide by the rules in the conventional code of society. Training and maintenance in the adult moral code and deviations from the code are delegated to individuals attached to various social agencies whose responsibility it is to help individuals to conform. Deviants are viewed as odd, neurotic, psychopathic, or criminal, depending on the transgressions and the accompanying circumstances.

Since the development of moral behavior from four to six years is our primary interest, we present in some detail the first moral code, as suggested by Doll's Social Maturity Scale (1948) and Havighurst's sequence of developmental tasks (1953).

1. Sexual behavior
   a. Moral—show sexual modesty by covering oneself properly; display appropriate sex-role behavior toward members of the opposite sex (boys help and defer to girls and women, and girls act "cute" with boys and men).
   b. Unmoral—expose sex organs; participate in sex play and sexual self-stimulation; behave without differentiation toward members of the opposite sex.
2. Behavior toward adults
   a. Moral—be differentially courteous and helpful to others, depending on whether they are parents, relatives, or friends; within limits, respond nonaggressively to frustrations imposed by others; comply with requests of parents, teachers, and other responsible adults.
   b. Unmoral—engage in impolite behavior; display physical and/or verbal aggression toward adults; ignore requests of or defy parents, teachers, and other responsible adults.
3. Behavior toward peers
   a. Moral—converse and play with siblings and peers in simple cooperative games; engage in competitive exercise and table games; participate in active, venturesome play with skates, wagons, tricycles, or sleds.
   b. Unmoral—do not engage in simple cooperative or competitive games and activities; be physically and verbally aggressive toward individuals or groups of peers.
4. Behavior toward property
   a. Moral—play with toys and other objects without willfully destroying them; treat toys and objects differentially on the basis of ownership labels (my toys and ours versus his, hers, yours, and their toys).
   b. Unmoral—destroy toys and property; disregard simple ownership rights.
5. Linguistic behavior
   a. Moral—use differential linguistic behavior to describe fantasy and reality; use respectful language for adults, and acceptable child language for peers.
   b. Unmoral—tell "lies" (two kinds: not discriminating between fantasy and reality, and misrepresenting situations to avoid aversive consequences); use inappropriate language with adults and peers (profanity, name-calling, etc.).
6. Adherence to rules of group activities

    a. Moral—adhere to simple rules of games and play activities; follow
       the rules of the social group.
    b. Unmoral—do not adhere to the rules of play or of group activities.

THEORIES OF MORALITY AND MORAL DEVELOPMENT

When the study of morality was the exclusive domain of theology and
philosophy, the origin of morality was usually attributed to the child's
inherent nature. Theologists such as St. Augustine held that a child is
naturally sinful and that adults, who represented sacred and peculiar
values, were duty-bound to save him through punishment; otherwise the
child would become a lost soul. Philosophers, such as John Locke for
example, maintained that a child is morally neutral—a *tabula rasa*—and
that whether a child's morality is considered sinful or good and pure
depends upon his training and experiences. Other philosophers, such as
Rousseau, held that a child is born morally good and pure and that
immoral behavior results from his contacts with corruptive adults; hence,
it was essential that adult moral influence be minimized, especially in the
early years.

It has been said with some justification that these three philosophical
doctrines have been carried over into the major contemporary psychological theories; namely, the psychoanalytic theory, the social learning theory,
and the cognitive-development theory (Hoffman, 1970). According to
orthodox psychoanalysis (Freud, 1949), the child is controlled by *inborn
primitive and self-fulfilling drives* (the "id" part of his personality
structure) that he is reluctant to give up but which he is forced to do
because of parental sanctions. External punishment becomes self-punishment through the development of the "superego" part of his personality,
and so a child behaves morally to avoid self-punishment, anxiety, or guilt.
This anticipation of future self-punishment following transgression of the
rules of society serves as a drive for behaving in ways consistent with these
internalized standards. When unmoral behavior does occur, it is said to be
motivated by the child's need for punishment and self-blame. Hence,
morality, according to psychoanalytic theory, is primarily motivational and
emotional. It is also unconscious. "Moral standards are the largely
unconscious products of powerful irrational motives and are based on the
need to keep antisocial impulses from becoming conscious awareness"
(Hoffman, 1970, p. 261).

Psychoanalytically oriented researchers have attempted to relate parents' childrearing practices as revealed by interviews, questionnaires, and rating scales to the personality and moral characteristics of their children, as measured by tests, rating scales, and observations. Because of loosely formulated definitions and inadequate research designs and procedures, few reliable findings have been produced (Becker, 1964; and Caldwell, 1964).

The social learning theory of moral development (Bandura & Walters, 1963; Hoffman & Saltzstein, 1967; and Sears, Maccoby, & Levin, 1957) follows psychoanalytic theory in stressing the motivational and emotional aspects of moral behavior, but subscribes to different assumptions about the hypothetical variables and processes involved. According to social learning theory, a child is born morally *neutral*. By dint of his parents' childrearing practices he gradually develops a conscience through the defense mechanism of *identification*. "To get rid of the anxiety and assure himself of the parent's continued love, the child strives to become like the parent—to incorporate everything about him including his moral standards and values" (Hoffman, 1970, p. 306). Lovell (1971) summarizes the social learning theory position in these words:

The expectations are that punishment given by parents under certain conditions will bring about feelings of anxiety and will inhibit wrongdoing quite independent of whether, in the current situation, the child is punished. Avoidance and inhibition learned in the home should be generalizable to any and every situation outside even when there is no supervision of the child. Thus the conscious buildup through reward and punishment will be taken into all situations (p. 102).

Social learning theory adherents have also attempted to relate parents' practices to their children's moral characteristics but they have used more rigorous research procedures than their psychoanalytic counterparts. In general, their research has followed two avenues of inquiry. One pertains to the relationship between parental practices measured by questionnaires and interviews, and children's moral characteristics measured by psychological tests, observations, and laboratory tests (Sears, Maccoby, & Levin, 1957). Most of the correlations reported are low; even if they had been reasonably high, however, their meaning would still be obscure because parental practices were inferred from interviews and questionnaires, a research procedure that leaves much to be desired (Yarrow, Campbell, & Burton, 1964 & 1968). It has become apparent that research using such indirect methods can best serve to survey the terrain and provide hunches for planning ecological and experimental studies involving direct observations of parent-child, older sibling-child, and teacher-child relationships. The second social learning theory line of study has attempted to relate childrearing categories, such as power assertion, love withdrawal, induction (giving explanations or reasons), and affection to resistance-to-temptation measures, taken as indicators of conscience. Here, too, the results have been unimpressive (Hoffman, 1970). The difficulties encountered may well be attributed to the lack of a sound data basis for categorizing such childrearing practices as power assertion and induction and to the use of arbitrary rather than functional definitions of concepts, especially in laboratory studies on the conditions influencing resistance-to-temptation.

The cognitive-developmental theory of moral behavior (Piaget, 1932; Kohlberg, 1963) assumes that the child is morally *good*, and at the same time, has a morality all his own, that is, he has standards that do not come from adults, peers, and teachers. Kohlberg (1968) considers that "the child is a moral philosopher." According to this view, external rules become transformed into internal rules through *cognitive processes*: a child perceives the environment as a social situation in which he increasingly understands rules of conduct by spontaneously restricting his experiences in order to make the situation meaningful to him. The cognitive-developmental theorists believe that motivational-emotional processes play a less important role than they do in psychoanalysis and social learning theory. The child, according to this formulation, goes through three major developmental stages (defined somewhat differently by Piaget & Kohlberg) which correspond to changes in his cognitive structure: (1) *heteronomy*—the stage in which rules and laws laid down by adults are treated as real things and are sacred and fixed for all occasions; (2) *equality*—the period in which rewards and punishments are distributed equally and punishments are related to misdeeds; and (3) *equity*—the phase in which judgments are based on real situations. Variations in the order of the three stages are attributed to extenuating circumstances and the operation of certain motives and needs.

Research generated by the cognitive-developmental approach has focused on the development of moral judgment and moral character, especially among children who have reached the stage of "mature" moral judgment (about 8 or 9 years), which is determined by analyzing their responses to stories with ambiguous moral situations ("What would you say about the moral behavior of a man who steals food because his wife and children are hungry?"). In this formulation moral behavior, usually referred to as moral conduct, receives little or no attention and the postulated relationship between moral judgment and character on one hand, and moral behavior on the other, has not as yet been specified. Furthermore, this view makes a distinction between early compliance and noncompliance behavior and later "true" moral behavior. True moral behavior occurs when the child's "natural" moral tendencies become manifest. Hence, according to this approach, moral training, which consists mainly of discussions about moral problems, issues, and implications, should be delayed until pre-adolescence when the child is morally "ready."

The major shortcoming of all three theories is that each concentrates on some hypothetical variable (conscience, superego, and moral character) as the main determiner of moral behavior. Data based on the behaviors of children have been interpreted as indicators of some facet of personality (superego) or of the cognitive structures (socioeccentricity) of a child. As a consequence, the study of moral behavior itself, from its inception to its mature stage, has been postponed, presumably until the inner workings of the personality, or of the mind, have been revealed. Considering the nonproductive state of this area of investigation, the strategy that is called for would analyze moral behavior as a function of observable conditions, both historical and those in operation at the time of the moral event.

BEHAVIOR ANALYSIS OF INITIAL MORAL DEVELOPMENT

In the survey of the original nature of the neonate, Bijou and Baer (1965) concluded that an infant is not born with tendencies to be either morally good or bad and that his moral behavior in the basic stage of childhood will be a function of his genetic history, his interactional history during infancy, and the parent-child, sibling-child, and teacher-child relationships. Although this formulation may sound like a variation of the *tabula rasa* doctrine associated with social learning theory, it is not. The *tabula rasa* concept likens a newborn's mind or soul to a "clean slate." Behavior analysis is not concerned with the initial status of a child's mind or soul but rather with the observable conditions that generate moral behavior at all levels of development.

Influences from Interactional History in Infancy

From the interactions in infancy come motivations (the social reinforcing powers of a mother) and self-care and social skills which play a part in the way moral behavior develops in later years. Let us elaborate.

For his survival, an infant requires someone who will minister to his needs. In a typical family, the mother devotes herself to preserving the infant's health, protecting him from danger, stimulating pleasant social interactions, and helping him to help himself. In the process, the baby becomes socially and emotionally dependent on the mother (Gewirtz, 1969; and Sears, 1963). (Although we most certainly recognize that the mother generally acquires strong affectionate ties with the baby, this aspect of the mother-infant relationship is not emphasized because the focus here is on the development of the child.) To say that a child becomes dependent on a mother is to say, from a behavioral point of view, that a mother acquires reinforcing functions (as well as discriminative functions) for a baby that play a critical role in the training that follows (see Bijou & Baer, 1965, on socialization).

A mother's training begins with helping the child to help himself and usually consists of providing the baby with opportunities to hold and manage objects, to creep, crawl, walk, and to interact with people. She weans him from the bottle or breast and teaches him to drink from a cup or a glass, to eat solid foods with the proper utensil, to urinate and defecate in the proper way and in the prescribed places, and to dress and groom himself to the extent he is able. All of this training takes place, of course, within the bounds of family living and the family's moral code. All this training involves incidental exercises in self-control, as pointed out by Bandura & Walters (1963).

In all cultures there are social demands, customs, and taboos that require a member to exhibit self-control. Biological gratifications must be regulated in relation to the time schedules of the culture and to prescribed routines. Feeding, elimination, and sleep routines are rigorously imposed by parents and involve delay of gratification of biological needs or interference with other rewarding activities. In conforming to these schedules and demands, the child has often to relinquish behavior that has previously led to immediate and direct reinforcement and to replace this by responses that are less efficient for obtaining immediate reinforcement for the agent. Thus, even the basic socialization processes involve the acquisition of a certain degree of self-control and the observing of social prohibitions and requirements (p. 165).

Custom does indeed meet us at the cradle.

Influences from Interactions in Early Childhood

Probably the most important single factor influencing parents of all socioeconomic classes in explicitly training their child to comply with the family's moral code is the way the parents themselves were reared ("That's what *my* mother did to me when I told a lie."). There are, of course, parents who adopt standards that are antithetical to their own parents' practices, especially in the group of those with upward social mobility, those who think their parents did a poor job, or those who advocate extreme permissiveness ("I will never spank *my* child no matter what he does."). Actually, because they arise out of various circumstances, it is difficult to detail the historical and current conditions that determine the moral training practices of parents. Findings from studies comparing groups of parents suggest that the following factors may be involved: parents' age and sex, training for parenthood, socioeconomic status, conformity to group-approved techniques, concept of adult role, emotional reactions to the various models of discipline (e.g., permissive versus authoritarian), concept of the morality (e.g., every child needs a good spanking now and then), sex and age of child, and the specific disciplinary situation.

The complexity of the problem should not discourage vigorous investigation with appropriate research instruments. If one wishes to know what a mother does in training her child in the initial do's and don'ts, one should start by observing her behavior in her daily relationships with the child. The observer would probably find that, incidental to her household and social activities, she instructs her offspring mainly by "explaining" the difference between desirable and undesirable behavior, repeating instructions, pointing out consequences, stating precepts, and engaging in other forms of "reasoning." The observer would also note that the mother labels the child's behavior as "good" or "bad" and frequently follows "good" behaviors with acceptance, praise or other positive comment, and desirable objects and activities, while "bad" behaviors evoke scolding, threats, isolation, deprivation, appeals, and spanking. Her behavior is similar to that of a kindergarten or elementary school teacher except that the teacher tends to use "right" and "wrong" rather than "good" and "bad." In general, the teacher's techniques are similar to those of the parents because her classroom practices are influenced more by the way she herself was reared than by her college training (Allen, 1971). We shall analyze, in some detail, the early moral training practices of parents, older siblings, and teachers in terms of the concepts and principles of behavior analysis. Before doing so, however, we must explain the behavioral meanings of three critical terms: decision making, problem solving, and self-management behavior.

Moral decision making and problem solving. Moral decision making and problem solving resulting in moral judgment are important aspects of moral behavior for at least two reasons: (1) Situations arise in which there are ambiguities and uncertainties about exactly what constitutes a moral act; and (2) The individual and society are served best when a child learns to respond to the family moral code, and as he grows older, the general moral code, in light of the specific circumstances in each instance. If one distinguishes immature moral judgment (like that of a young child) from mature moral judgment (like that of an average adult) and holds with Kohlberg (1964) that the child exercises mature moral judgment sometime between the ages of nine and twelve years one must wait until the child reaches pre-adolescence to teach him moral problem solving, primarily through the cultivation of his innate moral philosophy. However, if one does not accept such a distinction and contends that moral decision making and moral problem solving vary with the developmental status of the child and the specific situation at hand, then one seeks ways of improving the child's moral decision making and moral problem solving from the inception of moral training. The latter position is the one taken here.

Moral decision making and problem solving refer to behavior sequences that precede moral behavior in a situation in which a child is uncertain about the outcomes of alternate courses for action, or cannot make a response with a high probability of reinforcement. In moral decision making, the child engages in covert and overt behaviors that provide differential values to the alternative courses of action open to him and then makes a choice in favor of the most attractive or least aversive. In moral problem solving, as in intellectual problem solving, a child engages in behaviors that alter conditions in the external and internal environments so as to enable him to arrive at the response that solves the problem (see Chapter 4, pp. 70–74). A child's effectiveness as a moral problem solver depends on his repertoires of moral knowledge, his problem-solving skills, and the contingencies involved.

Research on moral decision making and moral problem solving in hypothetical situations and in actual situations requires separate analyses. In hypothetical situations, the researcher describes an ambiguous moral situation and asks the child to tell what he would do and why. Responses are usually reinforced with educational contingencies such as, "That's a good explanation." This kind of moral problem solving has been used by Piaget (1932), Kohlberg (1964), and their students to study the cognitive processes underlying moral judgment and moral character. In actual situations, moral problem solving may involve natural or contrived contingencies. An example of the natural type: A mother finds a broken cup and asks her four-year-old whether he had broken it. He is confronted with his reactions to the contingencies that might result from admitting his guilt versus those from telling a lie. He is not entirely sure what the contingencies will be for either response, but he is sure that whatever they are, they will be "real." An example of the contrived type: A child is brought into an experimental room and told how he can win prizes. The situation is arranged so that he will get more or better prizes by disobeying the rules. He is confronted with the choice between the immediate specified contingencies, such as a trinket for each response, or the consequences of behaving contrary to instructions and getting more reinforcers, such as several trinkets for each response.

Results from studies on moral behavior in relation to hypothetical situations (what a person says he will do) and in reaction to actual situations (what a person does) have not been in high agreement (e.g., Hartshorne & May, 1928–1930), a finding that seems surprising because it is contrary to our cultural concept of man as a rational being. But it is not baffling when one remembers that problem solving in relation to hypothetical moral situations is a function of circumstances, past and present, and that problem solving in relation to actual moral situations is also a function of circumstances, past and present, and that these two sets of determining conditions are usually quite different.

Moral self-management behavior.   Self-management behavior consists of interactions in which an individual reacts to the environment in ways that alter it, and the altered environment which, in turn, changes the individual's behavior in the desired direction. The various interactional systems that constitute one's behavioral makeup (personality) may interrelate just as individuals may interrelate: each may complement, inhibit, modify, or be insensitive to the other. In moral self-management behavior, the interactions are mainly inhibitory. At the beginning of training in moral behavior, many of a young child's previously reinforced responses now produce aversive consequences, and accordingly the child inhibits or changes his responses. For example, running around in the nude, which once brought forth smiles and laughter, now produces reprimands and the child soon refrains from public nudity. Likewise, the child must suppress many of his escape and avoidance responses because they are now punished, whereas his inhibitory behaviors are reinforced (not playing a game according to the rules is disapproved of; earlier this behavior was accepted "because he's only a baby"). Whether such switches in contingencies, which are a normal part of the environment of development, will lead to self-management behavior depends on the specific circumstances involving a child's ability (1) to respond to his own behavior, (2) to identify the conditions that precede, follow, and serve as a context for the behavior, and (3) to engage in behavior that alters one or more of these conditions (Thoresen & Mahoney, 1974). When the child responds to a tempting situation with a socially prescribed self-management reaction, he is described as behaving morally, or as having good self-control, at least for that class of circumstances.

In this analysis, self-management behavior originates in the external environment and is ultimately strengthened or weakened by conditions in the external environment (Skinner, 1969). Therefore, it is not necessary to postulate that something has been internalized, in the sense that an external punishing agent has been transformed, through identification or some other psychoanalytic or social learning theory mechanism, into an internal punishing agent which prohibits unmoral or immoral behavior.

BEHAVIOR ANALYSIS OF MORAL TRAINING PRACTICES

The analyses of the well-known practices of parents, older siblings, and teachers in training a young child in initial moral behavior are based on the empirical concepts and principles derived primarily from laboratory research (Bijou and Baer, 1961). They are presented under five headings: (1) reducing or eliminating transgressions on the family moral code, (2) strengthening positive moral behavior, (3) rearranging setting factors, (4) using physical conditions to prevent unmoral behavior, and (5) other procedures.

Reducing or Eliminating Transgressions

Transgressions, or instances of unmoral behavior, are reduced or eliminated by at least one of four procedures: (1) punishment, (2) instructions with conditioned aversive contingencies, (3) extinction, and (4) reinforcement of incompatible behavior.

Punishment. To a large extent, children are taught the prohibitions and taboos of the family moral code through punishment (Radke, 1946).

The reasons most frequently given for using punishment in moral training are the following: (1) it stops the undesirable behavior (if the punishment is strong enough); (2) it is the frustrated parent's "natural" reaction to the child's unmoral behavior; (3) it supposedly deters repetitions of the act; and (4) it is considered essential for moral training (a child cannot possibly develop a conscience and thereby become a good citizen unless he has been punished sufficiently for his wrongdoings).

According to behavior analysis punishment refers to five separate and distinct procedures: (1) the presentation of negative reinforcers (a spanking); (2) the presentation of conditioned negative reinforcers (threat of a spanking); (3) the withdrawal of positive reinforcers (making a child get off of his tricycle and taking it away); (4) the threat of withdrawal of positive reinforcers (threatening to take away the tricycle); and (5) the removal of opportunities for positive reinforcement, or "time-out" (taking a child out of an exciting play situation). Note that the behavior analysis of punishment differs sharply from the everyday meaning of the term, which is, according to *Webster's New Collegiate Dictionary* (1963), "retributive suffering, pain, or loss." Retribution is in no way involved in the behavioral meaning of punishment.

The conditions under which the presentation of negative reinforcers or conditioned negative reinforcers are administered—procedures (1) and (2) above—contribute to suppressing future instances of similar unmoral behavior. Among these conditions are the promptness with which the punishment is administered, the intensity of the punishment, and the schedule of the punishments. However, inadvertently aversive contingencies may be mixed with instances of nonreinforcement and reinforcement and thus create an intermittent schedule of reinforcement that *increases* rather than decreases the probability of future occurrences of the unmoral behavior (Bijou & Baer, 1961). If an aversive contingency is weak, it will not, by definition, alter the unmoral behavior; if it is very strong, it will not only stop the unmoral behavior, but it will generate powerful emotional behavior.

It is well known, mainly through the writings of clinical psychologists and psychiatrists, that severe and frequent punishment for transgressions of the moral code may have undesirable effects on behavior. Strong aversive-presentation contingencies may generate strong emotional behavior with escape and avoidance operants. Depending on the circumstances, these evasive behaviors take the form of counteraggressive or passive, shy, and withdrawn behavior. In either case, the child acquires avoidance behaviors not only in relation to the particular unmoral act but also in relation to other stimuli present at the time. Thus, it is possible that parents (the common social components in most punishment situations) who have acquired positive reinforcing properties during the child's premoral universal stage of infancy may lose them and acquire aversive properties in the basic stage of early childhood if they rely primarily on punishment to teach their child initial moral behavior.

An excessive use of aversive-presentation punishment to suppress unmoral behavior also affects the practices of parents. A parent seeing that punishment has "worked" may adopt a stereotyped way of treating all infractions of the family moral code, whether they are serious or trivial. Such rigidity tends to develop rapidly because this type of punishment can be both negatively and positively reinforcing to the one administering the punishment: it quickly terminates the behavior that is aversive to the parent, and more often than not, produces behavior that is deemed desirable even if the child's resulting behavior is nothing more than sitting quietly doing "nothing." This combined set of consequences often establishes strong behaviors in the person responsible for moral training, particularly if he or she believes that "real" moral training can be achieved only through punishment. Moreover, those who rely on aversive-presentation punishment to stop unmoral behavior and to prevent repetitions are apt to resort to stronger punishment when the previous dosage has proven ineffectual (Azrin & Holz, 1966). When extreme forms of such punishment fail to suppress unmoral behavior and instead engender extreme forms of escape and avoidance behaviors, parents have no alternative but to turn to outside agencies for assistance in managing the behavior of their child. (See Chapter 7.)

Another possible consequence of the excessive use of aversive-presentation punishment is a "guilt" reaction or an aversive self-reaction from the act of punishing (the parent who says, "This hurts me more than it does you."). Such conditioned aversive stimuli develop in the punisher's history through the association of aversive stimuli with the act of aggression. For example, according to the general adult conventional code, aggressive behavior, such as knocking down a woman and snatching her purse, is an immoral act; but aggressiveness toward a person for his own good, like pulling down and restraining someone who is violent, may be acceptable as a moral act. Statements about guilt reactions are maintained by the punisher's insistence to others and himself, that aggression under these circumstances is acceptable. However, in seeing the suffering he has caused, the punisher may show remorse, apologize, or compensate the victim by demonstrations of affection or generous gifts. Such "overreaction" may establish behavior contrary to the objectives of moral training by making punishment a discriminative stimulus for positive reinforcement.

It is entirely possible to teach a child to use aversive-presentation punishment to manage his own moral behavior. He may, for example, be shown how adding a second aversive contingency to an unmoral act, which ordinarily carries a weak aversive contingency, helps to prevent him from doing something that is prohibited. For example, a mother tells her child never to take ice cream from the refrigerator without permission. She also says she knows the ice cream is tempting, so she is going to ask him to promise he won't take ice cream without asking permission. Thus, if he were tempted to take ice cream without prior permission, he would incur not one but two infractions: taking forbidden food and breaking his promise to his mother.

The other punishment procedures of the five mentioned above used to suppress unmoral behavior—namely, the withdrawal or threat of withdrawal of positive reinforcers, and the removal of the opportunity for positive reinforcers (time-out) contingent upon a response—have been shown through research to generate less emotional behavior and fewer detrimental side-effects than the first two aversive-presentation procedures discussed. For example, Wahler (1969) and Patterson, Cobb, and Ray (1970) found that when parents use time-out from positive reinforcement for oppositional behavior, their positive reinforcement value seems to increase. These three procedures are in general more difficult to apply than the aversive-presentation methods discussed because they require the parents to exercise self-control, flexibility, and forethought, and in many instances, may inconvenience other members of the family. However, such inconveniences are not nearly so serious as some of the emotional byproducts and social disruptions caused by aversive-presentation methods (Azrin & Holz, 1966).

Instructions with aversive components.   There is a strong tendency for the prohibitions of parents, older siblings, and teachers to be couched in words, expressions, and gestures having emotional properties associated with aversive contingencies. They can therefore be viewed as training by conditioned aversive contingencies.

Sometimes a child is instructed in what he must not do ("We do not bite other children here.") and sometimes he is instructed in what he must not do and is told the contingency for such a transgression at the same time ("I don't want you to lie, and if I catch you telling a lie, I'll give you a spanking."). The effectiveness of this procedure depends on the functions of these words for the child and they in turn are dependent on the fidelity with which these rules or similar rules have been carried out in the past. Repeating the rule in training situations may be viewed as a kind of prompting technique, and as such, its effectiveness also depends upon how consistently such rule-giving has been followed up with appropriate contingencies.

Extinction. Weakening unmoral behavior by extinction—not responding to behavior, or reacting as though it had not occurred—has the advantage of possessing little or no aversive properties (Baer, 1962). However, extinction has limited value as a moral training technique because (1) it can be used only in instances in which the parents can afford to let the behavior go unchecked; (2) it ordinarily takes many repetitions over a relatively long time to work; and (3) it may be used to establish an intermittent schedule of reinforcement that strengthens rather than weakens the undesirable behavior (Bijou & Baer, 1961).

Reinforcement of incompatible behavior. Reinforcement of incompatible behavior, sometimes referred to as a distraction technique, and frequently resorted to because of the immediate results, consists of calling attention to, or setting the occasion for, another activity that competes effectively with the unmoral behavior in progress. A parent, seeing that her child is about to splash paint on the furniture, might terminate that activity by quickly suggesting that they dash off to the supermarket to get the dessert for tonight's dinner. Unlike other techniques of reducing or eliminating transgressions, this procedure does not weaken the unmoral behavior; it merely diverts the child to another activity, and the unmoral behavior retains its original strength.

Strengthening Positive Moral Behavior

Parental practices that strengthen positive moral behavior may be analyzed as including simple differential reinforcement, modeling or imitation, social role-taking, and stating the rules in positive terms.

Simple differential reinforcement. One way of training a young child in many of his family's moral standards is to give him ample opportunity to behave according to its moral code and reinforce him for doing so. Initially, situations can be arranged so that the child is free to play with all the toys and objects around, regardless to whom they belong. Next, the situation may include one or more taboo objects with attendant differential reinforcement training designating ownership, beginning with labels such as "mine" and "yours" and later extending to "his," "hers," "theirs," or "ours."

In the same spirit, situations can be arranged involving non-family adults and peers to give the child additional opportunities to engage in social behavior. The difference between these training situations and those that occur in the natural course of a mother's daily activities is that the training situations are specially designed for the child and are therefore carefully planned to provide the appropriate opportunities and carefully supervised so that the appropriate differential contingencies are delivered.

Modeling or imitation. Modeling, or its equivalent, imitation, is a powerful prompt for behavior—moral, unmoral, or immoral. Because at least two age-related moral codes are in effect in the home at the same time (one for the parents and one for the young child), the child quickly learns to discriminate the moral behaviors that will probably be reinforced from those that will probably not be reinforced. A young boy modeling his father's example of waiting until all the family is seated at the table before he starts to eat would almost without exception be reinforced; for modeling his father's cursing when he trips over a toy left lying around, he would probably be reprimanded.

Positive moral behavior is maintained according to the frequency and distribution of reinforcements. Since most of a child's moral training is incidental to family living, parents and other members of the household will respond inconsistently to instances of his moral behaviors. In other words, intermittent reinforcement and mixtures of positive reinforcement, nonreinforcement, and aversive contingencies characterize moral training. Moreover, variations in setting factors constantly influence the effectiveness of schedules of reinforcement. For example, when father is in a good mood, he tends to overlook his child's abuses of property; when he is irritable, he is apt to deal harshly with comparable or even less serious infractions of the rules governing the family's possessions. Likewise when friends or relatives are visiting, parents often relax or even abandon their usual practices in dealing with moral and unmoral behaviors. Depending on the schedule of reinforcement that these variations in parental practices generate, some forms of initial moral behavior become well established and highly resistant to change, while others remain tenuous and erratic.

Social role-taking. Roles are generalized ways of behaving toward categories of people (Brown, 1965). If a person possesses the defining characteristics of a particular category (discriminative stimuli), he is expected to behave according to the social prescription for that category— in other words, to assume that role. Sometimes the defining characteristics are biological (boys do this, girls do that; infants do this, children do that); sometimes they reflect a kind of training (intern, apprentice, student); sometimes they are occupational (teacher, doctor, office manager); and sometimes they are recreational (Little Leaguer, nature lover, tennis star). Training in role-taking, which usually supports training in moral behavior, consists primarily of training a child in the defining characteristics of a role, describing the behavior required for that category, and applying differential contingencies for compliance and noncompliance.

Training in role-taking begins in the universal stage of infancy with colors, names, clothing, toys, or hair style, and is related solely to biological criteria (male, female, son, daughter). In early childhood, roles are based on combinations of biological and social indicators. For example, in reprimanding her six-year-old for hitting his younger sister, the mother might admonish him by saying, "You should take care of your little sister and see that she doesn't get hurt instead of hurting her, and besides you should never hit a girl."

Stating the rules. Moral behavior instilled through positively stated rules, maxims, and precepts is a technique generally based on verbal imperatives such as: "Tell him the rules," "Let him know what is expected," and "Tell him what he ought to do."

Although stating rules is probably the most pervasive method used to develop positive moral behavior, its effectiveness is difficult to predict because it depends primarily upon the past relationships between the rule-giver and the child. If stating a rule leads a child to behave in accordance with that rule and his compliance is reinforced, it is likely, after several repetitions, that the procedure will be effective. In other words, under these circumstances stating a rule becomes a discriminative stimulus for the action prescribed by the rule (Schutte & Hopkins, 1970).

Stating the rules can also be taught to a child as a self-management technique, and we know that a child can use self-instruction at an early age. Stone and Church (1973) observed that preschoolers frequently instruct themselves by talking to themselves out loud but, like adults, they do not always do what they say. One approach to training a child in this technique is to encourage her to say aloud what she is going to do and to reinforce her as soon as she does it. For example, a mother might say to her daughter in a "let's play" manner, "First, say to yourself that you are going to put your blocks away and then join your mother in the kitchen for a dish of ice cream, and then do it." When the child does both, the mother reinforces her.

Rearranging Setting Factors

Setting factors, or the physical, social, and biological context in which an act occurs, may be arranged so that they strengthen moral acts and weaken unmoral acts. Because of their frequent use in animal research, the setting factors most often alluded to are deprivation of, and satiation for, the reinforcing stimuli. On a long car trip, for instance, children are restricted in physical activity (deprivation). Stopping to give them a chance to run and play until they have had enough (satiation) tends to reduce the aggressive behavior frequently evident during family outings.

Parents' conceptions about the origin of morality is another instance of a setting factor. If they consider a child to be inherently bad, sinful, or antisocial, they tend to be righteous in their belief that moral standards can be achieved only through aversive-presentation contingencies. ("He won't learn the things that are good for him unless he's given a good spanking now and then.") If, on the other hand, they hold the Rousseauian view that a child is inherently good ("He should be given every opportunity to realize his full potential."), they tend to use aversive contingencies sparingly.

Popular literature dealing with childrearing practices is a third example of a setting factor, especially for middle-class parents. It is well established that pediatricians, child psychiatrists, and child psychologists continually write how-to-do-it books on childrearing in sympathy with the *Zeitgeist* rather than basing their work on well-documented psychological principles (Stendler, 1950; and Wolfenstein, 1953). In the early 1970s the news media were reporting that "permissiveness" (which was said to be responsible for student unrest during the 1960s) is giving way to "individualism." These terms do not in the least describe what parents do in rearing their children. They are concepts based on many considerations, and particularly on the reporters' biases.

A fourth example of a setting factor is the competence and mental health of the parents. Obviously, retarded and emotionally disturbed parents have difficulty in defining and carrying out the kind of moral training that helps a child learn the behaviors that are required in a well-functioning family and outside his home, nor would they, in most instances, be cognizant of the need for such training.

The fifth and last example pertains to the conditions that control the emotional characteristics of a child. A family situation generating behaviors in a child that lead friends and neighbors to describe him as happy, angry, or fearful means, in terms of behavior analysis, that certain classes of his responses are highly probable and that certain others, usually the opposite types, are highly improbable. We say that the happy child tends to smile a great deal and to complain very little; the angry child tends to argue and fight often and to smile and joke rarely; the fearful child tends to avoid situations frequently and to smile and chat infrequently. The conditions that generate positive emotional predispositions in a child (a tendency to smile, laugh, banter, etc.) also facilitate acquisition of the family moral standards and do so on the basis of positive reinforcing contingencies. Among other things, the probability of imitative behavior of all sorts is greater.

A child can be trained to manage setting factors which influence his own behavior. Advising him to count to ten when he gets angry, and then to act, is still sound advice. When one is frustrated by a person or an obstacle of some sort, counting reduces the possibility of an aggressive response by providing time for the physiological component of the anger response to attenuate (Holland & Skinner, 1961).

Using Physical Conditions to Prevent Unmoral Behavior

Conditions may be arranged to restrain a child physically from engaging in unmoral conduct (locking a child in his room to prevent him from leaving the house when he was told that he may not). Physical restraints serve merely as a temporary expedient; they do not teach the child to engage in the approved forms of moral behavior. However, they may be used to prime initial moral behavior (get the desired behavior going) and thereby give the parents an opportunity to reinforce it.

A child can be taught to apply physical restraint to himself as a self-management skill. For example, it is simple for a child to learn to clap his hand over his mouth and refrain from calling a bigger boy a dirty name. This trick may keep him from getting hurt in a fight, as may have happened on a past occasion.

Other Procedures

The above analyses of moral training techniques used by parents, older siblings, and teachers—reducing or eliminating transgressions, strengthening positive moral behavior, rearranging setting factors, and using physical conditions to prevent unmoral behavior—constitute practically all the presently known possibilities garnered from experimental research. Some child psychologists would take issue with this contention. Hoffman (1970), for example, includes an "induction" category, consisting of methods in which persuasion, explanations, and reasoning are used to help a child to comply with the family moral code. An example of a technique in this category is "pointing out the physical requirements of the situation or the harmful consequences of the child's behavior for himself or others" (p. 286). Induction is inappropriate in a behavior analysis approach because the techniques it subsumes are covered in one or the other of the categories discussed, such as instructions with conditioned aversive contingencies, stating the rules in positive terms, rearranging setting factors—particularly those involving emotional predispositions—and reinforcement of incompatible behavior. This was illustrated in the results of a survey in which nursery school teachers were asked to describe how they would "reason" with a child who threw sand in another child's face. Over half gave responses with aversive overtones: "It's wrong," "You won't be allowed to play," and "You'll lose your friends." About one-third directed the child to change the emotional state of the victim: "Let's help him clean up" and "Say you're sorry." A small percentage directed the child to do something else: "Throw the ball" and "Pound the clay."

APPLICATION OF BEHAVIORAL PRINCIPLES
TO INITIAL MORAL TRAINING

Our analyses make it apparent, first, that initial moral training can be accomplished in a variety of ways, and second, that procedures should be selected to fit the circumstances, yet not be detrimental to the child's future development. Even with little understanding of applied behavior analysis, parents can incorporate some of the principles into their childrearing practices; however, they will be far more effective if they learn and apply these techniques in an orderly manner. True, this requires time and effort, but considering that the newly acquired training skills will influence practically all aspects of their child's behavior, it would be a worthwhile investment.

Application of behavior analysis to training in initial moral behavior, like the technology of teaching motor skills, self-care abilities, communication skills, and academic subjects (Shearer & Shearer, 1972), consists of five steps: (1) specify in behavioral terms the goal of moral training; (2) begin training at a level at which the child can succeed; (3) arrange conditions to facilitate learning the behaviors that will lead to the objective; (4) monitor progress and alter the procedures and goals as necessary to insure reasonable steady progress; and (5) maintain the acquired moral behavior. It is beyond the scope of this chapter to describe each step comprehensively; nevertheless a resume follows that will acquaint the reader with what is involved.

1. Specify the goal of training. Parents who aspire to train their child to be truthful, honest, considerate, and responsible are bound to have problems in knowing what to do to achieve these ends and in recognizing when they have accomplished their aims, for these terms refer not to behavior, but to personality traits. Both of these difficulties can be avoided if, first, the parents clearly identify in behavioral terms each moral goal they want their child to achieve, and second, by dealing with a single, specific, concrete instance as it arises (Mager, 1962). For example, instead of trying to train a child to be truthful, the parents should aim to have him report accurately on his own behavior even on instances that are contrary to the family moral code. Thus, parents may reinforce a child for telling the truth yet punish him for his transgression. Obviously, it is essential to arrange the differential contingencies in a way that encourages the child to continue to tell the truth.

2. Begin training at a realistic level for the child. Many parents decide that "it is time" to begin some form of moral training on the basis of the child's age, which, in turn, is presumed to be an indicator of some internal "readiness," such as neurological maturation (development of myelin sheath), mental ability (hypothetical mental structure), or timing (the "critical" period concept). But no matter what the rationale, most age-dependent indicators of "readiness" are not in the least tenable (Hunt, 1969). A more promising approach is to evaluate the child's actual performance in related tasks and start training at that level. (See Chapter 5 on criterion-referenced testing.)

3. Arrange conditions to facilitate learning. Arranging conditions to facilitate learning of the family moral code incorporates the techniques previously described for prohibiting unmoral behavior and strengthening positive moral behavior, with the long-range view of helping a child to comply with moral standards in the absence of a supervising adult; for example, training a child not to aggress against his younger sibling both in the presence and absence of a parent or parent surrogate. Although the specific conditions to be arranged, or the techniques to be used in training a child in any category of moral behavior depend on many factors, the most effective approach strengthens desirable behavior *and* weakens undesirable behavior. For example, a parent might use instructions to strengthen moral behavior and to prohibit unmoral behavior. Here, training involves telling the child in clearly stated terms what he ought to do and what he ought not to do, and applying differential contingencies for compliance and noncompliance.

4. Monitor progress and alter procedures as needed. Evidence as to how well or how poorly a child is learning the family's moral standards is generally gleaned from the frequency with which he has to be scolded for violations. Counting infractions, however, is a poor teaching technique if for no other reason than that it continually calls the child's attention to his mistakes, misjudgments, and oversights. Some kind of a monitoring procedure—even a crude one such as entering on a chart instances of positive behavior—is effective because it emphasizes and shows at a glance the child's progress and achievement in learning the moral behavior. An added advantage of such monitoring is that indications of progress reinforce the parents' efforts, and indications of little or no progress alert them to the need for alternative procedures.

5. Maintain the acquired moral behavior. Establishing initial moral behavior is the first goal of the training task; the second is maintaining the acquired behavior. Effective maintenance is often the more difficult task for it requires parents not only to be alert and to reinforce instances of moral behavior and to punish, or not reinforce, incidents of unmoral behavior, but to do so over an extended period and under a variety of circumstances. Although differential contingencies need not be given after each response, they should occur with sufficient frequency to maintain the acquired behavior.

AN EXAMPLE OF INITIAL MORAL TRAINING
BASED PRIMARILY ON POSITIVE REINFORCEMENT

In describing the steps involved in training early moral behavior, we included many brief examples. To emphasize the logic of the entire procedure, we present an example of training dealing with property rights. The procedures involve the presentation, withdrawal, removal, or non-occurrence of positive reinforcers rather than aversive-presentation methods. Because aversive-presentation punishment may lead to rigid parental practices, and because it does not always suppress unmoral behavior and may instead generate considerable "side-effects" (Goldiamond, 1968), a convincing case can be made for the positive approach.

If the mother in the example appears to be a paragon with few responsibilities other than to train her child, she has been pictured so in order to keep the situation as uncomplicated as possible. We recognize that the contingencies in family living are such that in the course of moral training parents lose their tempers or resort to dictatorial methods. In a comprehensive account of an actual training sequence, these reactions would also be analyzed in behavioral terms.

Mrs. Boller, an informed parent, has no objection to her five-year-old Rory's playing with things that belong to her friends and neighbors and their children (nor do they) but she tells him she would like him to ask the owner's permission first (instructions). One day she sees Rory in their neighbor's yard playing on the jungle gym and decides to set up a miniprogram she has read about which will help him learn the behavior she considers essential: obtaining prior permission. She knows that he has the required language repertory to benefit from such a program, that he understands the meaning of words like *his, hers, mine, theirs, belongs, owns,* etc.

Mrs. Boller calls Rory into the house (time-out from opportunities for positive reinforcement) and tells him that she knows he likes to climb and swing on the Hensons's play equipment, and as far as she is concerned, it is all right for him to do so. But, she continues, the jungle gym *belongs* to Mrs. Henson, so each time he wants to play on it, *he must ask Mrs. Henson for permission* (instructions with respect to his antecedent behavior). She adds that if he prefers that she ask Mrs. Henson for him, she would be willing to do that. After this talk, she makes a note in her diary of the date, the occasion, and the gist of her talk. The next day she sees Rory swinging on the jungle gym and learns from him that he has neglected to ask permission. She takes him into the house (time-out from a reinforcing activity), repeats her statement about the need for prior approval (instructions), and goes through the procedure with him to strengthen the required chain: (1) She takes him by the hand and they go into the neighbor's yard. There she again tells him that the jungle gym *belongs* to the Henson family and points out the fence separating their yard from the Hensons's yard. (2) She takes him back into their house, and instructs him to ask her to phone Mrs. Henson for permission for him to play. (3) He does so; Mrs. Boller telephones, and receives permission for him. (4) She then tells him that he now has permission and sends him on his way. She notes the incident in her book.

Two days later, Rory is once again playing on the jungle gym. His mother calls to him and asks whether he has obtained permission. When he says "yes," she asks whether it is all right to check with Mrs. Henson, to which he assents. Learning from Mrs. Henson that he did not ask, Mrs. Boller calls him into the house (time-out from positive reinforcement) and tells him what she was told. She tells him to go next door and ask for permission, and if permission is granted, he may go there to play. She records the occurrence. The next day, before going out, Rory asks his mother to phone Mrs. Henson for him. The mother expresses her delight and phones. He runs off to play and she makes another entry in the book. On each of the next three days, he asks his mother to phone and Mrs. Boller is satisfied that he has learned the "lesson." On the fourth day, the mother prompts him to ask permission himself and he does.

About a week later, Rory's mother sees him playing with a puppy in another neighbor's yard and goes to him. Although he admits that he neglected to ask permission, she compliments him for telling the truth and instructs him to go and ask the owner, Mrs. Taylor, for permission (time-out from positive reinforcement). Upon receiving permission, Rory resumes his play with the puppy. Mrs. Boller returns home, makes an entry in the diary, and goes back to doing the family laundry. She continues the monitoring practice until she is satisfied that her son "knows" what to do before playing with things that belong to the neighbor, that is, until the sight of, or the plan for playing with the possessions of others, becomes a discriminative stimulus for asking permission to play rather than for approaching and playing.

Such moral training practices, with a minimum of aversive-contingency punishment, have a number of positive implications for a child's development, three of which are noted here. First, a child trained in moral behavior in this way would probably not be afflicted with self-generated strong aversive stimulation—Freud's concept of superego or conscience.

There is no reason to believe that such a child would be deficient in moral behavior because moral behavior, like other classes of operant behavior, may be established reliably through positive reinforcing contingencies. A child reared primarily on the basis of positive reinforcement would acquire most of his moral behavior from what the psychoanalysts call the "ego-ideal" part of his personality.

A second implication is that he would probably be relatively free from self-generated aversive stimulation from committing an unmoral act (strong guilt or shame reactions). Self-generated aversive stimulation is like externally generated aversive stimulation: when presented contingently, it suppresses the antecedent behavior; when withdrawn, it reinforces behavior. There is a difference between self-generated and external stimulation, however. Self-generated aversive stimulation is an integral part of the child's internal environment, and as such, escape from its effects without physical intervention is impossible. The child's only behavioral recourse is to engage in other behaviors that are likely to remove or reduce its effects. These other behaviors are often detrimental to the social behavior of the individual.

A third implication of training based primarily on positive reinforcement is that it avoids operant and pain-elicited aggression or social disruption, both of which are a function of aversive-presentation contingencies (Azrin & Holz, 1966). In many instances, these forms of behavior are more harmful to the development of the child than the unmoral behavior for which aversive-presentation punishment was used.

A CONCLUDING NOTE

The development of initial moral behavior requires coordinated investigations in the home and in the preschool in order to learn the actual practices of parents and preschool teachers and how they affect the child in specific situations in and out of the home. The research methodology should involve direct observational measures that yield objective information on descriptive and functional relationships (Bijou, Peterson, & Ault, 1968; and Bijou, Peterson, Harris, Allen, & Johnston, 1969). Indirect evaluation methods, such as interviews and psychometric tests, must be set aside as inadequate for research in this area. Future studies on parent, older sibling, and teacher practices have the task of isolating and clarifying the conditions that facilitate the learning of initial moral behavior and eventually pinpointing those practices that are effective as well as those that are undesirable for the child from the long-range point of view. Such research, together with supplementary information from laboratory research, should yield, in relatively short order, a serviceable set of procedures for moral training practices because early child training is invariably and naturally individualized. The contingencies in effect are generally powerful; the behaviors involved are usually functional; and the child's history is so brief as to preclude prolonged remedial procedures.

From the point of view of practical application, parents can be trained to help their child acquire the initial moral behavior by behavioral procedures that have been successful in teaching parents how to help their child develop motor, self-care, communication, and academic skills (Shearer & Shearer, 1972). These approaches have been based on empirical concepts and principles derived from laboratory studies.

REFERENCES

Allen, D. "Implications of microteaching for inservice and preservice preparation of teachers." Microteaching Symposium, University of Kansas, May, 1971.

Aronfreed, J. The concept of internalization. In D. A. Goslin (Ed.), *Handbook of socialization theory and research.* Chicago: Rand McNally, 1969. Pp. 263–323.

Azrin, N. H. & Holz, W. C. Punishment. In W. K. Honig (Ed.), *Operant Behavior: Areas of research and application.* Englewood Cliffs, N.J.: Prentice-Hall, 1966. Pp. 380–447.

Baer, D. M. Laboratory control of thumbsucking by withdrawal and representation of reinforcement. *Journal of the Experimental Analysis of Behavior,* 1962, 5, 525–28.

Bandura, A. & Walters, R. H. *Social learning and personality development.* New York: Holt, Rinehart & Winston, 1963.

Becker, W. C. Consequences of different kinds of parental discipline. In M. L. Hoffman & L. W. Hoffman (Eds.), *Review of child development research.* Vol. 1. New York: Russell Sage Foundation, 1964, Pp. 169–208.

Bijou, S. W. & Baer, D. M. *Child Development: A systematic and empirical theory.* Vol. 1. Englewood Cliffs, N.J.: Prentice-Hall, 1961.

Bijou, S. W. & Baer, D. M. *Child Development: The universal stage of infancy.* Vol. 2. Englewood Cliffs, N.J.: Prentice-Hall, 1965.

Bijou, S. W., Peterson, R. F., & Ault, M. H. A method to integrate descriptive and experimental field studies at the level of data and empirical concepts. *Journal of Applied Behavior Analysis,* 1968, *1,* 175–91.

Bijou, S. W., Peterson, R. F., Harris, F. R., Allen, A. K., & Johnston, M. S. Methodology for experimental studies of young children in natural settings. *Psychological Record*, 1969, *19*, 177–210.

Brown, R. *Social psychology*. New York: Free Press, 1965.

Caldwell, B. M. The effects of infant care. In M. L. Hoffman & L. W. Hoffman (Eds.), *Review of child development research*. Vol. 1. New York: Russell Sage Foundation, 1964. Pp. 9–88.

Doll, E. A. *The measurement of social competence*. New York: Educational Publishers, 1948.

Freud, S. *Outline of psychoanalysis*. New York: Norton, 1949.

Gewirtz, J. L. Mechanism of social learning: Some roles of stimulation and behavior in early human development. In D. A. Goslin (Ed.), *Handbook of socialization theory and research*. Chicago: Rand McNally, 1969. Pp. 57–212.

Goldiamond, I. Moral behavior: A functional analysis. *Psychology Today*, 1968, *2*(4), 31–34.

Hartshorne, H. & May, M. S. *Studies in the nature of character;* Vol. I, *Studies in deceit;* Vol. II, *Studies in self-control;* Vol. III, *Studies in the organization of character*. New York: Macmillan, 1928–1930.

Havighurst, R. J. *Human development and education*. New York: Longmans, Green, 1953.

Hoffman, M. L. Moral development. In P. H. Mussen (Ed.), *Carmichael's manual of child psychology*. Vol. 2. (3rd ed.) New York: John Wiley, 1970. Pp. 261–360.

Hoffman, M. L. & Saltzstein, H. D. Parent discipline and the child's moral development. *Journal of Personality and Social Psychology*, 1967, *5*, 45–57.

Holland, J. G. & Skinner, B. F. *The analysis of behavior*. New York: McGraw-Hill, 1961.

Hunt, J. McV. *The challenge of incompetence and poverty: Papers on the role of early education*. Urbana: University of Illinois Press, 1969. P. 73.

Kohlberg, L. The development of children's orientations toward a moral order. *Vita Humma*, 1963, *6*, 11–33.

Kohlberg, L. Development of moral character and ideology. In M. L. Hoffman & L. W. Hoffman (Eds.), *Review of child development research*. Vol. 1. New York: Russell Sage Foundation, 1964. Pp. 383–432.

Kohlberg, L. The child as a moral philosopher. *Psychology Today*, 1968, *2*, 25–34.

Lovell, K. *An introduction to human development*. Glenview, Ill.: Scott, Foresman, 1971. Pp. 101–10.

Mager, B. F. *Preparing instructional objectives*. Palo Alto, Calif.: Fearson, 1962.

Patterson, G. R., Cobb, J. A., & Ray, R. S. A social engineering technology for retraining aggressive boys. In H. Adams & L. Unikel (Eds.), *Georgia symposium in experimental clinical psychology.* Vol. 2. Springfield, Ill.: Charles C Thomas, 1970.

Piaget, J. *The moral judgment of the child.* London: Kegan Paul, 1932.

Radke, M. J. *The relation of parental authority to children's behavior and attitudes.* Minneapolis: University of Minnesota Press, 1946.

Schutte, R. C. & Hopkins, B. L. The effects of teacher attention on following instructions in a kindergarten class. *Journal of Experimental Analysis of Behavior,* 1970, *8,* 117–22.

Sears, R. R. Dependency motivation. In M. Jones (Ed.), *Nebraska symposium on motivation.* Lincoln: University of Nebraska Press, 1963. Pp. 25–64.

Sears, R. R., Maccoby, E. E., & Levin, H. *Patterns of child rearing.* Evanston, Ill.: Row, Peterson, 1957.

Shearer, M. S. & Shearer, D. E. The Portage Project: A model for early childhood education. *Exceptional Children,* 1972, *38,* 210–17.

Skinner, B. F. *Contingencies of reinforcement: A theoretical analysis.* Englewood Cliffs, N.J.: Prentice-Hall, 1969.

Stone, L. J. & Church, J. *Childhood and adolescence.* (3rd ed.) New York: Random House, 1973.

Stendler, C. B. Sixty years of child rearing practices. *Journal of Pediatrics,* 1950, *36,* 122–34.

Thoresen, C. E. & Mahoney, M. J. *Behavior self-control.* New York: Holt, Rinehart & Winston, 1974.

Wahler, R. G. Setting generality: Some specific general effects of child behavior therapy. *Journal of Applied Behavior Analysis,* 1969, *2,* 239–46.

Wolfenstein, M. Trends in infant care. *American Journal of Orthopsychiatry,* 1953, *23,* 120–30.

Yarrow, M. R., Campbell, J. D., & Burton, R. V. Reliability of maternal retrospection: A preliminary report. *Family Process,* 1964, *3,* 207–18.

Yarrow, M. R., Campbell, J. D., & Burton, R. V. *Child rearing.* San Francisco: Jossey-Bass, 1968.

7

Child Behavior Treatment

The procedures for alleviating behavior problems that we discuss here apply to the treatment of young children with marked behavior deviations, such as those of a child who is so oppositional that he disrupts the daily activities of the entire family, or those of a child so grossly retarded that at age five has not yet begun to talk. Not included are mild problems—occasional temper tantrums, negativisms, and acts of aggression—which are generally handled by parents and teachers.

The chapter is in five sections: (1) historical background of child behavior therapy, (2) diagnosis and classification, (3) behavioral treatment techniques, (4) legal, ethical, and social issues, and (5) probable future trends.

HISTORICAL BACKGROUND

The treatment of young children's behavior problems by professionally trained specialists is a relatively recent social phenomenon. In the United States the first social agency devoted exclusively to the psychological treatment of children (although it was primarily for school-age children) was established by Leightner Witmer at the University of Pennsylvania in 1896 (Reisman, 1966). Witmer believed that most social and academic problems were caused by undetected physiological deficiencies. Hence, the diagnosis was based on physical and "mental" examinations, which included anthropometric measures, visual and auditory tests, and measures of reaction time; and treatment consisted of training or retraining in the defects discovered. The staff and consultants were mainly social workers, doctors, and teachers, with the remedial teacher as the central figure, since reeducation was the key treatment concept.

It remained for Freud, however, to pave the way for a psychological approach to the treatment of children's psychological problems. Freud's interest in treatment stemmed not from a conviction that his procedures were applicable to the problems of children but from an eagerness for data to support his theory of psychopathology. He claimed that neurotic disturbances in an adult originated in the sexual conflicts in childhood and therefore a child must have an active sexual life and vivid sexual fantasies. In 1909, he presented the case of a phobic four-year-old boy, the well-known case of Little Hans (Freud, 1925). The boy's father, a Viennese physician and a follower of Freud, kept anecdotal records of his son's fear of going outdoors because the boy was afraid he would be bitten by horses. The father took Hans to see Freud once, and carried on treatment in consultation with Freud through correspondence. The father learned that the child was particularly bothered by horses that "wore things in front of their eyes and black things around their mouths." Freud, believing that the child's description of the horses was actually a description of his father because he wore glasses and had a mustache, interpreted this to mean that the child was really afraid of his father. Through a series of discussions, the father tried to give his son "insight" so that he would understand that his fear was of the father and not of the horses. From the correspondence and a personal contact with the boy, Freud was convinced that this treatment was successful. Although the case cannot be considered either as supporting or as refuting Freud's theory of psychopathology (Wolpe & Rachman, 1960), nevertheless Freud's report was the first application of a modern psychological theory to a child's behavior problem.

Further explorations of psychoanalysis for the treatment of young children were made by psychoanalytically oriented teachers (Mahler, 1945). In 1913, Hug-Hellmuth (1919) developed teaching methods based on psychoanalytic principles and introduced play as a therapeutic tool. About ten years later, Anna Freud (1946) and Melanie Klein (1949), working separately, further refined and elaborated on the then current psychoanalytic techniques for children. Each wrote in some detail on the nature of transference, the symbolic character of play, the role of teaching procedures in treatment, and the ages and types of children who profit most from this type of treatment. On many points, they differed sharply with one another.

The efforts of these clinical teachers soon led to the treatment of children by psychiatrists, clinical psychologists, and social workers. In the United States, their influence was tailored to the needs of rapidly expanding child guidance clinics attached to mental hospitals, schools, courts, colleges, and social agencies. In these settings, and in private clinics and private practice, the trend was away from child analysis ("depth" analysis) requiring four or five visits a week and toward "brief" techniques requiring only one visit a week. Of the brief techniques, some were described as "free," wherein the child typically selected the materials and the form of his play (Pearson, 1949), and some as "controlled," with the therapist deciding on the material and the play setting and encouraging the child to react to the situations presented (Levy, 1939).

While psychoanalytic psychotherapy was being modified to fit the developmental characteristics of young children and data were being collected to evaluate its effectiveness, a different approach to child therapy was evolving from research in university-affiliated conditioning and learning laboratories. Foremost was a study by Mary Cover Jones (1924) on the reduction of fears. The claims of Watson and Rayner (1920) that fears in infancy are acquired by classical (Pavlovian) conditioning led Jones to investigate the methods of reducing fears in children from ages three months to seven years, who were residents of an institution for the temporary care of children. All the children were exposed to a fairly standardized range of situations: being left alone, being in a dark room, being with other children who showed fear, and the sudden presentation of a snake, white rat, frog, rabbit, false faces, and loud sounds. The majority showed no fears, and those that did, were treated. In the treatment process, Jones evaluated efficacy of numerous methods of eliminating fears: (1) disuse, (2) verbal appeal, (3) negative adaption (extinction), (4) repression (ridicule), (5) distraction, (6) direct conditioning, and (7) social imitation. Only the last two—direct conditioning and social imitation—proved to be effective. Direct conditioning of Peter, age 2 years 10 months, completely eliminated his fear of a rabbit by pairing candy with the presence of the rabbit, first at a distance and then close by. The power of social imitation was demonstrated in the case of Vincent, age 1 year 9 months, whose fear of a rabbit was accidentally established by seeing another child react fearfully to the rabbit (social imitation). The fear reaction, which persisted for over two weeks, was eliminated after another child playfully induced him to touch the animal.

Almost twenty years later Mowrer and Mowrer (1938) demonstrated that bedwetting could be eliminated by the application of learning principles. They devised a liquid-sensitive pad that was placed on the bed. As soon as the child began to urinate, a bell rang which woke him and alerted the parent who immediately took him to the bathroom to urinate in the toilet. The bell ringing device was then reset and the child returned to bed. Of the thirty children treated, all reached the criterion of fourteen consecutive dry nights within two months. Interestingly enough, the device, in a vastly improved form, is still being marketed forty years later by a large mail-order company.

During the next twenty years, roughly from the 1940s to the 1960s, many learning psychologists subscribed to the view that child therapy was basically a form of education or reeducation but few applied psychologists were concerned with developing treatment procedures based upon this conception. The application of psychoanalysis was in full swing. However, a few, such as Axline (1947), ventured into exploring procedures founded on Carl Rogers's client-centered approach (1939). The prevalent belief of psychiatrists and clinical psychologists was that conditioning and learning principles could be applied to the treatment of problems involving simple "habits" while psychoanalysis, which dealt with the inner workings of the personality, was required for the treatment of "deep-seated" emotional problems.

In the early 1960s, there was a resurgence of interest in the use of the learning-behavioral approach to the treatment of children's behavior problems. Three factors contributed to this movement: (1) the cumulation of data questioning the effectiveness of the psychoanalytic treatment of children (Levitt, 1957 & 1963); (2) the extension of experimental analysis of behavior from the animal laboratory to the study of young children (Bijou, 1955 & 1957); and (3) the appearance of Skinner's *Science and Human Behavior* (1953). In *Science and Human Behavior,* Skinner contended that psychological treatment should be concerned not with changes in hypothetical inner processes and states such as the relationship between the Freudian "id" or "superego" or between the conscious and unconscious, but with behavior itself. He further maintained that "therapy consists not in getting the patient to discover the solution to his problem, but in changing him in such a way that he is able to discover it" (p. 382).

An early study that kindled interest in the application of learning principles to the treatment of children demonstrated that "tyrant-like" tantrums in a twenty-one-month-old boy could be eliminated by extinction procedures (Williams, 1959). The study was carried out in the home under the supervision of the boy's father who was a psychologist. Because the child had a tantrum whenever his parents or his aunt left the room after putting him to bed, they spent from one-half to two hours each bedtime waiting for him to fall asleep. Following medical reassurance, the parents started the practice of putting him to bed in a normal, pleasant way and not responding to his tantrums when they left the bedroom. The frequency of tantrums decreased and by the tenth night, not only did the boy not cry, but smiled when his father, mother, or aunt left the room and made happy sounds until he dropped off to sleep. Inadvertently, the tantrums reoccurred and the extinction procedures were repeated. This time the tantrums were eliminated by the ninth night and none occurred during the next two years. Nor had any undesirable aftereffects been observed. In other words, the removal of a "psychological symptom" by direct procedures did not lead to a substitute psychological "symptom," which is what the psychoanalytic theory would have predicted. At four years old, the boy was described as friendly, expressive, and outgoing.

A second study demonstrating the applicability of behavior principles to the treatment of children's "emotional" problems were carried out by teachers in a nursery school setting (Harris, Johnston, Kelley & Wolf, 1964). Social reinforcement procedures were used to help a three-year-old girl, Dee, substitute well-developed walking for crawling, a form of locomotion she recently had reacquired, considered a sign of "regression" in psychoanalytic theory. The usual teacher approaches to her (friendly, warm, solicitous) resulted in strong withdrawal behavior. Treatment consisted of giving Dee attention when she was on her feet and withdrawing attention when she was off her feet, that is, when she was sitting, lying down, or crawling. The data from this procedure, together with data from two reversal procedures, showed that the attention of the teachers changed the child's behavior in the desired direction. Within five weeks of school attendance, Dee had made the kind of progress that would have been expected to take not less than five or six months under previous nursery school techniques. Post-treatment observational checks at irregular intervals over a year showed that Dee's improved behavior was stable.

The third study presented evidence that a mother could be trained to treat her child's problem behavior in the home (Hawkins, Peterson, Schweid, & Bijou, 1966). Four-year-old Peter was physically and verbally aggressive, his mother reported. He removed or tore his clothing, and hit himself to gain attention; he became enraged at the slightest frustration, and seldom cooperated with his mother. He had been previously diagnosed as hyperactive and of borderline intelligence, with possible brain damage. After the investigators observed Peter and his mother together for a little over two weeks, the treatment procedures were put into effect. The mother was told that the investigator would use three gestural signals that would indicate how she was to behave toward her son. Signal A meant she was to tell him to stop his objectionable behavior. This was used the first time a particular objectionable behavior occurred during a session. Signal

B meant she was to put Peter in his room and close the door. This was used only when he repeated a particular objectionable behavior. Signal *C* meant that she was to give him attention, praise, and affectionate physical contact. This was used when Peter was playing in a desirable way. Under this procedure, there was a striking decrease in all of the nine behaviors considered objectionable. The mother was then instructed to behave toward Peter as she had before the study began whereupon the rate of Peter's objectionable behavior increased. After a brief period, the treatment procedures involving hand signals were reinstituted, which again reduced Peter's objectionable behavior, demonstrating the reliability of the relationship between changes in the objectionable behavior and the contingencies used. The study, which took place over thirty-six weeks, was followed by twenty-four days without supervision of the mother. A post-treatment observational check showed that the improvement in behavior was still evident. The mother confirmed that Peter was reasonably well behaved and much less demanding and added that she had been using the time-out from opportunities for positive reinforcement only about once a week.

The fourth study involved a three-year-old boy with an assortment of problems, including a serious visual handicap resulting from the lens being removed because of cataracts (Wolf, Risley, & Mees, 1964). The subject, Dicky, was diagnosed variously as mentally retarded, diffuse and locally brain-damaged, and psychotic, with the possibility of additional anomalies including phenylprivic oligophenia and hyperthyroidism. The specific problems selected for treatment were reducing his temper tantrums (which included self-destructive episodes), training him to go to bed without emotional displays, teaching him to eat in a socially acceptable way, and training him to wear glasses. Treatment, which took leads from Ferster and DeMyer's work on autistic children (1961), was carried on under the supervision of a psychologist by the attendants and by the parents on their visits to the psychiatric hospital and in the home. Various techniques were used to treat the various problem behaviors. Tantrums and bedtime problems were reduced by a combination of extinction and time-out from opportunities for reinforcement for undesirable behavior, and positive reinforcement for desirable behavior. Acceptable eating behavior was developed by giving food and social reinforcement for eating with utensils and asking for food, and by removing food and reprimanding him for stealing and throwing food. Training in wearing glasses over a period of five months was accomplished by positive reinforcement of progressive approximations. Training in language skills was introduced to maintain Dicky's glasses-wearing behavior. In order to see pictures and make the necessary responses to questions, he had to wear his glasses. Social reinforcement was used mostly in this training. Six months after Dicky's return home, the mother reported that "he continues to wear his glasses, does not have tantrums, has no sleeping problem, is becoming increasingly verbal, and is a new source of joy to the members of his family" (Wolf, Risley, & Mees, 1964, p. 312).

Each of the four studies cited above had its special impact on subsequent research on the application of behavior principles to the treatment of problem behavior. The studies by Williams (1959) and Hawkins et al. (1966) on treating problem behavior in the home opened the way for a stream of studies on parent training, some in relation to social behaviors and others to cognitive behaviors (Shearer & Shearer, 1972). The work of Harris et al. (1964) in the nursery school suggested further research, both methodological and substantive, in preschool settings for normal and handicapped young children (Harris, Wolf, & Baer, 1964); and the study by Wolf et al. (1964) on the multiply-handicapped child inspired research, especially on social and language problems, on severely disturbed children in hospitals, clinics, and university-affiliated laboratores (Lovaas, Berberich, Perloff, & Schaeffer, 1966; Lovaas, Fritas, Nelson & Whalen, 1967; and Lovaas, Schaeffer, & Simmons, 1965). As new treatment procedures developed, it was inevitable that the problems of diagnosis and classification would have to be re-evaluated.

DIAGNOSIS AND CLASSIFICATION

The clinical diagnosis and classification of young children's behavior problems have always presented serious problems for therapists, teachers, and parents (Zubin, 1967). Aside from the almost insurmountable difficulties inherent in trying to relate clearly "psychological symptoms" (patterns of behavior) to presumed underlying psychopathic processes, there is the possibility that a diagnosis, such as psychoneurosis, made at one stage of a child's development will not apply at a succeeding stage (whether the child is treated or not). Moreover, a diagnostic label that suggests an underlying psychopathology often stigmatizes and further handicaps a child (Rosenhan, 1973; and Szasz, 1960). An almost classical abuse is that of the child who, having been diagnosed as mentally retarded, is not only cut off from most social interactions and contingencies that promote learning but is placed in an environment that tends to magnify any handicaps he may have. There is the additional danger of applying to a child a diagnostic label that has been derived from clinical experience with adult patients (e.g., schizophrenia). Although a behavior disorder of an adult and a child may have some features in common, each disorder would have a different history, require different treatment, and result in a different outcome. Finally, a traditional diagnostic category for children does not consist of a well integrated or homogeneous set of behaviors (Lorr, Klett, & McNair, 1963; and Zigler & Phillips, 1961) and is not linked to specific treatment programs (Kanfer & Phillips, 1970) (see page 96). At the very best, a diagnostic category indicates modal, "textbook," or idealized characteristics which, in an individual case, may have little resemblance to the child's behavior problems or to his repertory of functional behaviors. For these and other reasons, the children's diagnostic categories in the American Psychiatric Association's *Standard Nomenclature of Psychiatric Disorders and Reactions of the American Medical Association* have had less than wide acceptance, as evidenced by the fact that over forty alternate diagnostic schemes have been proposed by practitioners.

Behavioral Diagnosis and Classification

Among many child behavior therapists, the diagnosis of a child's problem is treated as a clinical *intake evaluation,* the main purpose of which is to help the therapist decide whether he or his agency can handle the problem. That is to say, from reports by physicians, teachers, and parents, and sometimes from direct observation, the therapist or case-worker *describes a child in observable behavioral terms* and decides whether the agency's facilities, staff, and caseload can accommodate him. If the agency's treatment program is carried out primarily through group activities (a remedial academic class or an activity treatment group), the initial categorization helps the staff to determine, for example, whether one more aggressive child in the class or treatment group would create an imbalance that would slow down the treatment program to the detriment of the other children.

A diagnostic classification scheme for intake evaluation may be completely descriptive; it need not be related to a presumed cause, etiology, or set of antecedent conditions. The problem behavior may be classified merely on the basis of its dominant form, or topography, as in the following:

1. *Behavioral excesses.* Children with behavioral excesses are de-

scribed variously as extremely hostile, aggressive, "acting out," hyperactive, incorrigible, and conduct problems (Bijou & Peterson, 1971; Kanfer & Phillips, 1969; Kanfer & Saslow, 1969; Reese & Lipsitt, 1970; Ross, 1971 & 1972; and Sherman & Baer, 1969). These behaviors are aversive to others and their severity is usually judged normatively in terms of their frequency and/or intensity.

2. *Shy, withdrawn, and fearful behaviors.* This category includes children with specific fears or phobias, children described as adjustment problems (Ross, 1972), or personality problems (Quay, 1972) in which timidity is an overriding feature.

3. *Behavioral deficits.* Children with behavioral deficits include those who are underdeveloped in self-care, language, social skills, moral behaviors, academic abilities, and basic knowledge (Bijou & Peterson, 1971; Reese & Lipsitt, 1970; Ross, 1971; Sherman & Baer, 1969; and Staats & Staats, 1963).

4. *Behavioral ineptitudes.* Although children in this category have many serviceable behaviors, they occur, from the point of view of society, at the wrong time or place (Bijou & Peterson, 1971 and Staats & Staats, 1963). This group includes children who can talk but do not direct their conversation to people; children who react to people as objects; children who do not always differentiate appropriately between imaginary and real events, and children who have acquired "manners" but do not apply them at the proper times. Those in the last group are often referred to as psychopathic or inept personalities.

Does such a descriptive behavioral classification scheme help the therapist determine the cause, or etiology, of a behavior problem? An adequate answer requires some preliminary comments about the nature of cause in the science and applied science of human behavior. From a behavioral point of view, any unit of psychological behavior, normal or deviant, is caused by, or is a function of (1) a child's genetic history, (2) his personal history, and (3) the current situation. A therapist seldom attempts to investigate a child's genetic history for possible causes of his behavior problem. Most often he views the child's genetic history as conditions that determine, in part, both his unique anatomical structure and physiological functioning, which, in turn, contribute some of the conditions influencing the child's behavior. On the other hand, a therapist usually explores a child's personal history for clues that may indicate the cause of the problem behavior. Ideally, he must analyze the entire sequence of interactions between the child's biological makeup and the *actual* (observable) environmental events. In other words, to know why a child behaves the way he does a therapist must know everything that could have produced that particular behavior. Obviously, such comprehensive information is impossible to obtain. Indirect sources of information, such as parents' recall of a child's behavior and situational events, and psychological tests, have proven to be of limited or of questionable value (Yarrow, Campbell, & Burton, 1968). Even if it were possible for the therapist to obtain accurate and detailed information on actual past interactions, would that information be indispensable? Obviously not, since the therapist's objective is not to undo or redo a child's history but to analyze the conditions that maintain the problem behavior and to help the child rearrange them so that he can learn socially desirable behavior. It seems, therefore, that it is potentially possible for the therapist to determine some approximation of the cause of a child's behavior problem but such information will be useless in planning an effective treatment program. From the point of view of the behavior analyst, it is the here and now of the problem that is most important.

To contend that a behavior therapist need not know the history of a problem does not mean that he should deliberately ignore the available information about a child's background. On the contrary, such information can serve other purposes, as we shall see.

Initial Assessment

The initial assessment provides the therapist with a description of the problem and the conditions that are maintaining it, enabling him to prepare a treatment program that meets the child at his current level of functioning in the problem area. The assessment is usually derived from (1) interview, (2) standardized norm-referenced psychological tests, and (3) criterion-referenced inventories of (a) the child's behavioral equipment, that is, the things he can do, and (b) the functional properties of people and objects, discussed in Chapter 5.

The interview, which may include checklists and questionnaires (Lazarus, 1971; and Wahler & Cormier, 1970), not only provides background and current information on the problem but also serves to develop a language system that promotes communication between the interviewee and interviewer, pinpoints the exact problem that requires treatment

(Lazarus, 1971), and in cases with multiple problems, provides a basis for determining treatment priorities (Wolf, Risley, & Mees, 1964).

Standardized norm-referenced tests of intelligence, school achievement, and personality are used for different purposes and to varying degrees by child behavior therapists. For some they aid diagnostic evaluation, therapeutic planning, baseline performance, and terminal evaluation; for others they provide information requested by school administrators, school psychologists, teachers, parents, and caseworkers. Still others find no need at all for such tests.

Criterion-referenced inventories of behavior are generally used to obtain answers to such questions as (1) What behavior assets does the child have that can be used as a basis for a treatment program? (2) What stimuli have strong conditioned aversive properties for the child and to what extent can he tolerate those stimuli? (3) What stimuli have strong positive reinforcing functions for him? (4) What conditions maintain the problem behavior? What the initial assessment inventory reveals in relation to the last question is particularly valuable. Describing maintaining conditions is particularly relevant when the therapy is to be conducted in a natural setting rather than in a clinical setting:

If social contingencies are to be therapeutically rearranged for the deviant child, one must know who provides these contingencies, in what behavior form they are provided, for what child behaviors they are provided, and in what specific settings or sub-setting they are provided. Given this information, the clinician is in a position to intervene—to train the significant "contingency dispensers" (e.g., parents and teachers) to modify their interactions with the child (Wahler & Cormier, 1970, p. 279).

TREATMENT TECHNIQUES

Plans for child behavior therapy generally include these steps: (1) setting the behavioral goals or objectives to be achieved, (2) preparing to begin treatment at the child's level of competence, (3) determining the recordkeeping procedure, and (4) applying the therapeutic technique. Steps 1 and 2 are tied in with initial assessment, as described in the previous section. Regarding step 3, we need only reiterate that recordkeeping or monitoring procedures utilizing objectively defined units are an indispensable part of this therapy. If the recordkeeping data show little or no progress, the therapist is cued to modify his procedures (and sometimes his materials) until change occurs in the direction of the therapeutic objective. Typically, procedural alterations mean adjustments of some component of the program, rather than setting up a new program. Monitoring therapeutic progress also provides information on when the behavioral goals have been attained. Step 4, applying therapeutic techniques, is the main substance of this section.

The treatment of a problem typically involves (1) weakening behavior that is aversive to others and strengthening prosocial (appropriate or desirable) behavior, (2) substituting shy, withdrawn, and phobic behavior with prosocial behavior, (3) extending and elaborating new discriminations and abilities, and (4) bringing inept or inappropriate behavior under appropriate stimulus control.

Note that the treatment categories listed above are related not to specific behavior problems but to procedures for effecting specific behavior changes. The traditional model of listing of problems, such as school phobia, enuresis, severe "acting-out" behavior, together with recommended treatment is not followed here because there is no set way of dealing with a given behavior problem. Each has its own history and is maintained by its own set of unique circumstances. Therefore, the therapist using this approach must look at each problem individually and must decide which procedure is most likely to be appropriate for moving the child from his current behavior situation (baseline) to the treatment goal (criterion performance). For example, in dealing with one child's enuresis the therapist may use extinction to remove behaviors that obstruct new learning and social reinforcers to strengthen the desired behavior. In dealing with another child's enuresis, he may use time-out reinforcement opportunities to remove undesirable behavior and contrived generalized reinforcers (tokens) to strengthen desirable behavior. Clearly, the treatment procedures for a problem must always be tailored to the child in relation to his particular set of circumstances.

Weakening Behavior Aversive to Others and Strengthening Prosocial Behavior

Behavior aversive to others may be weakened by extinction or by aversive contingencies, the latter including time-out from reinforcement opportunities, response-cost (removing positive reinforcers), and contingent physical aversive stimulation (physical hurt). When extinction, or nonreinforcement, procedures are used in conjunction with positive reinforcement to strengthen desirable behavior, the behavior selected to be strengthened is usually one that is incompatible with the aversive behavior. For example, in a study with six hyperactive mentally retarded children, hyperactivity, the undesirable behavior, was not reinforced but tokens exchangeable for candy were given contingent upon quiet, constructive behavior (Doubros & Daniels, 1966). In all cases, the level of hyperactive behavior was reduced.

Time-out from reinforcement opportunities, a form of aversive contingency, involves removing a child for a brief period from a positive reinforcement situation immediately following some form of unacceptable behavior. For example, in treating a four-and-a-half-year-old boy's aggressive biting, hitting, and kicking, the teacher reinforced cooperative behavior with praise and attention, but removed him from the nursery school classroom as soon as he became aggressive (Sloane, Johnston, & Bijou, 1967). The time-out procedure consisted of escorting the child to an adjacent room devoid of toys and objects that could provide reinforcement. The teacher, who observed his behavior during time-out from behind a one-way-vision screen, returned him to the classroom after he had remained quiet for two minutes. As the frequency of his aversive behaviors decreased, the teacher began to show him the techniques of playing cooperatively and arranged opportunities for him to generalize his newly learned social behaviors. Similar procedures have also been used successfully with older, retarded children (Vukelich & Hake, 1971).

Response-cost, which involves taking away positive reinforcers contingent on undesirable behavior, is frequently referred to as contingency contracting (Homme, Csanyi, Gonzales, & Rechs, 1969). The child may either receive or lose conditioned reinforcers depending upon his behavior. In group situations or "token economies," the participants earn money for good behavior and are fined for inappropriate behavior—the child loses tokens or points each time he engages in the prohibited behavior (Burchard, 1967; and Burchard & Barrera, 1972).

The use of contingent physical aversive stimulation is generally limited to cases in which the problem behavior is aversive to both the child and those who interact with him. Typically, contingent physical aversive stimulation, to weaken aversive behavior, and positive reinforcement, for incompatible prosocial behavior (Lovaas, Schaeffer, & Simmons, 1965; Lovaas & Simmons, 1969; and Risley, 1968), are combined in treatment. Suppose the problem behavior consists of a child's hitting his head against hard surfaces, vigorously punching himself in the stomach or scratching or biting himself until the blood runs. If extinction, time-out, or response-cost procedures were employed under these conditions, the child might seriously injure himself before those destructive behaviors had diminished to any appreciable degree. Whereas the usual institutional treatment procedure of restraining or inactivating the child, either by physical or chemical means, does indeed prevent him from hurting himself, it severely limits his opportunity to acquire new incompatible, prosocial behavior.

Replacing Shy, Withdrawn, and Phobic Behaviors with Prosocial Behavior

The treatment of shy and withdrawn behavior in preschool children, interestingly enough, requires changing the contingent social behavior of adults in his immediate environment. Children's prosocial behavior is generally followed by adult praise and attention; withdrawn behavior by withdrawal of adult praise and attention. For example, after having observed a four-year-old girl's social behavior for baseline data, the teacher initiated a program in which she paid attention to and praised the child only when she was interacting with other children and she ignored (extinction) the child, in ways that seemed natural to the circumstances, when she played by herself (Allen, Hart, Buell, Harris, & Wolf, 1964). Initially, any approximation of social interaction, such as even sitting near another child, was reinforced. As the child began to interact more readily with other children, the teacher increased the requirements for reinforcement and paid attention to her only when she was engaging in cooperative play, gradually reducing the frequency of reinforcement. The girl's interaction with other children, which was only fifteen percent of the time at the beginning of the study increased to sixty percent.

Another technique to increase social interaction is to reinforce those behaviors of which social interaction is a consequence, as in the case of a nursery school child who received teacher attention when she played with playground equipment that she had earlier avoided (Buell, Stoddard, Harris, & Baer, 1968). As in the previous case, the teacher first reinforced approximations of the target behavior and then gradually increased the requirements for reinforcement until the child was vigorously using the playground equipment. Since peer interaction was a part of the reinforced play behavior, there was a concomitant increase in social interaction. In a similar study, the teacher reinforced a shy and isolated five-year-old boy with nickels and praise for distributing candy and other treats to the children in the class in order to strengthen his social interaction (Kirby &

Toler, 1970). Following this training, the child's peer interactions increased in class as well as in other school settings.

Modeling or imitation techniques have also been employed to reduce shy, solitary behavior. First, the child is given the opportunity to observe another person engaging in a particular behavior he himself fears and to see the model reinforced for this behavior. Next, he is encouraged to do approximately what the model did and is reinforced for any effort to do so. This procedure is repeated until the child engages without hesitation in the once-feared behavior. A study exemplifying such a treatment technique is that involving an extremely withdrawn six-year-old boy (Ross, Ross, & Evans, 1971). In order to establish generalized imitative behavior, the therapist associated himself with various positive reinforcers, was warm and demonstrative, and launched the program by reinforcing the child for imitating simple motor responses. When the child responded with no hesitation, the therapist began to model positive social interaction and discuss the positive aspects of peer interactions. During subsequent play therapy periods, approximations of more outgoing desirable social behavior were reinforced. Treatment continued for seven weeks through a graduated series of social interaction phases until the child's social behavior approximated that of his peers. A follow-up evaluation two months later showed an appreciable reduction in the child's social-avoidance behaviors.

Another technique for weakening or eliminating troublesome fears and phobias is systematic desensitization, which involves gradually weakening the power of a stimulus to evoke a "neurotic-anxiety reaction" by conditioning to a positive stimulus. Wolpe (1958) who developed a systematic desensitization treatment technique for adults based his approach on the pioneering study of Jones (1924) whose work was mentioned in the historical background section. Because of its significance, her account is worth reproducing in full:

March 10, 10:15 A.M. Peter sitting in a highchair eating candy. Experimenter entered room with a rabbit in an open wire cage. The rabbit was placed on the table 4 feet from Peter who immediately began to cry, insisting that the rabbit be taken away. Continued crying until the rabbit was put down 20 feet away. He then started again on the candy, but continued to fuss, "I want you to put bunny outside." After three minutes he once more burst into tears; the rabbit was removed.

April 29, 9:55 A.M. Peter standing on highchair, looking out of the window. He inquired, "Where is the rabbit?" The rabbit was put down on the chair at Peter's feet. Peter patted him, tried to pick him up, but finding the rabbit too heavy asked the experimenter to help him in lifting him to the window sill, where he played with him several minutes (p. 389).

"Emotive imagery," a variation of systematic desensitization, has also been used to reduce phobic behavior (Lazarus & Abramovitz, 1962). In essence, it seeks to stimulate reactions to certain positive stimuli in the presence of the aversive or feared objects or events in order to reduce their strength or intensity. After listing a child's fears according to their severity (known as constructing the hierarchy of aversive stimuli) and listing the storybook characters and events the child enjoys most, the therapist tells the child a story weaving into it the least fearful stimulus on the list along with the child's favorite storybook characters. As treatment progresses, the story or stories include items that progress up the fear hierarchy. The child is told that if he feels frightened at any time, he is to tell the therapist who will then go back to a less fearful story or part of the story.

Another variation on systematic desensitization involves a combination of office treatment and natural setting treatment that has been used to treat school phobias, including feigning illness, throwing tantrums when taken to school, and simply refusing to go to school. In one case, initial sessions with a first-grade boy consisted of doll-play that was gradually changed to resemble his school setting (Patterson, 1965). Nonphobic responses to play representations of his school setting were reinforced with candy. After he freely played school in the therapist's office, he was taken to school by the therapist and was, of course, reinforced for what he had done. The time spent at school each day was progressively lengthened and the contrived reinforcers were gradually removed (faded) until the child regularly and willingly attended school.

Extending and Elaborating Abilities and Knowledge

Psychotherapy designed to extend and refine behavior repertories sometimes has to begin with training a child to pay attention. Since attending behavior is a prerequisite for any kind of learning, the establishment of eye-contact with the therapist is often the first task of training. Although eye-contact can be established by contingent adult attention, approval, and praise (McConnel, 1967), edibles are most commonly used because they serve well as a prompt. Typically, the therapist holds, say, a morsel of sweet cereal near the child's face and says, "Look at me." As soon as the child looks toward the object, and by necessity at the therapist, he is given the sweet. As the child responds more promptly and reliably, the sweet is gradually eliminated, until "Look at me" is all that is necessary for eye-contact.

A program for strengthening attending behavior is often the initial step in language training (Lovaas, Berberich, Perloff & Schaeffer, 1966). After attending behaviors have been established, other prerequisite behavior for language is introduced. For example, many language programs include extensive training in imitation. A five-year-old autistic child was taught, through progressive approximations, to imitate various sounds by reinforcement with food, music, and activities (Hewett, 1965). With this shaping procedure, the therapist gradually increased the response requirements for reinforcement until the child was saying recognizable words. In order to make the child's speech more functional, the therapist's verbalizations, which served as prompts, were replaced gradually with objects and printed words.

A child's ability to attend to another person and to imitate simple motor behaviors is also important in the acquisition of other complex behaviors. If he can imitate words and actions, training is simpler. Instead of having to shape each new behavior through a series of progressive approximations to the final response, the therapist can simply model (i.e., demonstrate) the new behavior and reinforce the child's imitative repertoire. An example of this procedure is the research on developing in autistic children complex social and intellectual behaviors, such as personal hygiene, nonverbal communication, writing, and playing games (Lovaas, Fritas, Nelson, & Whalen, 1967). Since these children displayed no ability to imitate simple behavior, they were trained to do so with the aid of prompts. But once imitation without prompts was learned, new behaviors were readily acquired.

The effectiveness of behavior therapy has been apparent in the teaching of self-help skills to children having the prerequisites of attending and imitating behaviors. Bensberg, Colwell, and Cassel (1965) prepared and evaluated individualized training programs for retarded children in feeding, grooming, toileting, and following simple instructions. Typically, each program begins by building upon the behaviors the child already has, as determined by the initial assessment. If the assessment indicates that certain prerequisite behaviors for acquiring a particular skill are absent, training is instituted to develop them. By prompting and then reinforcing successive approximations of the desired behavior, usually with edibles, the child gradually acquires self-help skills. This procedure ensures that the children associate the learning of self-help skills with positive objects and events since the reinforcement contingencies are specified in terms of successive approximations of the desired behavior. In order to generalize the reinforcers for self-help skills, the therapist systematically replaces the edible sweets with social reinforcers. At the beginning of the program, she praises the child each time she gives him an edible. After the target behavior has been acquired, the edible reinforcers are gradually discontinued and only social reinforcers are used. With each successive step in the program, longer and more complex units of behavior are required for a reinforcer. If a child fails to achieve a certain level of achievement at any point in the program, the therapist returns him to the preceding step. Monthly ratings on Doll's Vineland Social Maturity Scale (1948) showed that children trained by these methods made substantial improvements as compared with children who had not received this training.

Similar success was achieved with profoundly retarded children who were unable to feed themselves or to use eating utensils (Berkowitz, Sherry, & Davis, 1971). In the initial step of the program, the therapist guided a full spoon of food into the child's mouth. As the child learned to coordinate his hand and arm movements, the therapist progressively withdrew her help. Aversive contingencies were applied for eating with the hands, e.g., the child was removed from the table for a period or was not permitted to complete the meal. These training programs, coupled with reinforcement contingencies aimed at maintaining the newly acquired skills, resulted in marked improvement in the children's mealtime behaviors.

Bringing Inept Behavior
Under Appropriate Stimulus Conditions

Many children come to the attention of therapists because they engage in certain forms of normal behavior at the wrong time or in the wrong place. In other words, they fail to make certain kinds of discriminations that are important to society. For example, although the verbal behavior of an emotionally disturbed child may be adequate, it is not directed to people; hence the behavior is not reinforced in the usual way. In this instance, the therapeutic task is to help the child relate his behavior to appropriate circumstances, a task that is accomplished by providing differential reinforcement to responses to appropriate and inappropriate stimuli.

The classical features of an autistic child are his inappropriate use of speech and his lack of social responsiveness (Kanner, 1948). These features pose serious problems for the therapist because any treatment plan requires that a child be able to attend to instructions and demonstrations. Therefore, the first task for the behavior therapist working with children who do not relate appropriately to people is to establish the necessary prerequisite behavior. In some instances, he begins by establishing eye-contact and reducing incompatible disruptive behaviors; in others, he proceeds directly to training in stimulus control of verbal behavior. A therapeutic program designed to develop functional speech in echolalic children is an example of the latter approach (Risley & Wolf, 1967). In order to prevent the child's repeating the question, the therapist at once prompted and reinforced the first word in the reply. If the child began repeating the question, the therapist quickly turned away (a variation of time-out from opportunities for reinforcement) and removed the box of candy reinforcers. When the child reliably imitated the behavior, the therapist shifted from verbal prompts alone to prompts with objects and pictures, and the question "What is this?" Repetition of the question or echolalic speech resulted in withdrawal of the object or picture and turning away; correct responses were, of course, reinforced. Once the child had learned to respond to the therapist's question by naming objects without prompts, he quickly acquired an extended vocabulary. Single words were then expanded to phrases and sentences. Using the newly acquired skills in appropriate social situations was effected through initial prompting and immediate reinforcement. By gradually increasing the number and kinds of situations in which the child was required to use appropriate speech, the therapist increased the generalization of the acquired behaviors. To extend generalization still further, speech training was carried on in the home, with the parents serving as therapists.

Incontinence is another example of inappropriate stimulus control. Ellis (1963) suggested that appropriate toileting behavior requires making a series of discriminations. The physiological cues generated by a full bladder or rectum, for example, evoke alerting responses which, in turn, stimulate (after training) approach responses toward a lavatory and elimination.

One technique for treating enuresis in the home entailed training in the retention of liquids (Kimmel & Kimmel, 1970; and Paschalis, Kimmel & Kimmel, 1972). The child was instructed to tell his parents when he felt pressure and had to go to the bathroom. The parent told him to hold for five minutes, after which time, she gave him a cookie or favorite treat and then allowed him to go to the bathroom. The waiting period was gradually increased until the child could wait for thirty minutes before going to the bathroom. As the child learned to retain his urine during the day, there was a corresponding decrease in bedwetting. Of the thirty-one enuretic children who were treated, twenty-three showed significant improvement within twenty days. A nine-month follow-up study showed no relapses or new forms of problem behavior.

The most comprehensive program for toilet training institutionalized retarded children is based on precise programming of differential contingencies for voiding and elimination (Azrin & Foxx, 1971). Two monitoring devices were developed, one that the child wore in his training pants, and the other that was installed in a toilet bowl. If a child wet or soiled his pants, a tone sounded and the attendant immediately initiated a series of mildly aversive consequences: the child was told to shower and change his clothes, to wash his soiled clothes, and to mop up the area in which the "accident" had occurred. A one-hour time-out following each "accident" deprived him of drinks and candy and of the privilege of sitting in his favorite chair. To increase the number of opportunities for the attendant to reinforce elimination into the commode, each child was given quantities of liquids during each hour and was taken to the toilet every thirty minutes. If an elimination occurred, the sensing device turned on a signal and the child was reinforced with a big piece of candy and praised for his accomplishment. He was also reinforced once every five minutes that he sat on the toilet and tried to eliminate. In this program, modeling procedures were also employed. Groups of children were trained simultaneously so that they could observe each other being reinforced for correct toileting. The outcome of the program was impressive; the frequency of accidents was reduced by eighty percent within seven days. For some individuals, training required even less time than that.

Encopresis, or involuntary defection, has not received as much attention in the literature as enuresis. Programs for such training generally consist of ignoring (nonreinforcing) "accidents" and positively reinforcing each occurrence of the desired behavior (Keehn, 1965; Neale, 1963; Peterson & London, 1964; and Tomlinson, 1970).

LEGAL, ETHICAL, AND SOCIAL ISSUES

Whenever a society through one of its agencies authorizes a group of people with specialized training to utilize their knowledge and skills to affect the health, psychological functioning, or social status of its members, that society must at the same time make certain that safeguards are established to prevent abuse of this privilege. Often the specialists themselves impose the safeguards by setting up a code of ethics, and just as often society institutes safeguards through legislation and judicial decree. Our concern here is primarily with the safeguards in the psychological treatment of retarded and emotionally disturbed children in natural, clinical, and institutional settings.

Child behavior treatment, even more so than adult behavior treatment, is still in the formative stage and society is rapidly changing its concept of the rights of children. Consequently, our discussion of safeguards must be in terms of issues rather than well established practices. We shall present seven issues that pertain to all psychological treatment and remark on their application to the needs of children. They include: (1) informed consent for treatment or participation in treatment research, (2) involvement in establishing the goals of treatment, (3) protection against diagnostic labels that may be detrimental to the client's welfare and development, (4) protection against potentially injurious treatment procedures, (5) protection against inadequately trained and willfully malicious personnel, (6) accountability for the progress and outcome of treatment to the client, to others intimately involved, and to society, and (7) the right to treatment and habilitation.

Informed Consent

It has long been understood that a responsible patient's or client's consent is a requisite to treatment, experimental or otherwise. But in most routine treatment procedures permission is taken for granted. However, when treatment involves an obvious risk, as in a surgical operation, consent is usually made explicit. The question of what constitutes informed consent in the eyes of the law is not easily answered. The legal meaning of the term refers to knowledge of the treatment process, competence to give informed consent, and giving voluntary consent. Each of these requires a discussion of a workable definition, which is beyond the scope of this chapter. One thing is clear: retarded and disturbed young children are rarely considered competent to give informed consent. That right is delegated to the parents or guardian, or to a social agency, and in many instances a court is necessary to determine whether the surrogate is seriously interested and concerned with his welfare and is acting in his best interest.

Establishing Treatment Goals

The issue here is who sets the goals of psychological treatment. For an adult judged to be responsible for his own behavior, the goals are generally established through negotiation or contract between client and therapist with provision for periodic re-negotiations. With young children, many of the goals of treatment are determined by societal consensus because of their obvious desirability—for example, increasing self-help skills, or improving the ability to communicate—while other goals, such as reducing self-mutilating or severe oppositional behavior, are negotiated by the parents, guardian, or a social agency.

Diagnostic Terms

Diagnostic terms such as "minimal" brain damage, schizophrenia, and mental retardation have for a long time been applied to psychological problems because they presumably designate the causes (see page 96). The reality is that these labels do not pinpoint causes at all, and that the course of treatment embarked upon has been based on other considerations, such as the specific competencies of individuals. Moreover, many diagnostic designations carry unwarranted implications about the origin of the problem and its treatability, duration, and reversibility. This "side-effect" of diagnostic labeling may be detrimental to the welfare and development of the client, particularly with children, because we know so little about the developmental process in general and the potentialities of newly developed treatment procedures. Recently a group of psychologists spent two years trying to untangle the knotty problem of how to retain the benefits of classifying exceptional children while diminishing the stigmatizing consequences of such labeling (Hobbs, 1974). They recommended, among other things, the complete elimination of gross categories and the substitution of specific education or treatment requirements for individual children.

Potentially Injurious Treatment

Treatment procedures that include deprivation of basic needs and rights, and the utilization of aversive contingencies have received more attention than any of the other issues, for they involve the whole question, with all its emotional overtones, of whether or not physical punishment is ever justified. Extreme forms of deprivation and aversive contingencies to which children may be subjected are considered to be child abuse and a serious violation of the law. Yet both are used in treatment. The question then becomes: What safeguards must be instituted to ensure that the procedures are necessary and that the results achieved will be in the child's best interest? As a rule, the answer centers on the benefits and the risks in specific situations. In weighing the pros and cons of possible procedures, consideration is given to the kinds of stimuli involved, the feasibility of less drastic or restrictive methods, the demonstrated effectiveness of a specific procedure, the duration of treatment, the severity of the problem, and the short and long run consequences (Kazdin, 1975).

Unqualified Personnel

This issue is that of quality control, of protecting the client from being treated by an inadequately trained person no matter how sincere his intentions. It raises the question of certification and accreditation of clinical psychologists as well as others who consider themselves expert in the application of psychological principles. In recent years psychologists have established a professional board to certify applied psychologists (American Board of Professional Psychologists) and have worked to enact state laws to certify or register applied psychologists, particularly clinical psychologists. However, there is as yet no procedure for identifying those qualified to provide behavioral treatment. Whether it is necessary to specify the behavioral specialist within clinical psychology, as a way of establishing and maintaining quality control of personnel, is still very much a topic for discussion.

Accountability

Accountability here refers to procedures for providing the client, his family, or a representative of a social agency with information on the progress and outcome of treatment. The purpose of accountability is to assure the client that the psychologist will continue to provide him with appropriate treatment. When the client is considered to be responsible for his own behavior, progress reports of the treatment are usually included when the client and therapist renegotiate their treatment contract. If the client is young, retarded, or mentally disturbed, accountability is directed to those individuals responsible for his welfare.

Right to Treatment

In several recent court decisions (*Wyatt* v. *Stickney*, and *Welsch* v. *Liken*), a person's right to medical and psychological treatment or habilitation has been made explicit. This right pertains to children and adults in the home and in all social institutions including residential hospitals, training schools for the retarded, correctional schools, and prisons. According to these decisions, anyone who prevents or fails to help to provide treatment is violating the law.

The legal concept of the right to treatment has been extended to the right to education. In *Pennsylvania Association for Retarded Children* v. *Board of Education* and *Mills* v. *Board of Education* the courts decreed that individuals of all developmental levels have a right to the kind of education that will enable them to develop to their fullest potential and to enjoy a satisfying life.

PROBABLE FUTURE TRENDS

Future trends in the development of the techniques for treating children's problems are unpredictable because the future depends on the continued high productivity of basic and applied behavioral research (Drash & Freeman, 1973; Skinner, 1973). If for any reason these activities are curtailed, child treatment techniques will remain at their present level of sophistication; the field would probably resemble the current status of child psychiatry, which is based on psychoanalysis and its many variations.

A review of the changes in child psychiatry over the past two decades would suggest that although some minor shifts in attitude and orientation have occurred, putting an emphasis on different issues, the practice has remained relatively unaffected apart from the trial of different therapeutic maneuvers. The minimal research that has emerged in this period has had little impact on the establishment of a scientifically based body of knowledge . . . In fact, the art has flourished but the science has stood still (Anthony, 1973, p. 299).

On the other hand, if basic research on both animals and children and applied research on children continue to produce new findings, rapid changes would be expected in (1) treatment procedures, (2) diagnostic assessment and monitoring methods, and (3) prevention of serious problem behaviors. Let us expand on these possibilities.

Treatment Procedures

It is anticipated that future research will produce new knowledge on (1) increasing the size of treatment units in some areas and decreasing them in others, (2) selecting and varying contingencies of reinforcement, (3) transferring from contrived to natural reinforcers, (4) weakening undesirable behavior, and (5) arriving at treatment goals with parents and teachers through contractual procedures.

Although more cumbersome than treatment in clinical settings, treatment in natural settings will probably be the preferred format of the future for several reasons: (1) it reduces or eliminates the problem of maintaining gains made in treatment; (2) it helps parents, teachers, and others involved in treatment to deal more effectively with the child on other occasions and to deal with other children with similar problems; (3) it is consistent with the *Zeitgeist* of psychology. Accompanying this trend will be the further development of effective training programs for parents, siblings, and professionals, such as teachers, speech therapists, social workers, nurses, and pediatricians and paraprofessionals, all of whom will be involved in treatment. The training of such groups will follow the clinical-laboratory format. Lectures and reading assignments will more and more be replaced by demonstrations of the procedures and supervised practice sessions with a client. In such actual treatment situations, the trainee's skills can be assessed more carefully and accurately, and consequently, training can be more sensitively tailored to each individual's learning history.

As the treatment of children's behavior problems in natural settings becomes the common mode, *maintaining* the therapeutic changes will be given more consideration by arranging conditions so that the essential contingencies will continue after the desirable behavior is established and similar procedures will be applied to other problem behaviors, if necessary. Thus the teacher would have learned during training or consultation to persist in praising a child for his cooperative work long after his hostile-aggressive behavior has been eliminated, and would recommend that other teachers do the same. Similarly, the mother would continue to pay attention to her child's requests and would continue to ignore any tantrum-like behavior.

Diagnostic Assessment and Monitoring Methods

Along with improvements in treatment techniques are bound to come changes in diagnostic evaluations and in monitoring treatment progress. It is likely that the initial assessment of a child will utilize more criterion-referenced measures rather than standardized, norm-referenced tests, direct observation of behavior, and circumscribed interviews. These methods are accurate for identifying the problem and the conditions that maintain it and therefore provide essential information for treatment planning. (See Chapter 5.)

The trend in monitoring treatment progress may well be in the direction of recording *multiple response classes* in order to keep abreast of correlated changes that may occur in nontreated behaviors. For example, in monitoring a child's oppositional behavior toward his mother, his behavior toward his siblings might also be measured. Expanded information of this sort would be helpful in planning the steps that constitute the complete treatment program.

Prevention of Serious Problem Behaviors

Future advancements in child behavior treatment should naturally lead to programs designed to prevent serious problem behavior. This trend is expected to evolve from the fact that parents, siblings, teachers, childcare workers in institutions, and others who serve in a treatment capacity derive not only personal benefits from participation but also acquire skills and knowledge applicable to other children. Thus, the teacher can apply behavior principles in order to manage her class, promote prosocial behavior, reduce aversive behaviors, and encourage academic and social learning (Becker, Engelmann, & Thomas, 1971). Parents, on the other hand, can apply behavior principles to help their children acquire self-help skills, prosocial behaviors, and basic knowledge in ways that are mutually satisfying. Prevention of problem behavior is also expected as behavior principles are applied to those aspects of childrearing that bear on establishing the roots of moral behavior—a factor in preventing serious problem behavior—as was pointed out in Chapter 6.

REFERENCES

Allen, K. E., Hart, B. M., Buell, J. S., Harris, F. R., & Wolf, M. M. Effects of social reinforcement on isolate behavior of a nursery school child. *Child Development*, 1964, *35*, 511–18.

Anthony, E. J. The state of the art and the science in child psychiatry. *Archives of General Psychiatry*, 1973, *29*, 299–305.

Axline, V. M. *Play therapy.* New York: Houghton Mifflin, 1947.

Azrin, N. H. & Foxx, R. M. A rapid method of toilet training the institutionalized retarded. *Journal of Applied Behavior Analysis*, 1971, *4*, 89–100.

Becker, W. C., Engelmann, S., & Thomas, D. R. *Teaching: A course in applied psychology.* Chicago: Science Research Associates, 1971.

Bensberg, G. J., Colwell, C. N., & Cassell, R. H. Teaching the profoundly retarded self-help activities by behavior shaping techniques. *American Journal of Mental Deficiency*, 1965, *69*, 674–79.

Berkowitz, S., Sherry, P. J., & Davis, B. A. Teaching self-feeding skills to profound retardates using reinforcement and fading procedures. *Behavior Therapy*, 1971, *2*, 62–67.

Bijou, S. W. A systematic approach to an experimental analysis of young children. *Child Development*, 1955, *26*, 161–68.

Bijou, S. W. Methodology for an experimental analysis of child behavior. *Psychological Reports*, 1957, *3*, 243–50.

Bijou, S. W. & Peterson, R. F. The psychological assessment of children: A functional analysis. In P. McReynolds (Ed.), *Advances in psychological assessment.* Vol. 2. Palo Alto, Calif.: Science & Behavior Books, 1971. Pp. 63–78.

Buell, J., Stoddard, P., Harris, R., & Baer, D. M. Collateral social development accompanying reinforcement of outdoor play in a preschool child. *Journal of Applied Behavior Analysis*, 1968, *1*, 167–73.

Burchard, J. D. Systematic socialization: A programmed environment for the habilitation of antisocial retardates. *Psychological Record*, 1967, *17*, 461–67.

Burchard, J. D. & Barrera, F. An analysis of time-out and response cost in a programmed environment. *Journal of Applied Behavior Analysis*, 1972, *5*, 271–82.

Doll, E. A. *The measurement of social competence.* New York: Educational Publishers, 1948.

Doubros, S. G. & Daniels, C. J. An experimental approach to the reduction of overactive behavior. *Behavior Research Therapy*, 1966, *4*, 251–58.

Drash, P. W. & Freeman, B. J. *Behavior modification, behavior therapy, and operant conditioning: An historical survey and a bibliography of books in print 1900–1972.* Behavioral Information & Technology, 5407 East Drive, Baltimore, Md., 1973.

Ellis, N. R. Toilet training the severely defective patient: An S-R reinforcement analysis. *American Journal of Mental Deficiency*, 1963, *68*, 98–103.

Ferster, C. B. & DeMyer, M. K. The development of performances in autistic children in an automatically controlled environment. *Journal of Chronic Diseases*, 1961, *13*, 312–45.

Freud, A. *Psychoanalytic treatment of children*. London: Imago, 1946.

Freud, S. *Collected papers*. Vol. 3. Hogarth Press, 1925.

Harris, F. R., Johnston, M. K., Kelley, C. S., & Wolf, M. M. Effects of positive social reinforcement on regressed crawling of a nursery school child. *Journal of Educational Psychology*, 1964, *55*, 35–41.

Harris, F. R., Wolf, M. M., & Baer, D. M. Effects of adult social reinforcement on child behavior. *Young Children*, 1964, *20*, 8–17.

Hawkins, R. P., Peterson, R. F., Schweid, E., & Bijou, S. W. Behavior theory in the home: Amelioration of problem parent-child relations with the parent in a therapeutic role. *Journal of Experimental Child Psychology*, 1966, *4*, 99–107.

Hewett, F. M. Teaching speech to an autistic child through conditioning. *American Journal of Orthopsychiatry*, 1965, *35*, 927–36.

Hobbs, N. *The future of children*. San Francisco, Calif.: Jossey-Bass, 1974.

Homme, L., Csanyi, A. P., Gonzales, M. A., & Rechs, J. R. *How to use contingency contracting in the classroom*. Champaign, Ill.: Research Press, 1969.

Hug-Hellmuth, H. V. *A study of the mental life of the child*. New York: Nervous and Mental Disease, 1919.

Jones, M. C. The elimination of children's fears. *Journal of Experimental Psychology*, 1924, *7*, 382–90.

Kanfer, F. H. & Phillips, J. S. A survey of current behavior therapies and a proposed classification. In C. M. Franks (Ed.), *Behavior therapy: Appraisal and status*. New York: McGraw-Hill, 1969. Pp. 445–75.

Kanfer, F. H. & Phillips, J. S. *Learning foundations of behavior therapy*. New York: John Wiley, 1970.

Kanfer, F. H. & Saslow, G. Behavioral diagnosis. In C. M. Franks (Ed.), *Behavior therapy: Appraisal and status*. New York: McGraw-Hill, 1969. Pp. 417–44.

Kanner, L. *Child psychiatry*. (2nd ed.) Springfield, Ill.: C. C. Thomas, 1948.

Kazdin, A. E. *Behavior modification in applied settings*. Homewood, Ill.: Dorsey Press, 1975. Pp. 237–44.

Keehn, J. D. Brief case-report: Reinforcement therapy of incontinence. *Behavior Research and Therapy*, 1965, *2*, 239.

Kimmel, H. D. & Kimmel, E. An instrumental conditioning method for the treatment of enuresis. *Journal of Behavior Therapy & Experimental Psychiatry*, 1970, *1*, 121–24.

Kirby, F. D. & Toler, H. C. Modification of preschool isolate behavior: A case study. *Journal of Applied Behavior Analysis*, 1970, *3*, 309–14.

Klein, M. *The psychoanalysis of children*. London: Hogarth Press, 1949.

Lazarus, A. A. *Behavior therapy and beyond.* New York: McGraw-Hill, 1971.

Lazarus, A. A. & Abramovitz, A. The use of "emotive imagery" in the treatment of children's phobias. *Journal of Mental Science*, 1962, *108*, 191–95.

Levitt, E. E. Results of psychotherapy with children: An evaluation. *Journal of Consulting Psychology*, 1957, *1*, 189–96.

Levitt, E. E. Psychotherapy with children: A further evaluation. *Behavior Research & Therapy*, 1963, *1*, 45–51.

Levy, D. M. Release therapy. *American Journal of Orthopsychiatry*, 1939, *9*, 913–36.

Lorr, M., Klett, C. J., & McNair, D. M. *Syndromes of psychosis.* New York: Macmillan, 1963.

Lovaas, O. I., Berberich, J. P., Perloff, B. F., & Schaeffer, B. Acquisition of imitative speech by schizophrenic children. *Science*, 1966, *151*, 705–7.

Lovaas, O. I., Fritas, L., Nelson, K., & Whalen, C. The establishment of imitation and its use for the development of complex behavior in schizophrenic children. *Behavior Research & Therapy*, 1967, *5*, 171–81.

Lovaas, O. I., Schaeffer, B., & Simmons, J. Q. Building social behavior in autistic children by use of electric shock. *Journal of Experimental Research in Personality*, 1965, *2*, 99–109.

Lovaas, O. I. & Simmons, J. Q. Manipulation of self-destruction in three retarded children. *Journal of Applied Behavior Analysis*, 1969, *2*, 143–57.

McConnel, O. L. Control of eye contact in an autistic child. *Journal of Child Psychology & Psychiatry*, 1967, *8*, 249–55.

Mahler, M. S. Child analysis. In N.D.C. Lewis & B. L. Pacella (Eds.), *Modern trends in child psychiatry.* New York: International Universities Press, 1945.

Mowrer, O. H. & Mowrer, W. M. Enuresis: A method for its study and treatment. *American Journal of Orthopsychiatry*, 1938, *8*, 436–59.

Neale, P. H. Behavior therapy and encopresis in children. *Behavior Research & Therapy*, 1963, *1*, 139–49.

Paschalis, A. P., Kimmel, H. D., & Kimmel, E. Further study of diurnal instrumental conditioning in the treatment of enuresis nocturna. *Journal of Behavior Therapy & Experimental Psychiatry*, 1972, *3*, 253–56.

Patterson, G. R. A learning theory approach to the treatment of the school phobic child. In L. Ullmann & L. Krasner (Eds.), *Case studies in behavior modification.* New York: Holt, Rinehart & Winston, 1965. Pp. 279–84.

Pearson, G. H. J. *Emotional disorders of children.* New York: W. W. Norton, 1949.

Peterson, D. R. & London, P. Neobehavioristic psychotherapy; quasi hypnotic suggestion and multiple reinforcement in the treatment of a case of post-infantile dyscopresis. *Psychological Record*, 1964, *14*, 469–74.

Quay, H. C. Patterns of aggression, withdrawal, and immaturity. In H. C. Quay &

J. S. Werry (Eds.), *Psychopathological disorders of childhood.* New York: John Wiley, 1972. Pp. 1–29.

Reese, H. W. & Lipsitt, L. P. *Experimental child psychology.* New York: Academic Press, 1970.

Reisman, J. M. *The development of clinical psychology.* New York: Appleton-Century-Crofts, 1966.

Risley, T. R. The effects and side effects of punishing the autistic behaviors of a deviant child. *Journal of Applied Behavior Analysis,* 1968, *1*, 21–34.

Risley, T. & Wolf, M. Establishing functional speech in echolalic children. *Behavior Research & Therapy,* 1967, *5*, 73–88.

Rogers, C. R. *The clinical treatment of the problem child.* Boston: Houghton Mifflin, 1939.

Rosenhan, D. L. On being sane in insane places. *Science,* 1973, *179*, 250–58.

Ross, A. O. *Behavior disorders in children.* New York: General Learning Press, 1971.

Ross, A. O. Behavior therapy. In H. C. Quay & J. S. Werry (Eds.), *Psychopathological disorders in childhood.* New York: John Wiley, 1972. Pp. 273–315.

Ross, D. M., Ross, S. A., & Evans, T. The modification of extreme social withdrawal by modeling and guided participation. *Journal of Behavior & Experimental Psychiatry,* 1971, *2*, 273–79.

Shearer, M. S. & Shearer, D. E. The Portage Project: A model for early childhood education. *Exceptional Children,* 1972, *38*, 210–17.

Sherman, J. A. & Baer, D. M. Appraisal of operant therapy techniques with children and adults. In C. M. Franks (Ed.), *Behavior therapy: Appraisal and status.* New York: McGraw-Hill, 1969. Pp. 192–219.

Skinner, B. F. *Science and human behavior.* New York: Macmillan, 1953.

Skinner, B. F. Some relations between behavior modification and basic research. In S. W. Bijou & E. Ribes-Inesta (Eds.), *Behavior Modification: Issues and extensions.* New York: Academic Press, 1973. Pp. 1–6.

Sloane, H. N., Johnston, M. K., & Bijou, S. W. Successive modification of aggressive behavior and aggressive fantasy play by management of contingencies. *Journal of Child Psychology & Psychiatry,* 1967, *8*, 217–26.

Staats, A. W. & Staats, C. K. *Complex human behavior.* New York: Holt, Rinehart & Winston, 1963. Pp. 404–11.

Szasz, T. S. The myth of mental illness. *American Psychologist,* 1960, *15*, 113–18.

Tomlinson, J. R. The treatment of bowel retention by operant procedures: A case study. *Journal of Behavior Therapy & Experimental Psychiatry,* 1970, *1*, 83–85.

Vukelich, R. & Hake, D. F. Reduction of dangerously aggressive behavior in a severely retarded resident through a combination of positive reinforcement procedures. *Journal of Applied Behavior Analysis,* 1971, *4*, 215–25.

Wahler, R. G. & Cormier, W. H. The ecological interview: A first step in out-patient child behavior therapy. *Journal of Behavior Therapy & Experimental Psychiatry*, 1970, *1*, 279–89.

Watson, J. B. & Rayner, R. A. Conditioned emotional reactions. *Journal of Experimental Psychology*, 1920, *3*, 1–4.

Williams, C. D. The elimination of tantrum behavior by extinction procedures. *Journal of Abnormal and Social Psychology*, 1959, *59*, 269.

Wolf, M. N., Risley, T., & Mees, H. Application of operant conditioning procedures to the behavior problems of an autistic child. *Behavior Research & Therapy*, 1964, *1*, 305–12.

Wolpe, J. *Psychotherapy by reciprocal inhibition.* Stanford, Calif.: Stanford University Press, 1958.

Wolpe, J. & Rachman, S. Psychoanalytic "evidence": A critique based on Freud's case of Little Hans. *Journal of Nervous & Mental Diseases*, 1960, *130*, 135–48.

Yarrow, M. R., Campbell, J. D., & Burton, R. V. *Child rearing.* San Francisco: Jossey-Bass, 1968.

Zigler, E. & Phillips, L. Psychiatric diagnosis: A critique. *Journal of Abnormal and Social Psychology*, 1961, *63*, 607–18.

Zubin, J. Classification of the behavior disorders. *Annual Review of Psychology*, 1967, *18*, 373–406.

8

Preschool Education

The credo of future educators will be that *preschool is the most important educational experience in a person's life.* At present, educators and psychologists believe that the preschool years constitute one of the most important stages of human development. It follows then that when a truly effective approach to preschool is achieved, that period should be the most significant and influential in a child's life. According to this thinking, we should without further delay view the problems of preschool education in the light of the most reliable knowledge of human behavior and development. We do just that when we apply the concepts, principles, and methodology of behavior analysis.

The application of behavior principles to the preschool is by no means an innovation. It is, in fact, as old as the original behavioristic brand of functionalism as a school of psychology. At the turn of the century Patty Smith Hill (1916), a follower of John Dewey, John B. Watson, and Edward L. Thorndike, contended that the kindergarten curriculum should develop from the subject matter of the school, the developmental characteristics of the children, and the history and future potentialities of society. Furthermore, she maintained that the method of teaching should be based on "habit" training, such as that recommended by the founder of behaviorism, John B. Watson (1929). The present-day behavioral approach to preschool education is to be found in the work of many, including Becker and Engelmann (1969), Bushell (1973), Etzel, Bybel, Busby, Dixon, Spradlin, and Schilmoeller (1973), Risley, Reynolds, and Hart (1970), and Thomson (1972). It is also reflected in other parts of the academically-structured preschool program (Bereiter & Engelmann, 1966), the early training project of the Demonstration and Research Center for Early Education (DARCEE) (Klaus & Gray, 1968), and the Tucson early educational model (Hughes, Wetzel, & Henderson, 1973). In all instances, the theoretical view is based not on Watson but on Skinner (1953 & 1969) who integrated Thorndike's theory of trial-and-error learning and Pavlov's concept of classical conditioning into a system for the understanding of human behavior.

This chapter focuses on the behavioral approach to preschool education with respect to the (1) philosophy of preschool education, or the goals of teaching, (2) methods of teaching, or the means of achieving preschool goals, (3) supports essential for a teacher so that she may perform her job to the extent of her training, and (4) parent participation.

A brief sketch of the early development of preschool education, including the kindergarten, nursery school, and day-care center, will serve as a background for the discussion to follow. The first modern school for five-year-olds was founded in 1837 by Frederick Froebel, a German educator. Froebel was greatly influenced by Comenius, Rousseau, and Pestalozzi who championed the rights of children in the face of the prevalent notion that schools were places that trained children to serve society through serving their families. Why the then-revolutionary idea of preschool education was accepted at this particular time by German middle-class families is not entirely clear, except for the possibility that they had the means to pay someone to take charge of their children for part of the day. What is clear is that Froebel thought that the curriculum for five-year-olds should be based entirely on the "original nature" of the child and that the teaching and supervision should be carried on by young, single women. His concept of a five-year-old child's original nature was based on the horticulture analogy: A child has inborn tendencies for spontaneous self-generated activities and spiritual feelings, and therefore should be nurtured and protected like a flower in a well-tended garden. Hence, cultivating the child's natural tendencies in the kindergarten meant providing him with opportunities to play and to follow a regime insuring nourishment, care, rest, and protection from harm.

Froebel's philosophy of preschool education and his teaching methods for five-year-olds were introduced into the United States by Susan Blow shortly after the Civil War and before long, in 1874, a department of kindergarten was established by the National Educational Association, which recommended kindergartens as part of public school systems. In the past hundred years, kindergartens have become an integral part of education in the United States. During 1966–67 about 9,800 public school systems were reported to have kindergarten programs (Ream, 1968).

Not until fifty years after the appearance of kindergartens were nursery schools established in the United States. According to Mayer (1960), the first public nursery school was founded in 1919, and the parent-cooperative nursery school in 1923. Establishment of model nursery schools during the 1920s and 1930s, such as the Gesell Child Guidance Nursery School at Yale University, the Merrill-Palmer Institute in Detroit, Teachers College of Columbia University in New York, and the Child Welfare Station at the University of Iowa, accelerated the trend toward education for the prekindergarten-age child. Further impetus was provided by funds from the federal government during the Depression in the early 1930s and during World War II in the 1940s when many mothers of young children joined the work force. It is estimated that by the late 1960s there were about 816,000 children in nursery schools on the campuses of colleges and universities, in churches, homes, shopping centers, and civic buildings. The variations in the way these schools were, and still are, operated are endless. Based on a survey by Ream (1968), Evans (1971) describes the situation as of 1966–67:

Some are commercial; others are nonprofit. Some require professional credentials; others do not. Some are exclusively parent-cooperative ventures, while others may exercise no apparent commitment to parental involvement. Some accommodate three-, four-, and five-year-olds; others accept four-year-olds only. Some are limited to half-day programs; others include a full day. Some schools convene two or three days a week; others utilize the full five-day week. In short, variation is the rule rather than the exception. Exceptional, however, is the sponsorship of nursery school programs by public school systems. During the 1966–67 school year nursery programs were manned by only 148 public school systems as compared to nearly 9,800 which regularly mount kindergarten programs (p. 13).

PHILOSOPHY OF PRESCHOOL EDUCATION: THE GOALS OF TEACHING

Every parent, older sibling, relative, friend, or teacher who helps the young child to learn has a philosophy of education. For parents and older siblings (who are really parent aides), the goals are implicit or "natural" to the practices of the family and consist of helping the child learn self-care skills and achieve the rudiments of social, cognitive, and moral behavior. For relatives and friends, the goals are also implicit and "natural" to the practices of the extended family and the neighborhood, and consist of the achievement of broader social and recreational abilities and knowledge. On the other hand, the goals of preschool teachers are (or should be) explicit, have some kind of "child development" rationale, and are linked with educational materials and methods that form a curriculum focusing largely on the child's verbal abilities and knowledge and on his social-emotional "needs."

Preschool Goals Are Value Judgments

Regardless of who assumes the role of the teacher, what the setting for teaching, and the degree of explicitness of objectives, the goals of teaching are *value judgments* about what the behavior of a child should be; they are by no means the conclusions drawn directly from educational, sociological, psychiatric, or psychological research (Katz, 1973 and Spodek, 1973). The goals for preschool are founded on ideological or philosophical conceptions of the child, the family, society, and the role of preschool education in that society. Those responsible for selecting and articulating the goals are the parents, teachers, school administrators, boards of education, and governmental officials. Experts in early childhood education serve primarily as resource persons who provide the decision makers with information on human development, learning, the instructional process, the remedial instructional process, methods of evaluating educational programs, the workings and future directions of society, the benefits and risks of particular educational practices, and the principles of the decision-making process itself.

Advice from professional educators about preschool goals has been divergent, conflicting, and confusing, to say the very least (Katz, 1974). At one extreme, there are those who hold that the goals should be based entirely on the psychological needs of the child; at the other extreme are those who maintain that the needs of society should be the sole factor. Educators who espouse child-centered goals generally hold that a child is born with built-in, self-actualizing tendencies and that one should "leave him to his own devices" so that he may "unfold" and thereby realize his naturally constructive nature. Consequently, they favor "open" teaching situations. These present-day advocates of Froebel's doctrine include (1) the Piagetians with their hypothetical cognitive structures and processes evolving through predetermined stages (Kohlberg & Mayer, 1972); (2) the neo-Freudians with their concepts of the development of the personality (id, ego, and superego and the evolution of the sense of trust, autonomy, and initiative) (Erikson, 1963); and the Gesellians with their notions about the growth of the mind, manifested in motor, social, adaptive, and language development (Todd & Hefferman, 1970). Cognitive structures, the components of personality structure, and the divisions of mind are hypothetical internal causal entities, inferred from preconceptions about the original nature of man. They are constructs that exist only in the writings and lectures of the theorists. When it is demonstrated that preschool goals and the means of achieving them can be stated in clearly observable terms, rather than in terms of hypothetical constructs and relationships of personality theorists, nursery school programs based on these formulations will require revision.

Educators who hold that preschool goals must be based on the needs of society rather than the needs of the child contend that a child is naturally unsocial or antisocial and that if a child is not given a highly structured school situation, such as the Bereiter-Engelmann program (1966), he will fail to acquire the behaviors that are essential for societal living. Besides supporting certain religious doctrines that hold that a child is sinful by nature, this rationale is a carryover from the days when parents used their children to contribute to the economic needs of the family. In the preindustrial period, and prior to the delegation of education to a social agency, this constituted the most important aspect of a child's education and training. With the onset of the industrial age and the establishment of community schools, child labor on large-scale farms and in factories created serious physical and mental hazards for the children, which required federal laws forbidding such practices.

An acceptable general goal of the preschool, like the goal of any school, must take into account both the further development of the pupil and the characteristics and future development of his society. This position is not derived from an effort to "take the best of both worlds," but is, instead, an implication of the natural science approach which says that a child develops, or changes progressively, as a consequence of interactions with the environment. Therefore *the development of a child must be considered in terms of its interaction with the specific events that constitute his environment.* A child's organization of behavior ("personality") on entrance to nursery school is the result of the interactions between his unique biological makeup (including biological maturation) and the specific events he has encountered in family living since birth. By the end of nursery school his behavior is a function of his unique biological makeup in interaction with specific events in his home, nursery school, and immediate community. Watts (1972), who devoted his life to interrelating Eastern and Western thought, states the case for the interdependence of the individual and his environment.

I have tried to explain that the relationship between an organism and its environment is *mutual,* that neither one is the "cause" or determinant of the other since the arrangement between them is polar. If, then, it makes sense to explain the organism and its behavior in terms of the environment, it will also make sense to explain the environment in terms of the organism. (Thus far I have kept this up my sleeve so as not to confuse the first aspect of the picture.) For there is a very real, physical sense in which man, and every other organism, creates his own environment (pp. 89–90).

BEHAVIORALLY ORIENTED PRESCHOOL SUBGOALS

The implication of the concept that an individual and his environment are a unity is that the general goal of the preschool should be to help the child acquire behaviors that enhance his development, and contribute to the advancement of his society *at the same time*. To accomplish this end, we must state specific goals in the following areas: (1) the development of abilities and knowledge, (2) the extension of motivations, and (3) the enhancement of self-management skills. To fulfill the second requirement of the general goal, we must teach the specific goals in ways that promote the *individuality* of each child (as a means of contributing to diversity) and encourage *problem-solving motivations and skills* (as a means of contributing to socially meaningful innovations). The items under each heading, listed below, are not viewed as immutable but as alterable in light of new findings from an experimental analysis of behavior, child development research, and observations of change in our society—where the society is and where it is probably heading.

Development of abilities and knowledge. Abilities and knowledge goals aim to teach a child how to do things, and to acquire information about objects, people, occurrences, and about himself, i.e., his "self-concept" (see Chapter 3). These goals fall into ten subclasses. The first four pertain to the child's behavior primarily in relation to himself, and the last six to the child's behavior in relation to society.

1. Body management and control, including manual dexterity and locomotor skills.
2. Physical health and safety.
3. Self-care, including dressing, undressing, and toileting.
4. Recreation and play.
5. Social behavior, including all forms of communication.

6. Aesthetic knowledge and abilities in relation to art, crafts, music, and literature.

7. Everyday mechanical knowhow (e.g., how to turn the TV on and off, how to let water out of a tub, etc.).

8. How things work in the community (e.g., the transportation system, sanitation department, fire department, etc.).

9. Pre-academic and academic subjects.

10. Methods and content of science.

Extension of motivations. In technical behavioral terms, the extension of motives, in the form of attitudes, interests, and values, involves replacing appetitional and aversive contingencies with positive conditioned reinforcers: specific, generalized, extrinsic, and intrinsic. In psychoanalytical terms, the objective is to change behavior motivated by id forces to behavior motivated by ego and superego impulses. Goals in the behavioral sense include:

1. Preservation and extension of moral values in keeping with the family moral code *and* the moral code of the classroom as a subculture.

2. Preservation and extension of ecological (natural) reinforcers, and by definition, preservation and extension of exploratory behavior.

3. Development of positive attitudes and interests in people as individuals and as groups.

4. Positive attitudes toward, and interest in, attending school and in the activities of school and community.

Enhancement of self-management skills. The third category of objectives refers to the acquisition of self-management skills in the broadest sense. These skills are usually deemed desirable because they are said to enhance innovative behavior, self control, and problem-solving ability. They consist of the beginning stages of:

1. Personal self-management techniques including the development of desirable "personal habits," "moral habits," and "work habits," as well as the ability to concentrate on the subject at hand and work independently and systematically (development of autonomy).

2. Problem-solving (thinking) and decision-making skills, including creative and innovative behaviors.

TEACHING METHODS: MEANS OF ACHIEVING GOALS

Throughout history highly effective teachers have usually developed "on their own," or through the specific contingencies that constitute their personal histories. With the advent of an applied science of human behavior, competent teachers can be trained to be even more effective, and less competent teachers can be trained to perform at least adequately.

The notion that an effective teacher can be trained raises the question of the learning models offered in teacher training. Typical teacher training models are (1) the *experience model*, which emphasizes exposing a child to a large variety of stimulating experiences, (2) the *doing model*, which encourages all sorts of activity, especially exploratory behavior, (3) the *trial-and-error model*, which affords a child opportunities to interact with objects and people in order to learn from "feedback," or the consequences of his actions, and (4) the *open-situation model*, which provides a child with physical and social environments that encourage naturally evolving desirable behavior.

Each of these models stresses only one aspect of learning. In the experience model, the material or task to be performed is emphasized; in the doing model, the behavioral component receives most of the attention; in the trial-and-error model, the consequences of the behavior are paramount, and in the open-situation model, the setting for learning is stressed. A model based on modern behavior theory brings together all four of these components and defines teaching as the arrangement of these four classes of conditions to facilitate learning (Skinner, 1969). The antecedent component includes the selection and sequencing of the material or procedure, and the techniques of presenting them (e.g., priming, modeling, fading, and rule-giving); the behavioral aspect pertains to the shaping of behavior or the development of motor and verbal abilities and skills. The consequences of behavior relate to the management of reinforcing contingencies, including their proper selection and use in developing personal traits (e.g., autonomy) and new reinforcers (new "interests"). And finally, the setting or contextual component pertains to managing the entire situation to promote educationally desirable behaviors throughout the school day.

Of course, a child is perfectly capable of learning without a teacher and should be given ample opportunity and encouragement to do so. However the learning of many abilities and knowledge does require a teacher because the reinforcement contingencies involved do not ordinarily occur naturally (as in concept formation), or because they are too remote to influence appropriate behavior (as in learning to avoid poisonous plants).

The General Teaching Strategy

The application of learning principles to the teaching situation might correctly be called the applied behavior analysis general strategy. We have discussed this approach in teaching the family moral code to a young child (Chapter 6) and in the treatment of severe problem behaviors (Chapter 7). The same five basic steps apply; namely, (1) specifying the goals of teaching in observable terms, (2) beginning teaching at the child's level of competence, (3) arranging the teaching situation (materials, procedures, instructions, setting factors, and contingencies) to facilitate learning in directions that enhance the individuality of a child, (4) monitoring learning progress and altering the situation to advance learning, and (5) following practices that generalize, elaborate, and maintain the behaviors acquired.

Before commenting on each of these steps, we wish to make two points that will clarify the subsequent discussion. First, the fact that applied behavior analysis has a well-recognized strategy does not mean that we now know all about teaching, or in other words, that the behavioral approach to teaching is a closed system. It signifies merely that the essential elements of effective teaching have been identified. The details for carrying out each of the five steps will be modified constantly, as long as basic and applied research continues to supply new information. Because the present system is built entirely on objectively defined concepts and relationships, the changes will be revisions and extensions, rather than turnabouts and abandonments. The need for new findings from basic and applied research to keep educational practices in a healthy state should be obvious. Second, the behavior analysis strategy will work only when teaching is *individualized*. Instruction must be individualized so that the educational materials and the teaching procedures can be tailored to fit each child's competencies and motivational structure (the relative strengths of reinforcing and eliciting stimuli and their hierarchical relationships). Individualization does not mean that all school activities are to be carried out on a one-teacher-to-one-child basis; but it does mean arranging each teaching situation so that a child is practically always responding to material at his own level of competence, or somewhat above, and is always responsive to the contingencies being employed. Nor does individualization mean bringing the child up to his mental age, chronological age, grade placement, or some other arbitrary standard. It means helping him to achieve in the programs designed for him under positive contingencies and positive setting factors. Interestingly enough, a panel reviewing federal programs for young children recommended individualizing procedures for preschool children with special needs (White, 1973). The panel should have recommended individualizing procedures for all children.

1. Specifying teaching goals. We have stated that the goals of preschool teaching are, or should be, established by a representative group of people with parents having a clear and strong voice, and that the goals stem from their philosophy of the child, the society, and the role of preschool education in that society. The teacher's main function is to make decisions about dividing each goal into its subdivisions and subgoals. For example, she may divide the teaching of art into (a) art appreciation, (b) art discrimination involving aesthetic comparisons and differences in relation to color, line, shape, and texture, (c) art mechanics, including skillful use of pencil, crayons, scissors, paste, brushes, and clean-up procedures, and (d) the artistic aspects of crafts, with concentration on different types for different children depending on each child's repertories and "needs."

2. Beginning teaching at the child's level of competence. In order to begin a teaching program at a child's level of competence, the teacher must first assess each child's preinstructional behavior (competencies) in the relevant areas, that is, the teacher makes an educational diagnosis. For this purpose she uses criterion-referenced tests rather than norm-referenced tests so as to obtain information relating to social and cognitive learning rather than to a child's mental age, social age, IQ, or grade achievement. (See Chapter 5.)

3. Arranging conditions to facilitate learning. The teacher selects the materials, activities, and situations that will probably lead to reaching the preestablished goal. As an example, in planning art experiences, she takes into account three kinds of art activities: (1) those that allow freedom to combine elements; (2) those that deal with the development of skills and discriminations; and (3) those that are craft-oriented, and use techniques that encourage original productions in the light of a child's personal history. She also encourages a child to interact with the materials, her instructions, and the reinforcers (Thomson, 1972).

4. Monitoring and modifying materials and procedures. To have a systematic account of his progress, the teacher keeps records of the child's productions, such as samples of handwriting, and of instances of social behaviors, such as initiating conversation with a peer. On the basis of these data, she reevaluates her programming of the material, the physical setting, the instructions, and the effectiveness of the reinforcers. Thomson (1972), for example, provides the teacher with an observational code, an inventory schedule of social, physical, and conceptual skills, and a form on which to record each child's entering repertories, assigned tasks, and progress notes to help her observe and record behavior systematically. The teacher is also given material on how to develop positive social reinforcers and guidelines for reprogramming materials.

5. *Generalizing, elaborating, and maintaining learned behavior.* The teacher incorporates in her daily teaching plans activities that generalize, elaborate, and maintain the abilities and knowledge the child has acquired. She does this by posing problems and questions in contexts that differ from the learning situation and by reinforcing instances of related learned behaviors that occur "spontaneously," that is, not arranged by her. She also works with the child's mother and demonstrates how to help her child generalize, elaborate, and maintain school-learned behavior at home. We will discuss parent participation and cooperation later in this chapter.

A further note on generalization, elaboration, and maintenance. Behavior acquired in the learning situation generalizes to other situations; stated more precisely, learned behavior automatically comes under the control of stimuli similar to those in the learning situation. Effective teaching, by teachers and parents alike, increases the probability of generalization, mainly through practices that strengthen the learned behaviors. For example, contingencies are arranged to teach cooperative behavior in the preschool during group activities, recess, snack time, or art class, and in the home, during play, clean-up, mealtime, or chore time. When we speak of elaborating learned behavior, we refer to the arranging of contingencies so as to transform learned behavior into more complex forms, such as extending walking to hopping, skipping, and jumping, and extending one-word sentences, such as "Drink" or "Mine," to phrases and longer sentences.

Maintaining learned behavior, often referred to as improving memory or retention, consists of arranging reinforcing contingencies so that the learned behavior preserves its strength. Once a child is taught to take off his coat and hang it up he should be encouraged, by a pleasant remark or a pat on the back, to continue this practice whenever he enters the room from the outdoors. The key principle underlying this aspect of the applied behavioral analysis teaching strategy is to distribute reinforcement on a schedule that will keep the behavior vigorous, starting, as we know, with frequent reinforcement and gradually reducing the frequency.

Techniques for generalizing, elaborating, and maintaining learned behaviors have been the last features to be incorporated into the applied behavior analysis strategy. They have been last because educators and psychologists have been reluctant to accept the notion that traits, like all other behaviors, are established and maintained by environmental contingencies. For example, stable traits mean that the individual is interacting with stable environments, and changing traits mean that he is interacting with changing environments, some described as progressive (as in the early stages of development), some as regressive (as in old age), and some as fluctuating.

Application of the Behavioral Teaching Strategy to the Preschool

We take the position that the effectiveness of the application of the behavior strategy to teaching specific objectives ultimately depends upon the dedication of the teacher to achieving the curriculum goals, her training in applied behavior analysis, and her skill and art in applying these principles to develop the individuality of each child in her class. Although it is agreed almost unanimously that the teacher is the most important factor in any teaching situation since she is the one who has direct contact with the child, research shows that there is practically no relationship between teacher characteristics and pupil accomplishment and achievement. This astonishing fact calls for new ways of conceptualizing the teacher and the teaching process (Spodek, 1972). One way of evaluating a teacher's effectiveness is how well she applies the principles of behavior and development. If she is skillful, a substantial positive relationship between her teaching behavior and pupil achievement and school attitudes is predictable for the reason that she continually rearranges the teaching situation according to the child's progress, recorded in objective terms.

Development of abilities and knowledge. Teaching both the abilities and the knowledge required to deal with the ten behavior subgroups mentioned earlier (namely, body management, physical health and safety, self care, recreation and play, social and communication behaviors, aesthetic behaviors, mechanical skills, how things work in the community, preacademic and academic subjects, and the methods and content of science) involves the effective management of reinforcing contingencies. The key procedure for teaching the *ability* categories is *differential* reinforcement of successive approximations to the form of the goal response. For example, working with a young child learning how to draw a circle, the teacher reinforces him, first, as he learns more and more efficient ways of holding the pencil, then for drawing curved lines and closer and closer approximations of a circle, and then for drawing an acceptable circle. This procedure is referred to as response differentiation, or, in the vernacular, shaping. (See Chapter 3.) To say that the key principle in teaching abilities and skills involves reinforcing successive changes in response form does not imply that the occasion (discriminative stimulus or cue) and context (setting factor) can be ignored. As indicated in Chapter 3, an ability is always taught in relation to some situation (ability to draw is taught in relation to a pencil or crayon and a sheet of paper) and a favorable context (a quiet and relaxed setting) for performing that task.

The fundamental procedure for teaching the *knowledge* categories is discrimination training or differential reinforcement on the basis of an *occasion* (discriminative stimulus or cue), as explained in Chapter 4. Sometimes the occasion for differential reinforcement is the action of a person, such as extending his hand in a gesture of greeting; sometimes it is one or more aspects of two stimulus complexes, as in teaching a child to discriminate between an apple and an orange; and sometimes it is abstraction, as in teaching spatial relations concepts, such as "in front of" (Dixon, Spradlin, & Etzel, 1973). The form of knowledge behavior, which ranges from a simple pointing response to a complex verbal structure (interactional chain), and the setting factors for learning are also taken into account in the teaching of knowledge.

An additional significant and essential point about the teaching of abilities and knowledge is this: *the achievement of the other two categories of goals—motivations and self-management skills—depends to a large extent on the techniques used to teach the abilities and knowledge categories.* In other words, abilities and knowledge taught according to the principles described here serve to extend and elaborate motives and to strengthen self-control and self-management skills.

Extension of motivations. Ineffective procedures used by the teacher in teaching abilities and knowledge can make the activity, the situation, and the teacher distasteful to a child. Even though the teacher works diligently at presenting, explaining, repeating, and reviewing the subject matter and even though the child responds as required, ineffective teaching may encourage indifference on the part of the child. In contrast, effective teaching procedures arouse the child's enthusiasm for the activity, the situation, and the teacher, with predictable progress in learning.

Teaching designed to extend moral values and positive attitudes toward peers and adults, school, and ecological (natural) reinforcers involves the skillful management of positive reinforcers in ways that establish new positive conditioned reinforcers for a child (Bijou & Baer, 1961 & 1965).

The extension of moral values depends largely on clearly specifying the behaviors classified as "good" and applying positive contingencies when they occur, and specifying "bad" behaviors and applying either no contingencies at all or techniques of self control including mild reprimands when they take place (Skinner, 1953). The teaching of new moral values and extensions of old moral values follows the procedures outlined in Chapter 6.

Teaching a child positive attitudes toward peers and adults, both as an individual and as a member of groups, involves pairing the activities of peers and adults with social and/or physical stimuli (including activities) that are meaningful (functional) for a child. Since most children enter nursery school with positive attitudes toward their peers, teacher, and aides, training for a child with negative attitudes is usually categorized as remedial.

To teach positive attitudes toward attending school, reinforcers must be paired with coming to school. The first step in planning the program is an assessment of a child's school attendance. His "liking for school" might be evaluated by his rate and regularity of school attendance, his frequency of crying (or length of crying episodes) upon arrival at school, how often he is smiling when he arrives, the parents' report of the child's eagerness (or reluctance) to go to school, or whether the opportunity to attend school could be used to reinforce other low frequency behavior in the home, such as eating breakfast, putting away pajamas, or helping to make his bed. The desired goal for a child who cries each time he comes to school would, of course, be to have him arrive at school cheerful and eager.

The principle involved in developing a child's interests in nonpreferred school activities is the establishing of *intrinsic* reinforcers, those reinforcers that come from participation in the activity. Again, the first step is an assessment—in this case the conditioned reinforcing properties of school activities—when a child first enters school by measuring the time he persists at a given task without prompts, primes, or reinforcement from the teacher, or by recording his choice or preference when given an opportunity to select his own activity. The second step is to provide social or other contrived reinforcers to responses to school tasks; the third step is to fade these response contingencies on a *percentage* reinforcement schedule, that is, on a schedule that starts with 100 percent pairing and is gradually reduced to some value, such as 30 percent, so that the activity itself—and in some cases, its products—develop conditioned reinforcement properties. For example, performing an activity, such as painting "art" products, approved of by the teacher, teacher's aide, and parents will, after such training, become automatically reinforcing, providing the approval is functionally reinforcing for the child. To maintain this behavior, occasional social reinforcers are required.

The strengthening of ecological (natural) reinforcers requires that the child has opportunities to engage in *exploratory behavior* in physical environments highly responsive to his overtures and at times when he is alert, rested, and has no need for food, drink, or toileting, that is, when he is free from appetitive and aversive stimulations (see Chapter 2). Whenever possible ecological reinforcers should be used in the teaching of any school subject. In teaching rhythms, for example, it is simple to arrange conditions so that the sounds the child produces are exciting and naturally reinforcing.

Enhancement of self-management skills. The enhancement of self-management skills, it will be recalled, includes the development of personal "habits" (self-control) and problem-solving (thinking) abilities. The teaching of these behaviors, which help a child to respond in ways that increase the probability of avoiding future aversive stimuli and coming into contact with future positive reinforcers, relies heavily on a teacher's ability to teach self-management techniques.

In the teaching of personal (self-control) techniques, contingencies must be arranged so that they strengthen desirable work and play "habits," such as concentrating on the task at hand, working independently for reasonable periods, and proceeding with a task in an orderly and systematic manner. The teaching of these behaviors is highly dependent on the artful use of increasing and decreasing interval and ratio schedules of reinforcement (Bijou & Baer, 1961 & 1965). For example, a decreasing ratio reinforcement schedule may be used to teach a child to work steadily on larger and larger blocks of arithmetic problems on a single sheet of paper. At the beginning of training, he might be reinforced for doing one or two problems on a page. Shortly, he would be reinforced for doing three, then four, and so on. The rapidity with which he reaches the set goal of doing, say, six problems on a page without assistance, depends on his previous training and the teacher's ability to reinforce and sustain longer and longer interactional chains.

The goal of teaching problem solving and thinking, including creative behavior, is to help a child learn how to cope with any situation—personal, social, physical, or biological—for which he does not have an immediate response that is likely to result in an appropriate reinforcer. Unfortunately, limited information from research makes problem solving a difficult subject to teach at the preschool level and it is only recently that this behavior has been cast in terms of observable objectives and methods in the areas of number operations (Parsons, 1973) and art (Goetz & Baer, 1971; Goetz & Baer, 1973; Holman, Goetz, & Baer, in press; Goetz & Salmonson, 1972; and Rosen, 1975). We do know, however, that teaching problem solving includes (1) helping a child to develop rich repertories of abilities and knowledge, (2) developing positive attitudes and motivations for problem solving, (3) providing him with a wide variety of opportunities to engage in problem-solving behavior, (4) giving him guidance, in the form of prompts and primes and reinforcement support, in approaching problems and in acquiring techniques that rearrange the external environment and his own behavior (e.g., concentrating and recalling) in making the solution response more probable, and (5) withdrawing or fading guidance and support so that reinforcers are generated from the problem-solving behavior itself, that is, problem solving becomes intrinsically reinforcing. It should be apparent from this list that all the preschool goals described here interrelate and augment each other.

The systematic teaching of problem solving and creative behavior as presented here is practically nonexistent in the typical preschool. Currently, attempts at teaching these skills consist mainly of providing a child with unstructured situations in the hope that he can achieve these complex goals "naturally," or merely exposing him to situations that are said to generate creativity, originality, and exploratory behavior. Evans's (1971) comments about the teaching of creativity are interesting here:

Early childhood educators have traditionally paid lip service to the development or cultivation of children's creativity. Only occasionally, however, does one observe any specific delineation of behaviors that constitute creative expression or productivity. Many classroom activities described as "creative" are found when observed carefully to be convergent in nature; that is, they require children to meet uniform standards such as cutting patterns from manila paper or coloring pictures "by the numbers." Further, creative activities are often limited to art and music, with little attention given to creative thinking in areas such as science and social studies (p. 317).

ESSENTIAL SUPPORTS FOR THE TEACHER

We stated that teaching effectiveness depends on the teacher's competence in arranging specific conditions of the educational environment so as to facilitate learning. In order to perform her job, she must not only have a solid grounding in the technology of teaching and a thorough knowledge of each of the children in her class but she must also have support from aides, administrators, and most of all, from parents.

Support from Aides

A nursery school teacher generally has several aides; the exact number is relative to the number of children in the school. The competence of these assistants depends to a large extent on the objectives of the school, the methods used to achieve them, and the thoroughness with which they are carried out. Preschools that provide more than the usual babysitting services attempt to select aides who are committed to teaching young children and who are willing and able to profit from training and supervision. In such schools, aides perform more than housekeeping chores; they teach in accordance with the techniques practiced by the teacher and the philosophy of the school.

Since the teacher-child ratios in behaviorally oriented preschools are determined not only by health and safety factors but also by the personnel requirements for achieving the prescribed goals for each child, these schools usually have a relatively greater number of aides. Obviously, more personnel increases budgetary problems, a potentially serious problem if all the assistants had to be full-time paid personnel. However, carefully selected, properly trained part-time volunteers have served well as teacher assistants. Volunteers from the ranks of high school and college students and from the retired citizens' population make up a teaching resource that has barely been tapped. In the past these volunteers have been relegated to child watching and housekeeping activities, certainly an unimaginative use of manpower. Fortunately, the whole area of the training and utilization of paraprofessionals is now being reassessed, particularly in the light of advances in the behavioral technology of teaching (Ayllon & Wright, 1972; and O'Leary, 1972).

Support from Administrators

Principals, superintendents, and supervisors play a critical role in the success or failure of a behaviorally-oriented preschool program. First of all, they have the responsibility of selecting the teachers, and of seeing to it that the teachers' efforts are adequately supported, financially, professionally, and personally.

Financial support means more than supplying funds for personnel, materials, equipment, and transportation. It also means providing a physical environment tuned to the behavior objectives of the school: the provision of rooms conducive to free play, academic learning, dramatic play, art activities, music, and mechanical activities. Research is beginning to show how the physical aspect of the preschool plays an important role in achieving preschool goals (Doke & Risley, 1972; and LeLaurin & Risley, 1972).

Administrative support for a teacher's professional growth must include opportunities to learn more about new developments in the behavioral approach as well as freedom to put them into effect. This requirement, comparable to what in business circles is known as maintaining quality control, is equally important in teaching and is achieved through updating practices derived from applied behavior research findings and demonstration projects. Furthermore, administrative support presupposes responsibility for perpetuating the program. All too often behavior programs that showed exciting promise at first have been abandoned because quality control had not been maintained or because new personnel had been given inadequate training.

And finally, it behooves administrators to demonstrate by word and deed that the teacher's efforts are appreciated. They must reinforce her achievements (even the small ones) and show understanding and sympathy for her occasional reactions to frustrations and disappointments that inevitably occur in the demanding task of trying to help each child enjoy and profit from school to the fullest extent.

PARENT PARTICIPATION

All approaches to preschool education include a program for parents, which ranges from simply attending childrearing discussions to serving as a teaching assistant, to acting as resource persons.

As we pointed out previously, parent participation in nursery school affairs is essential in developing the philosophy of preschool education. The mechanism for accomplishing this end is parent-teacher discussions that go beyond enumerating children's problems and family problems and possible solutions. It means describing family practices, manners, codes of moral behavior, interests, and aspirations for the child; it means open discussions about family customs and the desirability of incorporating them, along with others, into the practices of the preschool. This frank airing of firmly held family views is one way of dealing with the current controversy over whether the value systems taught in the preschool should be those of the family, the teacher, or the administrator.

Parent participation is also requisite for maximizing the effect of the preschool program, particularly with respect to generalizing, elaborating, and maintaining learned behaviors (Bronfenbrenner, 1974). For parents to be successful in extending the behaviors to the home situation, they must be willing, even at the price of some inconvenience, to arrange the home conditions so that the responses required of the child are similar to those he learned in school. Parents must be taught, and they in turn must teach other family members, to be sensitive to the occurrences of desirable new behaviors and to reinforce them, rather than to take them for granted. The best way for parents to acquire teaching techniques is through actual supervised participation in the nursery school program. The old saying is true: "Skill to do comes of doing." A substantial byproduct of this training is the parents' improvement in childrearing practices, which spills over to benefit the other children in the family.

Research and demonstration projects concerned with helping parents improve their childrearing practices have yielded a variety of suggestions for parent training. In the late 1960s several field experimental studies (Hawkins, Peterson, Schweid, & Bijou, 1966; Shah, 1969; and Zeilberger, Sampen & Sloane, 1968) demonstrated that mothers can readily be taught techniques to cope with their young children's conduct problems. Since then, many behaviorally oriented how-to-do-it books have appeared. Some are programmed texts (e.g., Becker, 1971; Ney & Ney, 1972; and Patterson & Gullion, 1968) and some have followed the usual book format (e.g., McIntire, 1970). At the same time, social workers, teachers, nurses, and psychologists were exploring approaches to the direct (face-to-face) training of parents, as exemplified by the Regional Intervention Program for Preschoolers and Parents (Ora, 1971), and the Portage Project (Shearer & Shearer, 1972). Although the Portage Project was designed to teach parents to teach their handicapped children at home, it can with some modification serve as a basis for parent participation in a preschool program. We shall therefore describe it in some detail.

The Portage Project intimately involves parents in the education of their children by training them to arrange contingencies for effective learning, and to observe, and record behaviors. Instruction of parents takes place in the home and is done by teachers who are trained in applied behavior analysis of child development and assessment techniques. The children range in age from birth to six years and have been diagnosed as behavior problems, emotionally disturbed, mentally retarded, physically handicapped, or economically deprived.

When a child is referred to the Project, a teacher visits the home to determine whether he is eligible for the program. The assessment instruments include the *Developmental Skill Age Inventory* (Alpern & Boll, 1972), the *Stanford-Binet Intelligence Scale* (Terman & Merrill, 1960), and the *Infant Scale* (Cattell, 1947). These test results are also used as one of the baselines for determining achievement.

After the initial assessment, the teacher visits the home each week with any materials that might be needed to carry out the teaching activities. The heart of the teaching program is the *Curriculum Guide* (Shearer, Billingsley, Frohman, Hilliard, Johnson, & Shearer, 1970) which consists of (1) a *Developmental Sequence Checklist* with 450 behaviors from birth to five years of age in five developmental areas: cognitive, language, self-help, motor, and socialization, and (2) a set of curriculum cards that match each of the behaviors in the *Checklist*. Each curriculum card describes a skill in behavioral terms and suggests materials and activities to assist in teaching it. The parents are also encouraged to contribute their own ideas to the planning and implementation of the curriculum for their child. The *Checklist* is used to determine the child's entering repertory in each of the five developmental areas and to provide a second baseline. In the first teaching session, the teacher prescribes the next behavior on the *Checklist*, often dividing it into smaller units so that the established goal can be achieved by the child within a week. In subsequent sessions, the teacher begins by assessing the previous week's progress, and on the basis of her findings, alters her previous prescriptions and/or introduces new activities in the sequences. Each assigned task is pretested to determine whether the child is capable of making the responses required for that task. As the parent gains experience and confidence in teaching and in recording the child's progress, the teacher increases the assignments from one or two to three or four a week in several areas of development.

The teaching of a new task is first demonstrated by the teacher who then observes the parent working with the child and uses prompts, primes, and fading methods to help sharpen teaching skills. As an aid, an activity chart, which describes the goal to be achieved, how often the skill is to be practiced, what reinforcers are to be used, and how the response is to be reinforced, is left with the parent each week. The parent is instructed to record on the chart the child's behavior each day for each prescription. When the teacher returns the following week, she checks the child's progress on the previous week's activity and discusses the findings with the parent, always reinforcing both parent and child for work well done.

After a year's operation, the Portage Project was evaluated in terms of changes in intelligence test scores and number of assignments completed. The data from the Cattell and Stanford-Binet Intelligence Tests indicated that the average child gained 13 mental-age months in an 8-month period, which is 7 mental-age months higher than the mean predicted from the tests given during the initial assessment. The mean number of prescriptions written for each child was 128; the records showed that the average child successfully fulfilled 91 percent of them. Another finding, not objectively measured, was the pride and the involvement the parents felt in their effectiveness in bringing about desirable changes in the behavior of their child.

REFERENCES

Alpern, G. D. & Boll, T. J. Manual for developmental profile. Unpublished manuscript, Indiana University School of Medicine, Indianapolis, Ind., 1972.

Ayllon, T. & Wright, P. New roles for the paraprofessional. In S. W. Bijou & E. Ribes-Inesta (Eds.), Behavior Modification: Issues and extensions. New York: Academic Press, 1972.

Becker, W. C. Parents are teachers. Champaign, Ill.: Research Press, 1971.

Becker, W. C. & Engelmann, S. Academic Preschool, Champaign, Illinois; One of a Series of Successful Compensatory Education Programs. It Works: Preschool Program in Compensatory Education. Washington, D.C.: U.S. Government Printing Office, 1969.

Bereiter, C. & Engelmann, S. Teaching disadvantaged children in the preschool. Englewood Cliffs, N.J.: Prentice-Hall, 1966.

Bijou, S. W. & Baer, D. M. Child Development: A systematic and empirical theory. Vol. 1. Englewood Cliffs, N.J.: Prentice-Hall, 1961.

Bijou, S. W. & Baer, D. M. *Child Development: Universal stage of infancy*. Vol. 2. Englewood Cliffs, N.J.: Prentice-Hall, 1965.

Bronfenbrenner, U. A report on longitudinal evaluations of preschool programs. Vol. 2. *Is early intervention effective?* Washington, D.C.: U.S. Dept. of Health, Education, & Welfare, Office of Human Development, Office of Child Development, Children's Bureau, 1974.

Bushell, D. The behavior analysis classroom. In B. Spodek (Ed.), *Early childhood education*. Englewood Cliffs, N.J.: Prentice-Hall, 1973. Pp. 163–75.

Cattell, P. *The measurement of intelligence of infants and young children*. New York: Psychological Corp., 1947.

Dixon, L. S., Spradlin, J. E., & Etzel, B. C. A study of stimulus control procedures to teach an "in-front" spatial discrimination. Paper presented at the biennial meeting of the Society for Research in Child Development, Philadelphia, Pa., 1973.

Doke, L. A. & Risley, T. R. The organization of daycare environments: Required versus optional activities. *Journal of Applied Behavior Analysis*, 1972, 5, 405–20.

Erikson, E. *Childhood and society*. (2nd ed.) New York: Norton, 1963.

Etzel, B. C., Bybel, N. W., Busby, K. E., Dixon, L. S., Spradlin, J. E., & Schilmoeller, K. J. Experimentally demonstrated advantages of "errorless" (programmed) learning procedures in children's learning. Assessment, cue relevance, generalization and retention. Symposium presented at the 1973 biennial meeting of the Society for Research in Child Development, Philadelphia, Pa., March 29–April 1, 1973.

Evans, E. D. *Contemporary influences in early childhood education*. New York: Holt, Rinehart & Winston, 1971.

Goetz, E. M. & Baer, D. M. Social reinforcement of "creative" blockbuilding in young children. In E. A. Ramp & B. L. Hopkins (Eds.), *A new direction for education: Behavior analysis—1971*. Lawrence: The University of Kansas, Department of Human Development, 1971.

Goetz, E. M. & Baer, D. M. Social control of form diversity and the emergence of new forms in children's blockbuilding. *Journal of Applied Behavior Analysis*, 1973, 2, 209–17.

Goetz, E. M. & Salmonson, M. M. The effects of general and descriptive reinforcement on "creativity" in easel painting. In G. Semb (Ed.), *Behavior analysis and education—1972*. Lawrence: University of Kansas, Department of Human Development, 1972.

Hawkins, R. P., Peterson, R. F., Schweid, E., & Bijou, S. W. Behavior therapy in the home: Amelioration of problem parent-child relations with the parent in a therapeutic role. *Journal of Experimental Child Psychology*, 1966, 4, 99–107.

Hill, P. S. Kindergartens of yesterday and tomorrow. *National Education Association of the U.S. Journal of Proceedings and Addresses*, 1916, 294–97.

Holman, J., Goetz, E. M., & Baer, D. M. The training of creativity as an operant and an examination of its generalization characteristics. In B. C. Etzel, J. M. LeBlanc, & D. M. Baer (Eds.), *Contributions to behavioral research: Festschrift in honor of Sidney W. Bijou,* in press.

Hughes, M. M., Wetzel, R. J., & Henderson, R. W. The Tucson early education model. In B. Spodek (Ed.), *Early childhood education.* Englewood Cliffs, N.J.: Prentice-Hall, 1973. Pp. 230–48.

Katz, L. G. Where is early childhood education going? Urbana: College of Education Curriculum Laboratory, University of Illinois, 1973.

Katz, L. G. Policy formation and early childhood pedagogy. Paper presented at the Annual Conference of the American Education Research Association, Chicago, Ill., April 1974.

Klaus, R. A. & Gray, S. W. The early training project for disadvantaged children: A report after five years. *Monographs of the Society for Research in Child Development,* 1968, *4* (33).

Kohlberg, L. & Mayer, R. Development as the aim of education. *Harvard Education Review,* 1972, *42,* 449–96.

LeLaurin, K. & Risley, T. R. The organization of daycare environments: Zone versus "man-to-man" staff assignments. *Journal of Applied Behavior Analysis,* 1972, *5,* 225–32.

McIntire, R. W. *For love of children.* Del Mar, Calif.: CRM Books, 1970.

Mayer, F. *A history of educational thought.* Columbus, Ohio: Merrill, 1960.

Ney, P. & Ney, M. *How to raise a family.* Victoria, British Columbia: Pioneer Publishing, 1972.

O'Leary, K. D. The entree of the paraprofessional into the classroom. In S. W. Bijou & E. Ribes-Inesta (Eds.), *Behavior Modification: Issues and extensions.* New York: Academic Press, 1972.

Ora, J. P. Instructional pamphlet for parents of oppositional children. Unpublished pamphlet. George Peabody College, Nashville, Tenn., 1971.

Parsons, J. A. Development and maintenance of arithmetic problem-solving behavior in preschool children. Ph.D. dissertation, University of Illinois at Urbana-Champaign, 1973.

Patterson, G. R. & Gullion, M. E. *Living with children.* Champaign, Ill.: Research Press, 1968.

Ream, M. A. *Nursery school education—1966–67.* Washington, D.C.: Research Division, National Education Association, 1968.

Risley, T. R., Reynolds, N., & Hart, B. The disadvantaged: Behavior modification with disadvantaged preschool children. In R. H. Bradfield (Ed.), *Behavior Modification: The human effort.* San Rafael, Calif.: Dimensions Publishing Co., 1970. Pp. 123–57.

Rosen, H. S. The development of creative easel painting and generalization to drawing in preschool children. Master's Degree thesis, University of Illinois, 1975.

Shah, S. A. Training and utilizing a mother as the therapist for her child. In B. G. Guerney (Ed.), *Psychotherapeutic agents: New roles for non-professionals, parents and teachers.* New York: Holt, Rinehart & Winston, 1969. Pp. 401–7.

Shearer, D. E., Billingsley, J., Frohman, S., Hilliard, J., Johnson, F., & Shearer, M. S. *Developmental sequence checklist.* Unpublished manuscript. The Portage Project, Cooperative Educational Agency, No. 12, Portage, Wisc., 1970.

Shearer, M. S. & Shearer, D. E. The Portage Project: A model for early childhood education. *Exceptional Children,* 1972, *38,* 210–17.

Skinner, B. F. *Science and human behavior.* New York: Macmillan, 1953.

Skinner, B. F. *Contingencies of reinforcement: A theoretical analysis.* Englewood Cliffs, N.J.: Prentice-Hall, 1969.

Spodek, B. Staff requirements in early childhood education. In *Early childhood education,* the 71st Yearbook, National Society for the Study of Education. Chicago: University of Chicago Press, 1972. Pp. 339–65.

Spodek, B. *Early childhood education.* Englewood Cliffs, N.J.: Prentice-Hall, 1973.

Terman, L. M. & Merrill, M. *Stanford-Binet intelligence scale. Manual for the third revision: Form L-M.* Boston: Houghton Mifflin, 1960.

Thomson, C. L. *Skills for young children.* Unpublished manuscript. Edna A. Hill Child Development Preschool Laboratories, Department of Human Development, University of Kansas, 1972.

Todd, V. E. & Hefferman, H. *The years before school: Guiding preschool children.* (2nd ed.) London: Collier-Macmillan, 1970.

Watson, J. B. *Psychology from the standpoint of a behaviorist.* Philadelphia, Pa.: Lippincott, 1929.

Watts, A. *The book: On the taboo against knowing who you are.* New York: © Pantheon Books, a Division of Randon House, Inc., 1972.

White, S. H. *Federal programs for young children: Review and recommendation-summary.* Vol. 4, Washington, D.C.: U.S. Dept. of Health, Education and Welfare, U.S. Government Printing Office, 1973.

Zeilberger, J., Sampen, S. E., & Sloane, H. N., Jr. Modification of a child's problem behaviors in the home with the mother as therapist. *Journal of Applied Behavior Analysis,* 1968, *1,* 47–53.

9

Summary—and a Look Forward

Development of the preschool-age child has been analyzed theoretically in terms of behavioral concepts and principles described by Bijou and Baer (1961), Kantor (1959), and Skinner (1953 & 1969). The analysis focuses on selected progressions in behavior, interesting in their own right and interesting as precursors of behaviors in the succeeding period; namely, exploratory behavior, or curiosity, cognitive behavior, intellectual behavior, play, and initial moral behavior.

Exploratory behavior is analyzed in terms of a child's interactions with the physical environment and the physical aspects of the social environment and of himself, the ecological reinforcers that evolve, and the appropriate setting factors. Exploratory behavior produces repertories that serve as entering behaviors ("readiness") for subsequent complex behavior, and as a basis for developing a hierarchy of powerful conditioned reinforcers. A behavior analysis of exploratory behavior calls attention to the fact that a large share of a child's repertory is acquired and maintained by nonappetitional reinforcers—that is, by stimuli not traceable to biological "needs."

Cognitive, or knowing, behavior consists of knowing how to do things (abilities), knowing about things (knowledge), and problem-solving skills. All of these classes of behavior are complex interactional sequences involving attending, perceiving, and effecting behaviors. The tremendous increase in the repertory of a preschool child may be attributed to the extension and elaboration of cognitive behaviors developed in the previous stage.

Intelligence, in the normative, psychometric sense, is analyzed as a child's performance on a carefully drawn sample of cognitive tasks selected primarily on the basis of their correlation with school achievement. Hence, a child's score on a standardized intelligence test is, or should be, interpreted as his aptitude for school work and is accounted for in terms of a child's interactional history with objects and people. Competence is also measured in terms of performance on a sample of cognitive tasks. However, items on a test of competence are selected on the basis of their relevancy to some practical task, such as self-care, language, or writing. Findings on a test of competence are used to suggest beginning points for teaching the target task. Thus, scores on intelligence tests provide information for educational selection and classification; scores on a competence test provide guidelines for teaching and training.

Play refers to a child's activities when someone, including the child himself, says that he is playing. Because it is such a comprehensive term, play cannot be analyzed as an independent technical term. The most strategic way to study play, within the theoretical framework presented here, is to analyze in functional terms what the child is doing when he is said to be playing. Such analyses reveal that the behavior called play may result in new knowledge or may maintain previously acquired knowledge. Moreover, play may establish new abilities, motivations, imaginative activities, and problem-solving skills, or maintain those already in his repertory. Parents and the preschool teachers can easily arrange situations at home and in school that will encourage a child to engage in the kind of play that will develop any one of these behaviors.

Initial moral behavior is viewed here as a child's behavior in relation to the moral code of his family. Through incidental learning and deliberate instruction a child learns to comply with the moral standards and practices of his family. Because members of the family label behaviors as "good" or "bad," accompanying each class with the appropriate contingencies, the child acquires techniques to manage his own behavior so as to avoid aversive consequences for transgressions. The acquisition and maintenance of self-management techniques replace the notion that moral behavior develops through the "internalization" of moral practices.

All of these analyses may be applied to childrearing practices, treatment of severe behavior problems, and preschool education. The childrearing practices that evolve emphasize setting clearly defined objectives, keeping records, and positively reinforcing desirable behavior. The treatment approach stresses that each problem has its own unique history and any attempt to link a behavior problem with a specific treatment program is an exercise in futility. Furthermore, a behavioral approach to treatment focuses on specific problem behavior (e.g., the lack of speech development) without labeling it a mental disease or disorder such as autism, childhood schizophrenia, or mental retardation. Finally, the application of behavior analysis to preschool education aims to help parents, teachers, and school officials determine the overall preschool goals and to help teachers translate these goals into specific objectives and to employ effective procedures for carrying them out.

The next objective is to apply behavior analysis to the development of a child in the middle childhood years, the period that begins with entrance to kindergarten or first grade (a marked alteration in a child's social environment) and ends with the emergence of the biological indicators of adolescence (a significant change in a child's organismic environment). This epoch, known variously as the gang age, the school years, or the (sexual) latency period, is referred to here as the societal stage of middle childhood. All the names for this span of development suggest that this period is dominated by social interactions.

Compared to the basic stage of early childhood (as well as the subsequent adolescent stage), the societal stage of middle childhood is the time in which physiological growth slows down, body proportions change (e.g., the head is about 90 percent of the size it is at maturity), replacements occur (e.g., "milk" teeth are succeeded by permanent teeth), and level of physical energy increases. Taken together, these organismic changes set the stage for more vigorous and sustained activities.

During the middle childhood years, opportunities for social interactions broaden. Typically, a child joins a school group and becomes a member of a peer group which brings him into direct contact with more people and objects. Expansion of the social horizon beyond the boundaries of the family may lead to conflicts because the values of the school or the peer group may be incompatible with those in the home. The nature of the conflicts (and their resolutions), the changes in moral behavior, and the prescribed differences in the social behavior of boys and girls are of particular interest.

During the middle childhood years the child attends elementary school, which is designed to help him acquire the basic communication skills (reading, writing, and arithmetic), which expand his knowledge and abilities in practically all aspects of life. During middle childhood cognitive repertories increase rapidly and assume highly complex forms.

Practical application of the analysis of the middle childhood years should center on the goals and teaching methods in the elementary school grades, and the procedures for treating developmental retardation, extreme shyness, excessive aggressiveness, and school learning problems.

The analysis of the societal stage of middle childhood is followed by the

next objective: an analysis of phase II of the societal stage of adolescence
—the doorway to adulthood.

REFERENCES

Bijou, S. W. & Baer, D. M. *Child Development: A systematic and empirical theory.*
Vol. 1. Englewood Cliffs, N.J.: Prentice-Hall, 1961.

Kantor, J. R. *Interbehavioral psychology.* (2nd rev. ed.) Bloomington, Ind.:
Principia Press, 1959.

Skinner, B. F. *Science and human behavior.* New York: Macmillan, 1953.

Skinner, B. F. *Contingencies of reinforcement: A theoretical analysis.* Englewood
Cliffs, N.J.: Prentice-Hall, 1969.

GLOSSARY

Ability. See *Constructed response.*

Abstract behavior. The control of behavior through one aspect or a combination of aspects of a stimulus, such as color, shape, location, pattern, or size. Also called *concept formation* or *conceptualizing behavior.* Example: A child is told to collect all the blocks that are green. In doing so, he ignores the shape and size of the blocks.

Accidental reinforcement. The strengthening of a response due to the coincidental reinforcing of an operant and a reinforcer. Synonymous with superstitious, spurious, or adventitious operant conditioning. Example: Wearing a brown shirt to a football game because the last time your team won, you were wearing that brown shirt.

Acquired reinforcement. The strengthening or weakening of a response by the occurrence of a stimulus that was initially neutral (i.e., nonreinforcing) but has gained reinforcing functions through a history of conditioning.

Acquired reinforcer. A social or nonsocial stimulus that acquired a reinforcing function for an operant by being paired with a primary reinforcer, or as a result of having been a discriminative stimulus. Same as a *learned, conditioned,* or *secondary reinforcer.*

Adaptation. A decrease in the strength of a response as a result of continuous stimulation or closely-spaced stimulations. It is a natural desensitization to the presented stimulus. Example: The strength of the response to a small electric shock decreases as the number of electric shocks of a given voltage increases. (Compare *Adaptation* with *Operant extinction* and *Respondent extinction.*)

Anxiety reaction. An emotional reaction characteristic of all stimuli, that leads to avoidance behavior. It includes (1) respondent behavior, (2) operant behavior, (3) operant predispositions, and (4) facial and postural changes. Example: Waiting in the dentist's office—sweating palms, holding a magazine but not reading it, searching for an excuse to leave, and looking apprehensive.

Appetitive reinforcer. Stimuli that are reinforcing without a history of acquisition of reinforcing power and related to biological functioning. Often referred to as primary reinforcers. Examples: Food, water, temperature, rest, oxygen, and pressure.

Applied behavior analysis.   The application of behavior concepts and laws to the practical problems of education, therapy, industry, rehabilitation, counseling, guidance, childrearing practices. Used interchangeably with *Behavior modification.*

Attending behavior.   An operant response that focuses on or actualizes a stimulus. It is usually the first part of an operant interactional chain. Example: Looking, listening, reaching, or turning, before making the next required response.

Aversive stimulus or *event.*   An observable physical, chemical, biological, or social event that inherently, or through conditioning, *strengthens* behavior as a consequence of its termination (negative reinforcer), or *weakens* behavior as a consequence of its presentation (inhibition). A negative reinforcer strengthens either avoidance behavior or escape behavior. All negative reinforcers are aversive stimuli but not all aversive stimuli are necessarily negative reinforcers. The latter must be demonstrated.

Avoidance behavior.   Behavior that increases in strength because it avoids the occurrence of an aversive stimulus. Example: Ducking to avoid a blow to the face. In contrast, *escape behavior* terminates an ongoing aversive stimulus. Example: Putting your hands over your ears to escape the deafening sound of a pneumatic drill.

Back-up reinforcer.   A reinforcer exchange for a token. See *Token* and *Token economy.*

Basic stage.   The period from the end of infancy to the time a child enters kindergarten or first grade. It is the period during which a child develops his unique organization of behavioral equipment through interactions that are relatively free from earlier organismic limitations. Example: Being able to walk rather than crawl, feeding oneself instead of being fed.

Baseline.   Some index of the strength of an operant response (usually its frequency of occurrence) before an experimental procedure is introduced.

Behavior.   See *Response.*

Behavior analysis.   The study of behavior (organism-environment interactions) wholly in terms of empirical concepts and laws for understanding, predicting, and controlling behavior. Also referred to as *Experimental analysis of behavior* or *Functional analysis* of behavior.

Behavior modification.   See *Applied behavior analysis.*

Behavioral technology.   See *Applied behavior analysis.*

Behaviorism.   A philosophy of science that holds that the subject matter of psychology is the observable interactions between a total functioning individual and environmental events.

Biological reflex. Respondent behavior or behavior that is coordinated with antecedent stimulation in an invariant manner. They are *not* conditionable. Example: Knee jerk.

Chainbreaking. An operation or event resulting in the breaking of a chain of interactions, producing emotional behavior. Example: In driving your car to school (an operant chain), you have a flat tire (a chain-breaking event).

Chaining. Developing a sequence of operant interactions in a backward order. The terminal response is strengthened first, the next to last response second, etc. Example: Teaching a child to eat with a spoon by guiding his hand, starting with a spoonful of food in his mouth and working back to scooping food with the spoon from a plate.

Concept formation. See *Abstract behavior.*

Conditioned reinforcer. See *Acquired reinforcer.*

Conditioned response. A response to a conditioned stimulus in respondent behavior. Example: Salivating to the smell of food, especially under conditions of food deprivation.

Conditioned stimulus. A stimulus event not initially coordinated with a respondent (a neutral stimulus) but acquiring the power to evoke a respondent after consistent association (pairing) with an unconditioned stimulus. Example: A "fear" reaction to going into the water after an experience of having almost drowned.

Conflict. The simultaneous action of a stimulus with opposing functions, i.e., a response produces positive and negative reinforcement probabilities at the same time. Example: Being offered delectable candy when on a strict diet.

Constructed response. A response with a specified form or sequence. Referred to as an *Ability* or a *Skill.* Example: A verbal answer to a question.

Continuous schedule of reinforcement. A procedure in which reinforcement follows each response. Reinforcement may come only after a certain delay or low rate (differential reinforcement of low rate), or after a very short interval or high rate (differential reinforcement of high rate). Hence, differential reinforcement of low rate is a slowing down process, and differential reinforcement of high rate is a speeding up process. Same as *continuous reinforcement.*

Cue. See *Discriminative stimulus.*

Cumulative record. A record, showing the number of responses against time, made by adding each response to the sum of all the previous responses. When graphically presented as a cumulative curve, it shows the rate of change of responses over time.

Decreasing interval schedule of reinforcement. As teaching or training progresses, the interval between reinforcements is gradually shortened.

Decreasing ratio schedule of reinforcement. As teaching or training progresses, the number of reinforcements is gradually increased.

Delay of reinforcement.   See *Temporal gradient of reinforcement.*

Deprivation of stimuli.   A setting event in which the absence of a class of reinforcers (stimuli) results in increased effectiveness of those reinforcers for related behaviors when they are available. Example: Food is more appetizing after a long period without food.

Development.   Progressive changes in the interactions between a total biological functioning organism and sequential environmental events.

Developmental stage.   A period in the psychological development of a child which is identified by observable organismic, social, or physical events.

Differential reinforcement.   A procedure in which reinforcement is given for one occasion and not for another, as in *discrimination training;* or reinforcement is given for one form of response and not another, as in *response differentiation* or *shaping.*

Differential reinforcement of other behavior.   Reinforcement of any response except the pre-selected target response. It serves to weaken the pre-selected response.

Differentiation.   See *Response differentiation.*

Discriminated operant.   See *Discriminated response.*

Discriminative stimulus (S^D).   A stimulus event that marks the occasion on which a class of operants will probably be reinforced.

Discriminated response.   A response controlled by an antecedent stimulus (S^D) in the presence of which that response is reinforced. Example: Getting up and walking out of the classroom when the bell rings.

Duration of response.   A measure of the strength, or topography, of a response based on the units of time (seconds, minutes, etc.) that elapse between the beginning and end of the response.

Ecological reinforcer.   A stimulus that derives its reinforcing property from interactions with the physical environment under specified setting factors. Example: A toddler banging pots and pans together.

Emotional behavior.   Observable operant and respondent behavior patterns (physiological, facial, and body reflexes) related to observable conditions.

Environmental control.   The fact that past environmental events (conceptualized as *stimulus and response functions*) and present environmental events determine the frequency and form of sequences of interactions.

Escape behavior.   Behavior that is followed by the withdrawal of an aversive stimulus or a conditioned aversive stimulus (negative reinforcer). Example: Turning off the heat when a room is too hot. Compare this definition with that of *Avoidance behavior.*

Experimental analysis of behavior.   Same as *Behavior analysis* and *Functional analysis.*

Fading. The procedure in discrimination or ability training in which a particular dimension of a stimulus is made more and more conspicuous (e.g., increasing in brightness), or less and less conspicuous to the point of elimination (e.g., the word *red* written with red-colored letters and gradually faded to black-colored letters).

Fixed interval schedule of reinforcement. Reinforcing a response after a specified interval and allowing all intervening responses to go unreinforced. Example: One reinforcement every five minutes. After extensive training, performance follows a pattern: slow at the beginning and fast at the end of the interval.

Fixed ratio schedule of reinforcement. Presentation of reinforcement according to some predetermined ratio of response to reinforcement. Example: One reinforcement to every fifteenth response. After extensive training, performance is usually slow at the beginning of the number of responses required and fast at the end.

Four-term contingency. The interrelationships among the discriminative stimulus (S^D), response (R), reinforcement (S^R), and setting event (SE). A critical concept since *all* operant interactions are analyzed in terms of the four-term contingency.

Functional analysis. Same as *Behavior analysis* and *Experimental analysis of behavior.*

Functional relationship. An observable relationship among antecedent stimulus functions, response functions, consequence stimulus functions, and setting factors. A functional relationship is demonstrated if behavior systematically changes when any one of the other components is systematically changed.

Generalized reinforcer. An acquired reinforcer that is effective under a wide range of setting factors or events. Examples: Money, attention, and praise.

Heredity. Factors in prenatal and postnatal development attributable to the genetic composition of the fertilized egg, which furnishes the internal environment of an organism.

Homeostatic reinforcement. The strengthening of a response by a stimulus event that maintains or restores biological functioning following deprivation of a class of stimuli. Example: Water after deprivation of water.

Homeostatic reinforcer. See *Appetitive reinforcer.*

Hypothetical construct. A term or process created by a theorist in an attempt to account for causal events not directly observable. Same as *hypothetical concept.* Examples: Drive, ego, habit, strength, internalization, and cognitive structure.

Imitative behavior. A class of discriminative operant behavior in which the behavior of one individual provides the discriminative stimulus (in this case, model) for the *same* behavior by the other. It is the same as *modeling* and *echoic behavior.*

Incompatible behavior. Behaviors are incompatible with one another when it is impossible for both behaviors to occur at the same time. Example: Talking and drinking a glass of water simultaneously.

Increasing interval schedule of reinforcement. As teaching or training progresses, the interval between reinforcements is lengthened.

Increasing ratio schedule of reinforcement. As teaching or training progresses, the number of reinforcements is decreased.

Interactional chain. A sequence in which two or more responses are linked together by common stimuli having both reinforcing and discriminative functions. These stimuli have the power both to reinforce the preceding response and to be discriminative for the succeeding response. The stimuli in a chain may also elicit respondent behavior.

Interactional history. The history of an individual's interactions with environmental events. Such a history establishes stimulus and response functions for the individual. Example: Interactions with boxes make it possible for an individual to do many things with boxes (stack them, stand on them, etc.) and to know many things about the properties of boxes.

Intermittent reinforcement. Contingent reinforcement of an operant response based either on the interval between reinforcements (e.g., reinforcement every ten seconds), or on a ratio of responses to reinforcement (e.g., reinforcement every fifth response). Pertains to schedules of reinforcement.

Instructional program. A sequence of material, together with instructions, prepared in graded steps so as to enable the learner to start at the level of his repertory and progress to some terminal behavior. A part of the technology of teaching.

Knowledge. Stimulus control consisting of a series of interactions with an attending phase, a perceiving phase (including perceptual reaction) and a doing-something-about-it, or affecting, phase.

Neutral stimulus. A stimulus event that neither strengthens nor weakens an operant over its baseline rate, nor does it evoke respondent behavior.

Operant behavior. Behavior that is sensitive to consequences. Example: Walking, talking, reaching, etc. are acquired and maintained by consequences.

Operant conditioning. Increasing the strength of a response through the presentation or withdrawal of contingent stimuli.

Operant discrimination. Control of an operant response class by an antecedent stimulus (S^D) in whose presence the response class is reinforced. Example: When presented with a blue and a yellow card, a child selects the blue when the teacher says, "Give me the blue card."

Operant extinction. The weakening of a conditioned response when it consistently produces only neutral stimulus consequences until it decreases to or below operant level. Example: Decrease of requests for a drink of water at bedtime after requests have been consistently ignored.

Operant interaction.   See *Operant behavior.*

Operant level.   The degree of strength characterizing a response before the introduction of an experimental reinforcer.

Operant-respondent relations.   Interactions between operants and respondents in a complex chain in which stimuli may have discriminative, reinforcing, and eliciting functions and responses may have both operant and respondent properties.

Intrinsic reinforcer.   A conditioned reinforcer that is automatically derived from performing an act. Example: Reading for pleasure.

Latency of response.   A measure of the response strength of an operant or respondent based upon the promptness with which it occurs in reference to the antecedent stimulus event. The antecedent stimulus event may be a discriminative stimulus, an unconditioned stimulus, or a conditioned stimulus.

Magnitude.   In respondent conditioning, the magnitude of the stimulus controls the magnitude of the response. In operant conditioning, the magnitude as well as the form of the response is arbitrary and depends on which responses are selectively reinforced.

Mand.   A function of verbal behavior in which a response is produced by deprivation or aversive stimulation and is reinforced by an event that reduces these setting events. A mand "specifies" its reinforcement. Example: "May I borrow your pen?"

Modeling.   See *Imitative behavior.*

Moral behavior.   Behavior that complies with the moral code of a person's social group (e.g., the family, classroom, or community).

Natural science.   The systematic search for lawful relationships among observable events in the natural environment, using the characteristic method of manipulating the conditions and observing related changes in the phenomenon under study.

Negative reinforcement.   Strengthening operant behavior by the termination of an aversive stimulus. Example: Jumping into the water to cool off.

Negative reinforcer.   See *Aversive stimulus.*

Neonate.   An infant from birth at full term to the end of the second week of development during which the normal effects of birth subside.

Organismic events.   Biological events in the organism coordinated with changes in behavior. Example: Having a pain in the stomach and saying, "My stomach hurts."

Organismic stimulus.   A stimulus event arising from biological and physiological processes within the organism that produces observable changes in behavior. Examples: Earache, holding ear, and seeking something warm to ease pain.

Percentage reinforcement schedule of reinforcement.   Pairing an effective reinforcer with a neutral reinforcer a certain portion of the time. Example: Pairing candy with praise fifty percent of the time. The percentage may be decreased or increased over the course of training.

Pavlovian conditioning. See *Respondent conditioning.*

Perceptual (perceiving) behavior. A specialized sequence of operant interactions consisting of: (1) attending to a discriminative physical stimulus (e.g., turning toward the source of a sound); (2) discriminative responding to aspects of the stimulus (e.g., "seeing" which was responsible); (3) discriminative operants (consummatory responses) produced by stimuli from the previous discriminative act (e.g., reporting what was "seen").

Positive reinforcement. The strengthening of an operant response by presenting a positive reinforcer, contingent upon that response.

Positive reinforcer. A stimulus event presented immediately following some operant that increases the probability of the response class on future occasions.

Primary reinforcer. A stimulus that is demonstrated to be reinforcing without any history of acquisition of this reinforcing power. Example: Food, water, warmth, oxygen.

Priming. Increasing the probability of an operant by manual guidance so that the desired behavior may be reinforced. Example: Gently setting a reluctant child on a tricycle and pushing it.

Problem solving. Interactions in which a person cannot respond immediately either to reduce ongoing deprivation of reinforcing stimuli or to avoid or escape aversive stimuli and sets about to alter the situation so he can make a reinforceable response.

Progressive approximation. See *Successive approximation.*

Prompting. Increasing the probability of an operant by adding a relevant discrimination stimulus or cue. Example: Giving a hint to an answer or to a solution to a problem.

Private events. Events taking place inside the individual that are a part of behavior itself. Example: "Thoughts." In behaviorism, public and private events, such as "thoughts," are assumed to have the same physical dimensions.

Psychological interactions. Interactions between stimuli and setting events on the one hand, and changes in behavior in a total functioning biological organism on the other.

Psychological reflex. Respondent behavior that is coordinated with an antecedent stimulation in an invariant manner. It is conditionable. Same as the behavior in *classical* or *Pavlovian conditioning.* Example: Salivary responses.

Punishment. The weakening of a response due to either the presentation of an aversive stimulus following that response (a reprimand for pinching the baby) or the withdrawal of a positive reinforcer (response cost) following that response (taking a child away from his easel because he called another child a dirty name).

Reinforcement. The strengthening of a response by the occurrence of a stimulus event that either accompanies another stimulus (the conditioned stimulus and unconditioned stimulus in respondent, reflex, classical, or Pavlovian conditioning), or follows upon the organism's own behavior (consequent stimulus in operant conditioning). The concept is used in both respondent and operant conditioning.

Reinforcement contingency. The relationship between the reinforcement and the exact properties of the behavior it follows. See *Reinforcement.*

Reinforcing function. The function of a stimulus class to change the probability of occurrence or the form of operant behavior or to establish conditioned respondent behavior. See *Reinforcement* and *Stimulus function.*

Reflex. See *Respondent behavior* and *Psychological reflex.*

Repertory or *repertoire.* The catalog of responses an individual is capable of displaying on specific occasions. (*Repertory* is Anglicized from the French *repertoire.*)

Respondent behavior. Behavior that is sensitive to preceding stimulus events and insensitive to consequences. Same as *Reflex.* Example: Eye blink.

Respondent conditioning. The process of changing a neutral stimulus to a conditioned stimulus through frequent pairing of the neutral stimulus with an eliciting stimulus. Also referred to as *classical, reflex,* and *Pavlovian conditioning.*

Respondent extinction. The process by which a conditioned stimulus ceases to coordinate with a respondent when the conditioned stimulus is no longer paired with the original unconditioned stimulus.

Response. Any countable unit of an individual's behavior that can be observed to interact with stimulus events. Used interchangeably with behavior.

Response cost. The withdrawal of a positive reinforcer contingent upon a response. Since it weakens the response class, it is a punishment procedure.

Response differentiation. Discriminative stimulus control of the topography of chains of stimulus-response units due to the selective reinforcement of some response topographies and the extinction of others. It is the same as *Shaping,* and is involved in training abilities and skills. Example: Walking.

Response generalization. The fact that responses other than those in the interaction take on the same functional relationship to a stimulus as those in the training situation, to the extent that they resemble each other (or share common properties). Often referred to as transfer of training.

Response strength. The measure of the rate (probability of occurrence), latency, magnitude, resistance to extinction, or vigor of a response.

Response topography. The form of a reinforceable response in terms of vigor, speed, duration, tempo, or pattern involving a combination of dimensions. Example: Hand movement in opening a lock: inserting key with forward movement, stopping, and turning key to the right.

Satiation of stimuli. A setting event in which the abundance of a class of reinforcers (stimuli) results in decreased effectiveness of those reinforcers for related behaviors when they are not available. Example: Food is not appetizing after a sumptuous meal.

Secondary reinforcer. See *Acquired reinforcer.*

Self-control (self-management). A special case of an interactional chain. The responses of an individual that produce or manipulate environmental stimulus variables, which, in turn, change the frequency of his own behavior. Example: To lose weight, an individual trains himself to leave uneaten half the food on his plate.

$S^D(S\text{-}\textit{"dee"})$. A symbol for a discriminative stimulus or a stimulus in the presence of which an operant response is reinforced.

$S^\Delta(S\text{-}\textit{delta})$. A symbol for a stimulus in the presence of which an operant response is not reinforced.

Self-produced stimulus. A stimulus event generated by the behavior of the individual which is capable of influencing subsequent behavior. Example: Telling oneself repeatedly that it is time to get out of bed.

Setting factor or *event.* One of the conditions that is taken into account in any analysis of behavior because it influences the functional properties of the stimuli and responses in the interaction. See *Deprivation of stimuli* and *Satiation.*

Shaping. See *Response differentiation.*

Skill. See *Constructed response.*

Social reinforcer. A behavioral consequence that is mediated by a person who has acquired a reinforcing stimulus function. Another person is the reinforcing agent. Example: Mother who praises, laughs, or plays with her child.

Social stimulus. A stimulus event in the form of the appearance and action of other people.

Socialization. The development of behavior to social stimuli.

Societal stage. The period from the end of early childhood to adulthood consisting of expanding contacts with social and cultural environments outside the family. May be subdivided into middle childhood, adolescence, adulthood, and old age.

Spontaneous recovery. A temporary breakdown in extinction when an extinguished response gains strength above the operant level in the absence of effective stimulus functions. Also refers to the increase in strength of a punished response when the punishment is no longer in effect.

Stimulus. An observable physical, chemical, biological, or social event which is coordinated with changes in observable behavior.

Stimulus control. The differential form or frequency of a behavior in the presence of one stimulus which is not evident in the presence of another. The stimulus in stimulus control performs the function of a discriminative stimulus (S^D). Same as *Discriminated response.*

Stimulus function. The classification of stimulus events according to their observed relationships with responses. Example: Stimuli may have a discriminative function, a reinforcing function, an eliciting function, or a neutral function. In an interactional chain, a stimulus usually has several functions. See *Interactional chain.*

Stimulus generalization. The fact that stimuli outside the training situation take on the same functional relationship to a response as those in the training situation, to the extent that they share common properties. Also referred to as *induction.* Example: A child learning to call a red ball "red" may also call an orange ball "red." Contrast with *Response generalization.*

Successive approximation. A technique used to condition a behavior not currently in the repertory. It involves initially reinforcing all responses that are approximate to the desired response, then subsequently reinforcing only the more well-defined target response.

Symbolic behavior. Discriminative operant behavior to symbols of objects, people, and events. Examples: Responses to models, pictures, drawings, words, numbers, etc.

Tact. The name for one of the functions of verbal behavior. It is a verbal discriminative operant in which a given response is strengthened by a particular object or event (or property of an object or event) when a *history* of *social reinforcement* for the response has been provided. The reinforcement is generally social, such as "That's right." Example: On presentation of an apple, a child says, "That's an apple."

Temporal gradient of reinforcement. The temporal relationship between the occurrence of an operant and the reinforcing consequences.

Threshold. The smallest magnitude of a stimulus sufficient to produce a response, either operant or respondent.

Time-out. A period of time during which the positive reinforcers are no longer in effect and invoked contingent on an undesirable response. Since time-out decreases the frequency of the antecedent behavior, it is a class of punishment such as *Response Cost.*

Token. A conditioned reinforcer, usually a metal or plastic disc, which can be exchanged for privileges, food, or other items. Example: Money. See *Generalized reinforcer.*

Token economy. A social system in which tokens are systematically provided to strengthen desirable behavior.

Unconditioned response. In respondent conditioning, the response elicited by an unconditioned stimulus. Example: Goose pimples on the arm.

Unconditioned stimulus. An antecedent stimulus event that is invariably coordinated with the respondent it precedes. Example: Cold air on a warm arm producing goose pimples.

Universal stage. The period from prenatal development through infancy characterized by respondent interactions, uncoordinated movements, and ecological behavior.

Variable interval schedule of reinforcement. Presentation of reinforcement at irregular intervals, irrespective of response output during the intervening periods. Performance after extended training is usually regular, even, and steady.

Variable ratio schedule of reinforcement. Reinforcement of an operant on the basis of a ratio of responses to reinforcement that changes irregularly in value from one reinforcement presentation to the next. Example: From five responses required for one reinforcement to eight responses for one reinforcement. Performance after extended training is usually regular, even, and steady.

Verbal behavior. Social behavior that is reinforced through the mediation of another person or group of persons.

INDEX